The Versatile PIANIST

Arranged by Richard Bradley

Richard Bradley is one of the world's best-known and best-selling arrangers of piano music for print. His success can be attributed to years of experience as a teacher and his understanding of students' and players' needs. His innovative piano methods for adults (*Bradley's How to Play Piano* - Adult Books 1, 2, and 3) and kids (*Bradley for Kids* - Red, Blue, and Green Series) not only teach the instrument, but they also teach musicanship each step of the way.

Originally from the Chicago area, Richard completed his undergraduate and graduate work at the Chicago Conservatory of Music and Roosevelt University. After college, Richard became a print arranger for Hansen Publications and later became music director of Columbia Pictures Publications. In 1977, he co-founded his own publishing company, Bradley Publications, which is now exclusively distributed worldwide by Warner Bros. Publications.

Richard is equally well known for his piano workshops, clinics, and teacher training seminars. He was a panelist for the first and second Keyboard Teachers' National Video Conferences, which were attended by more than 20,000 piano teachers throughout the United States.

The home video version of his adult teaching method, *How to Play Piano With Richard Bradley*, was nominated for an American Video Award as Best Music Instruction Video, and, with sales climbing each year since its release, it has brought thousands of adults to—or back to—piano lessons. Still, Richard advises, "The video can only get an adult started and show them what they can do. As they advance, all students need direct input from an accomplished teacher."

Additional Richard Bradley videos aimed at other than the beginning pianist include *How to Play Blues Piano* and *How to Play Jazz Piano*. As a frequent television talk show guest on the subject of music education, Richard's many appearances include "Hour Magazine" with Gary Collins, "The Today Show," and "Mother's Day" with former "Good Morning America" host Joan Lunden, as well as dozens of local shows.

Contents by Category

POPS:

STANDARDS:

Contents by Category

JAZZ:

CLASSICS:

Alphabetical Contents

Alphabetical Contents

Show Me The Meaning Of Being Lonely

Recorded by BACKSTREET BOYS

Words and Music by
MAX MARTIN and HERBERT CRICHLOW
Arranged by Richard Bradley

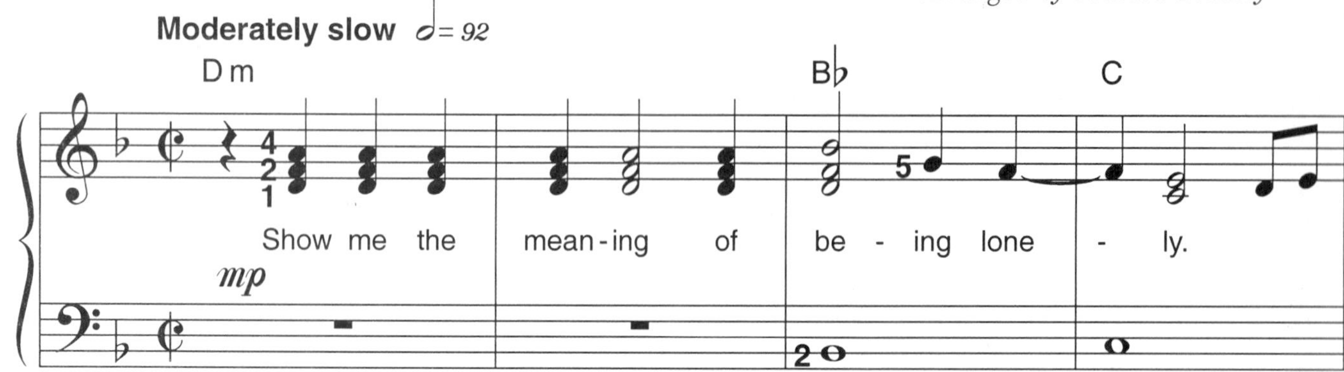

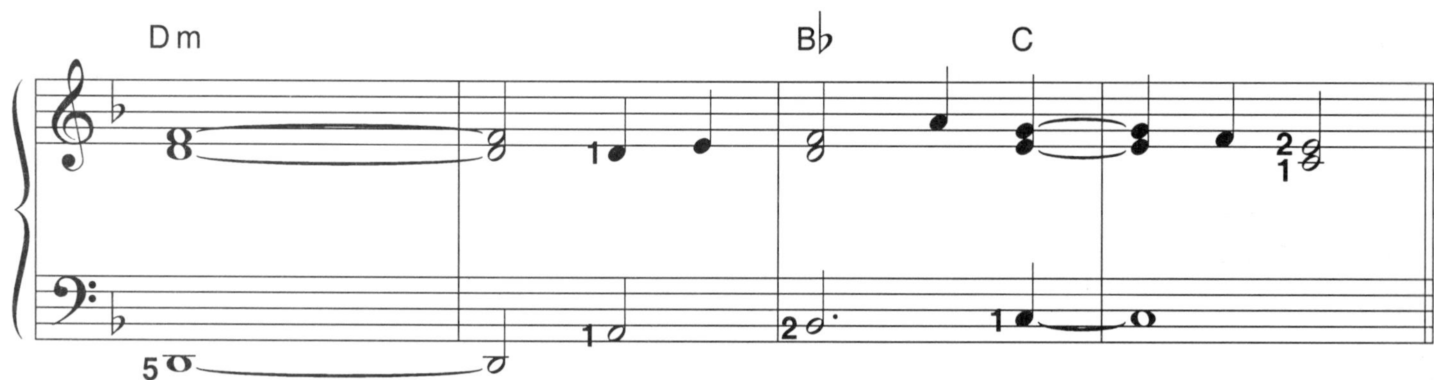

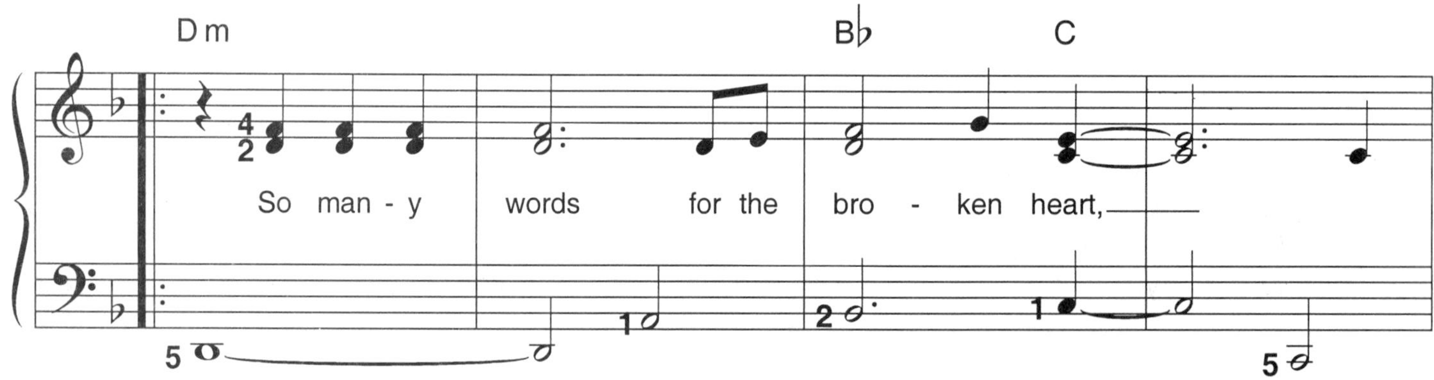

B♭
Asus4
A7
hard to breathe.
Walk with me and may - be
Dm
B♭Maj7
C
nights of light so soon be - come
Dm
B♭Maj7
C
wild and free I could feel the sun. Your
B♭
Asus4
A7
ev - 'ry wish will be done, they tell me...
Dm
B♭
C
Show me the mean - ing of be - ing lone - ly.
mf

Dm
Bb
C
Is this the feel - ing I need to walk with?
F
A7
Tell me why I can't be there where you are.
Dm
1.
There's some - thing miss - ing in my heart.
mp
2.
Em
some - thing miss - ng in my heart. There's no - where to run,

C
D
Em
I have no place to go. Sur - ren - der my heart,
C
D
G
CMaj7
bod - y and soul. How can it be you're ask - ing
B7sus4
B7
Em
me to feel the things you nev - er show?
C
D
Em
C
D
Em

C
D
Em
C
D
G
You are miss - ing in my heart.
B7
Em
Tell me why
I can't be there where you are.
Show me the mean - ing of
mf
be - ing lone - ly.
Is this the feel - ing I

Verse 2:
Life goes on as it never ends.
Eyes of stone observe the trends,
They never say, forever gaze.
If only guilty roads to an endless love,
There's no control.
Are you with me now?
Your every wish will be done, they tell me. . .

Bye Bye Bye

Recorded by *NSYNC

Words and Music by
KRISTIAN LUNDIN
JAKE and ANDREAS CARLSON
Arranged by Richard Bradley

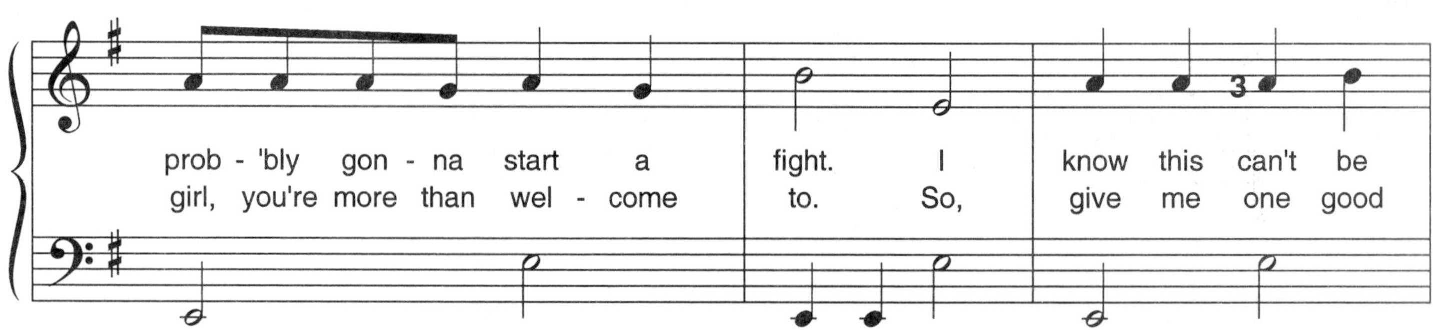

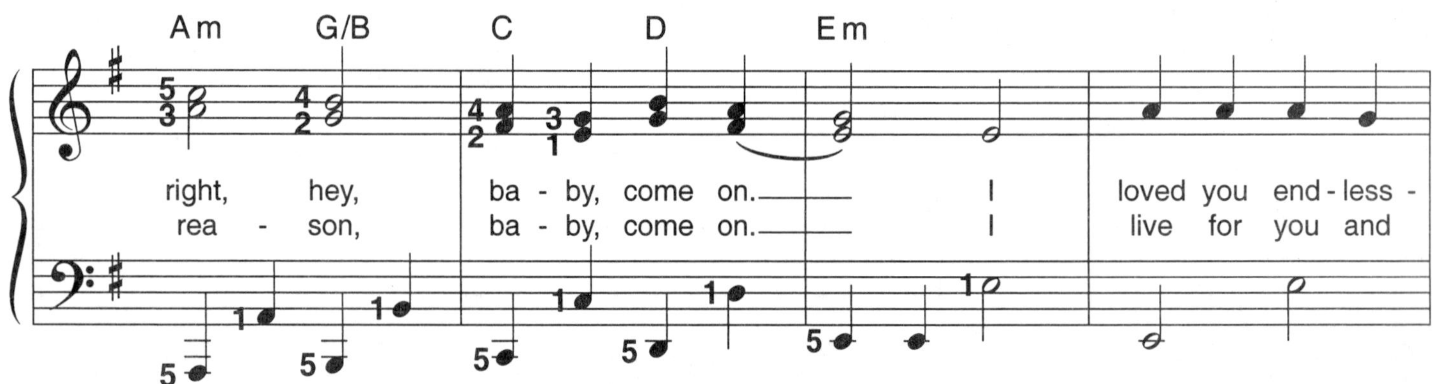

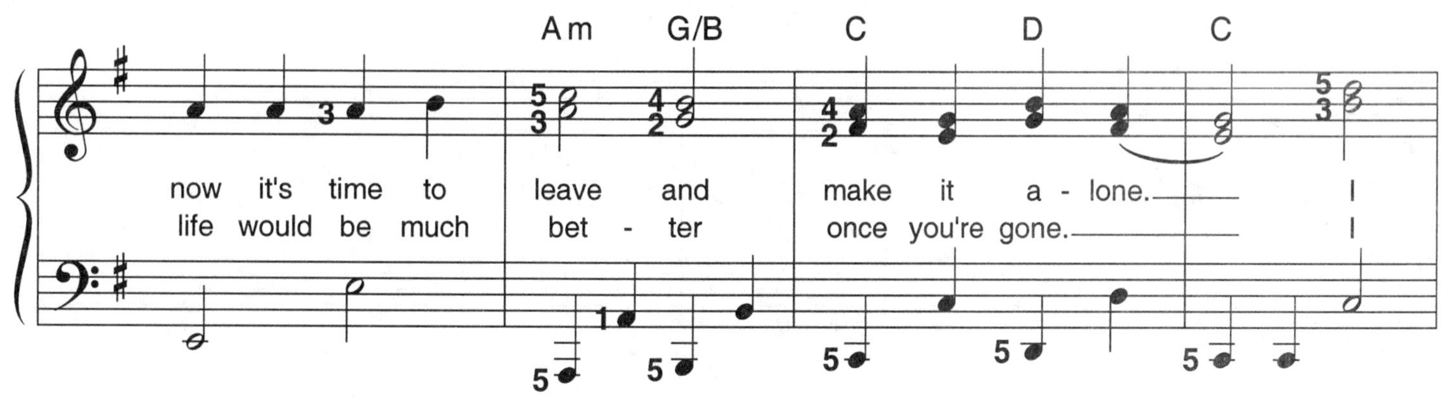
Am G/B C D C
now it's time to leave and make it a - lone. I
life would be much bet - ter once you're gone. I

D C
know that I can't take no more. It ain't no lie. I

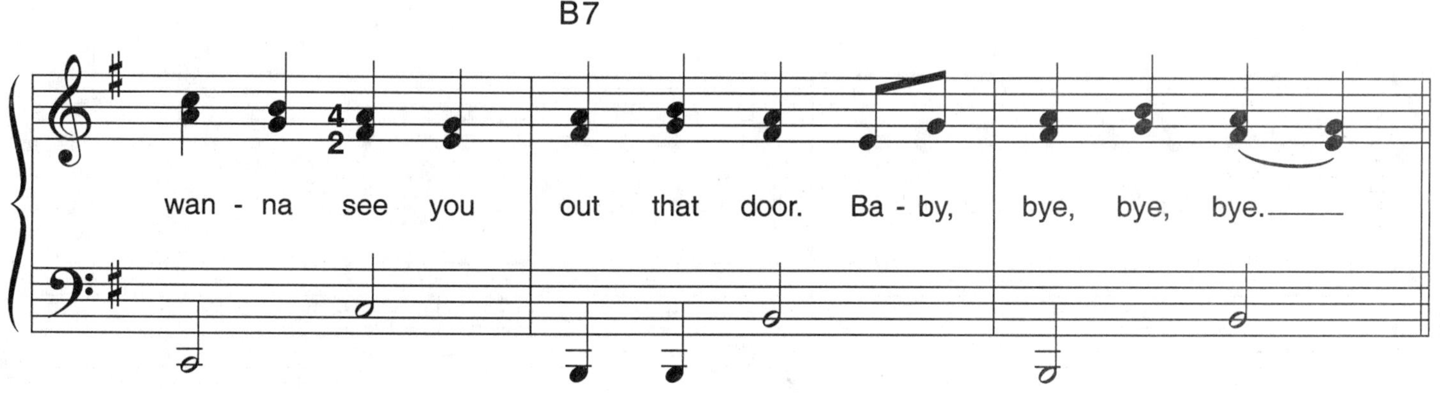
B7
wan - na see you out that door. Ba - by, bye, bye, bye.

Em D
I don't wan - na be a fool for you, just an - oth - er play - er in your

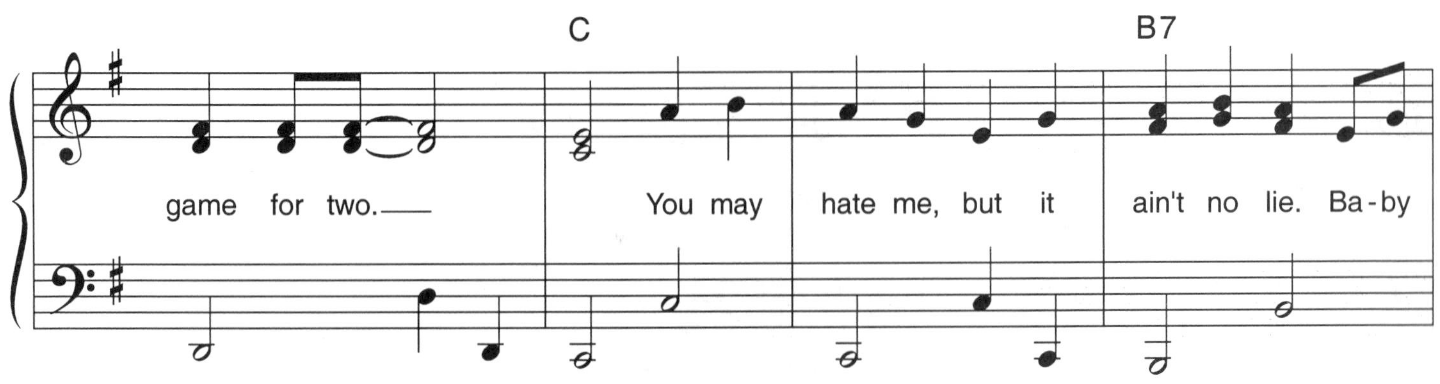
C
B7
game for two.
You may
hate me, but it
ain't no lie. Ba-by

Em
bye, bye, bye.
I don't real - ly wan - na
make it tough,

D
C
I just wan - na tell you that I
had e - nough.
It may sound

To Coda
1.
B7
C
D
cra - zy, but it
ain't no lie. Ba - by,
bye, bye, bye.

Em
2.
B7
C
D
4
2
3
1
4
2
1
ain't no lie. Ba-by,
bye, bye, bye.

Em
Em
I'm giv-ing up, I
know for sure. I don't

wan-na be the rea-son for your
love no more.
I'm check-ing out, I'm

sign - ing off. I don't
wan-na be the los-er and I've
had e - nough.

Em
D
I don't wan - na
be your fool in this
C
B7
Em
game for two,
so I'm
leav - ing
you be - hind.
D
C
I don't wan - na
make it tough,
but I
had
e - nough,
B7
D.S. al Coda
and it
ain't no
lie. Bye, bye.
Coda
B7
C D Em
8va
ain't no lie. Bye, bye,
bye.

I Need To Know

Recorded by MARC ANTHONY

Words and Music by
MARK C. ROONEY and MARC ANTHONY
Arranged by Richard Bradley

E7
Am
want to hear,
wan-na be.
but that's just talk un-till you
The on-ly thing's I need you
take me there.
here with me.
Oh,

E7
if it's true, don't leave me all a-lone out here,
won-d'ring if you're ev-er gon-na

Am
E7
take me there.
Tell me what you're feel-ing 'cause I
need to know.

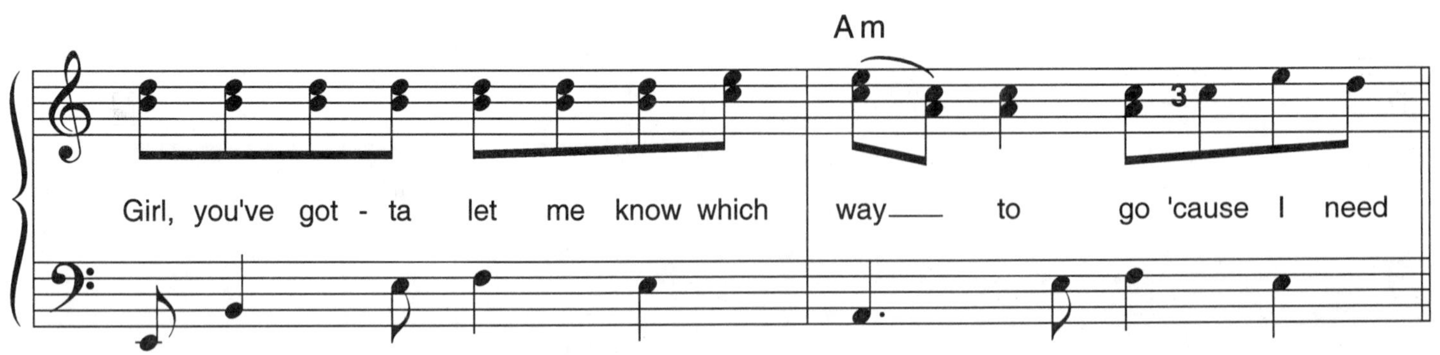
Am
Girl, you've got-ta let me know which
way to go 'cause I need

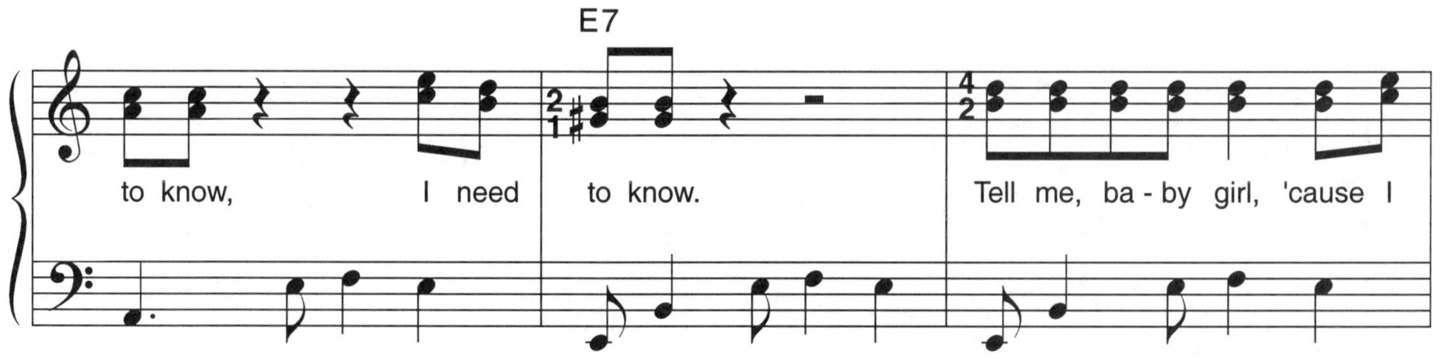
E7
to know, I need
to know.
Tell me, ba - by girl, 'cause I

Am
E7
need— to know, I need
to know, I need
to know.

1.
Am
2.
Am
Tell me, ba - by girl, 'cause I
need— to know.
need— to know.
Don't leave me here a -

E7
Am
lone.
'Cause I need
Don't leave me here a -

E7
5
to know, I need
lone.
to know.
Tell me, ba - by girl, 'cause I

Am
E7
need— to know, I need
to know, I need
to know.

Am
4
2
Tell me, ba - by girl, 'cause I
need— to know.
If it's true, don't leave me all a -

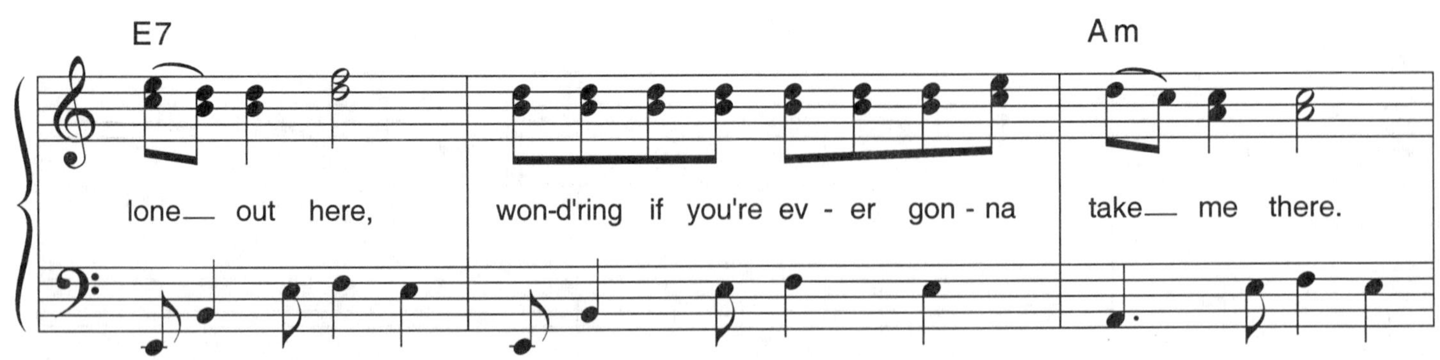
E7
Am
lone— out here,
won-d'ring if you're ev - er gon - na
take— me there.

E7
Tell me what you're feel - ing 'cause I
need to know.
1.
Am
Girl, you've got - ta let me know which
way to go 'cause I need
2.
Am
N.C.
way to go 'cause I need
to know, I need
to know.
Tell me, ba - by girl, 'cause I
need to know, I need
to know, I need
to know.
Tell me, ba - by girl, 'cause I
need to know.

Breathe

Recorded by FAITH HILL

Words and Music by
STEPHANIE BENTLEY
and HOLLY LAMAR
Arranged by Richard Bradley

Am7
G/B
C(9)
G/B
I watch the sun-light dance a-cross your face and I've

Am7
Dsus4
D
nev-er been this swept a-way.

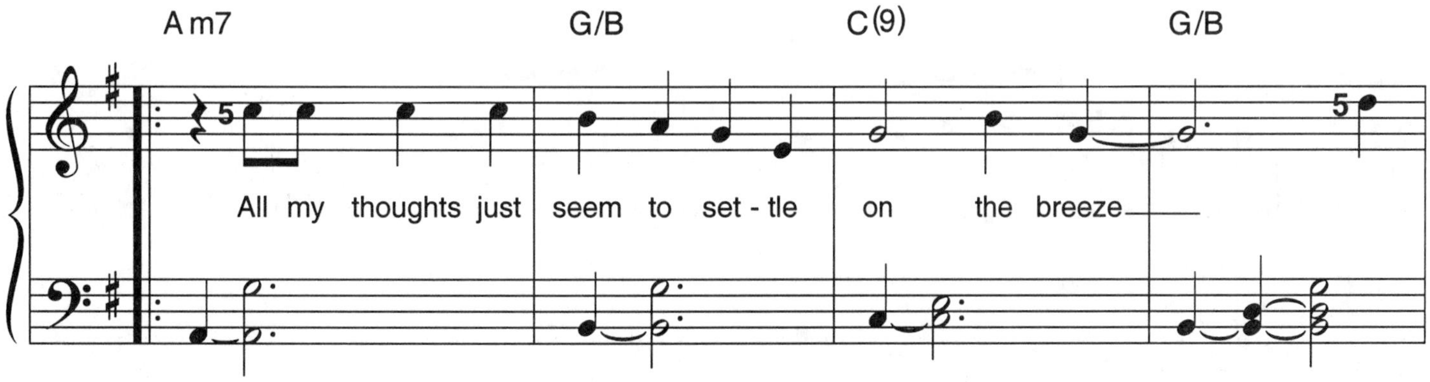
Am7
G/B
C(9)
G/B
All my thoughts just seem to set-tle on the breeze

Am7
G/B
C(9)
when I'm ly-in' wrapped up in your arms.

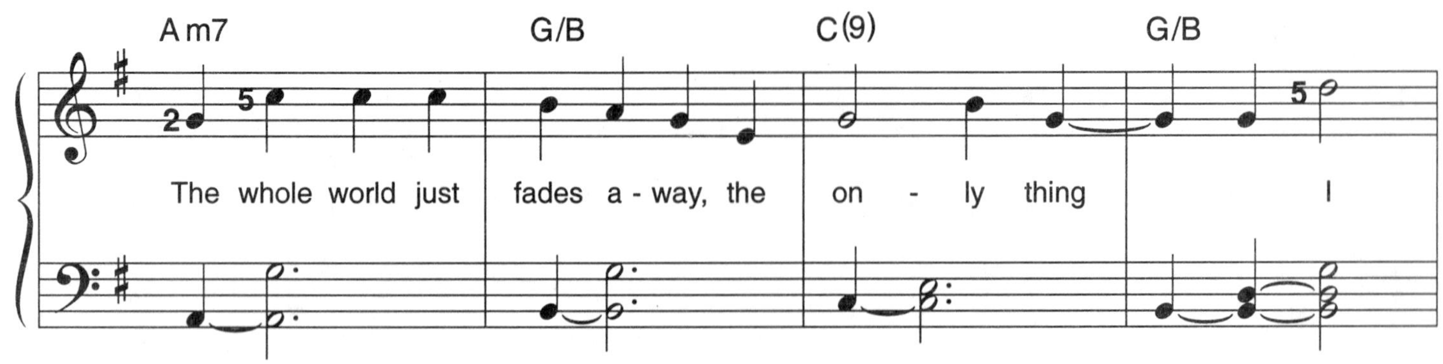
Am7
G/B
C(9)
G/B
The whole world just fades a - way, the on - ly thing I

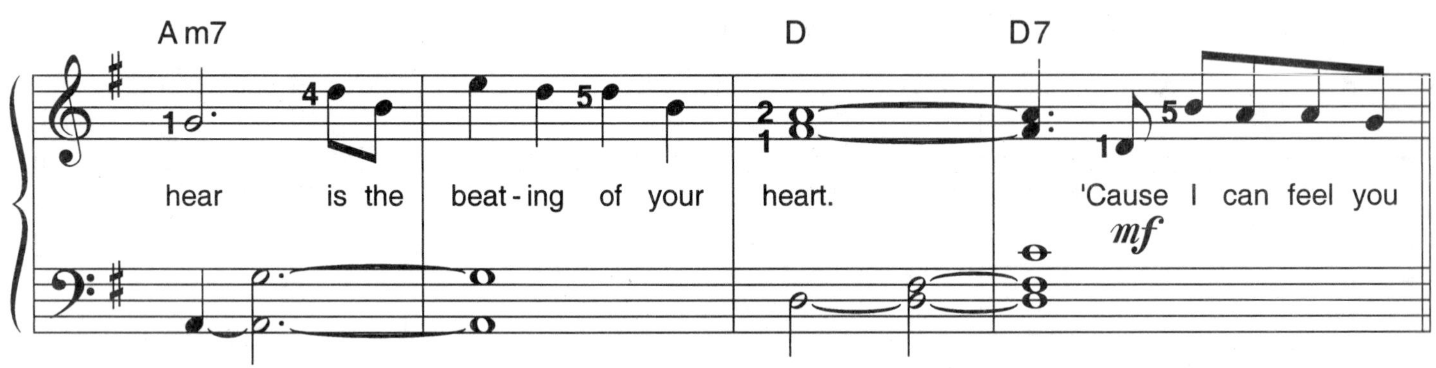
Am7
D
D7
hear is the beat - ing of your heart. 'Cause I can feel you
mf

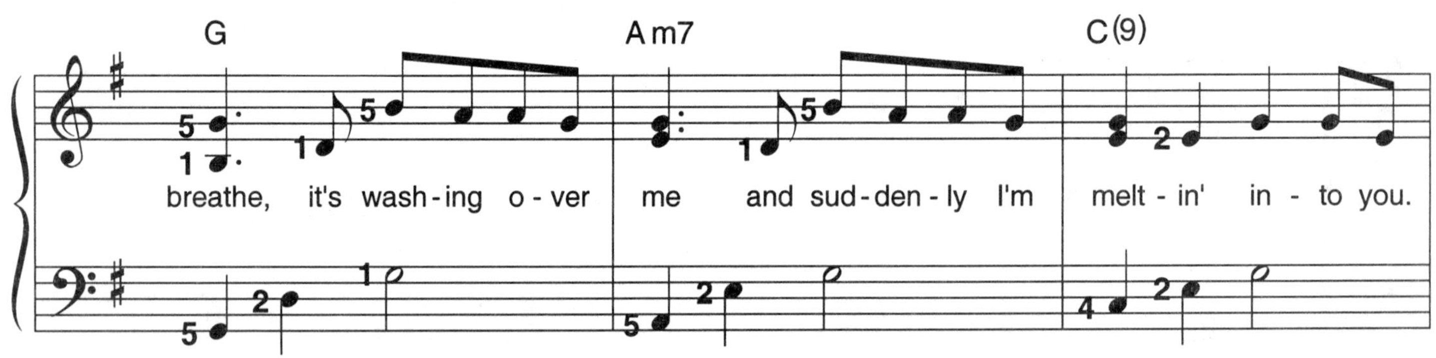
G
Am7
C(9)
breathe, it's wash - ing o - ver me and sud - den - ly I'm melt - in' in - to you.

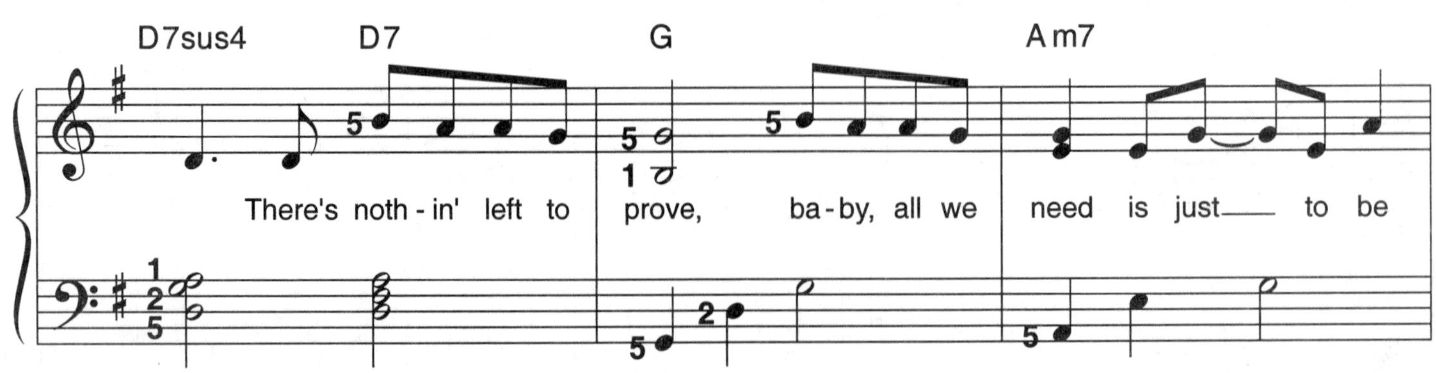
D7sus4
D7
G
Am7
There's noth - in' left to prove, ba - by, all we need is just to be

C(9)
D7sus4
D7
G
caught up in the touch, the slow and stead - y
Am7
C(9)
G/B
rush. And ba - by, is - n't that the way that love's sup - posed
Am7
D7sus4
D7
to be?
I can feel you
mp
C(9)
G/B
Am7
D7sus4
breathe.
mf
Just
To Coda
G
Am7
C(9)
D7sus4
D7
breathe.

Verse 2:
In a way, I know my heart is waking up
As all the walls come tumblin' down.
Closer than I've ever felt before
And I know and you know
There's no need for words right now.

I Don't Want To Miss A Thing

From the Motion Picture *Armageddon*
Recorded by AEROSMITH

Words and Music by
DIANE WARREN
Arranged by Richard Bradley

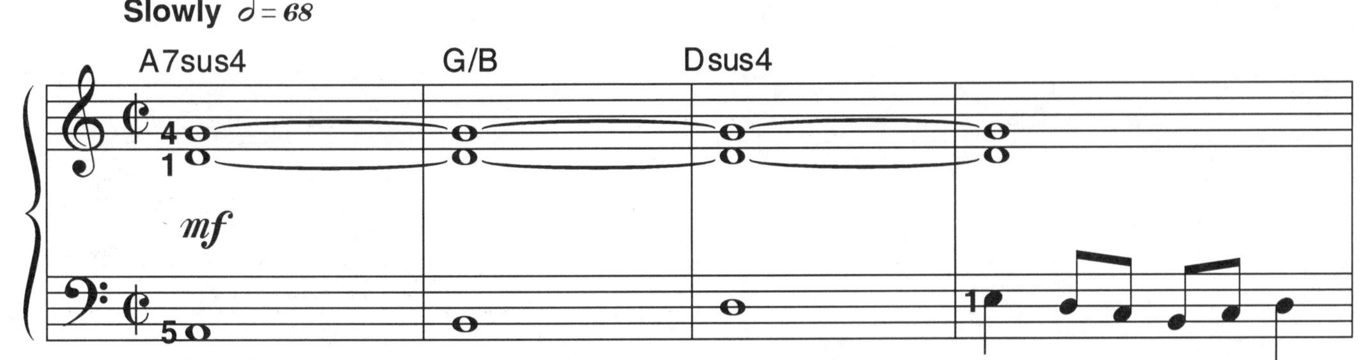

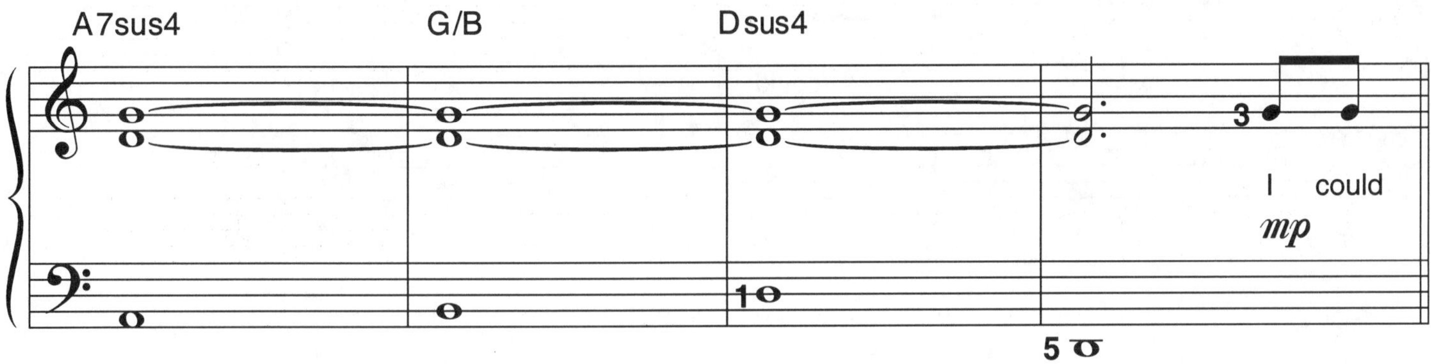

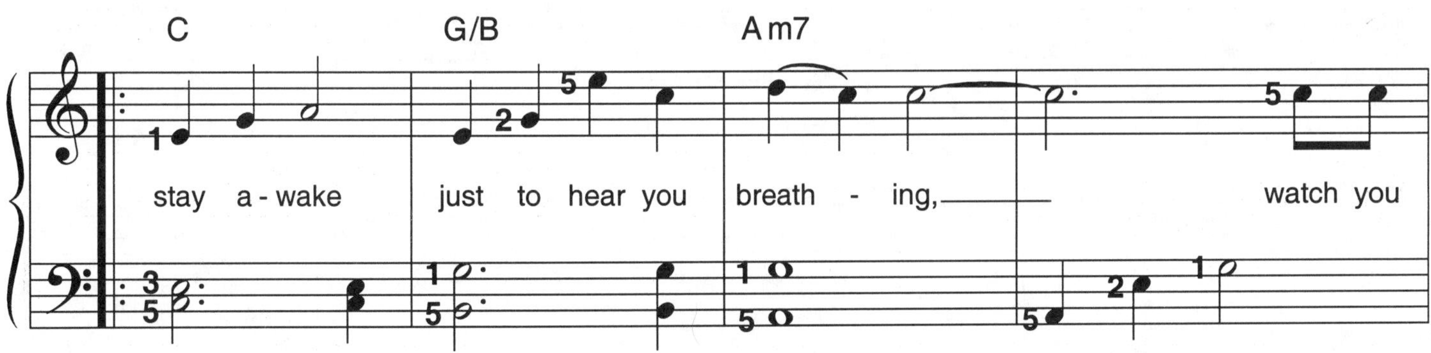

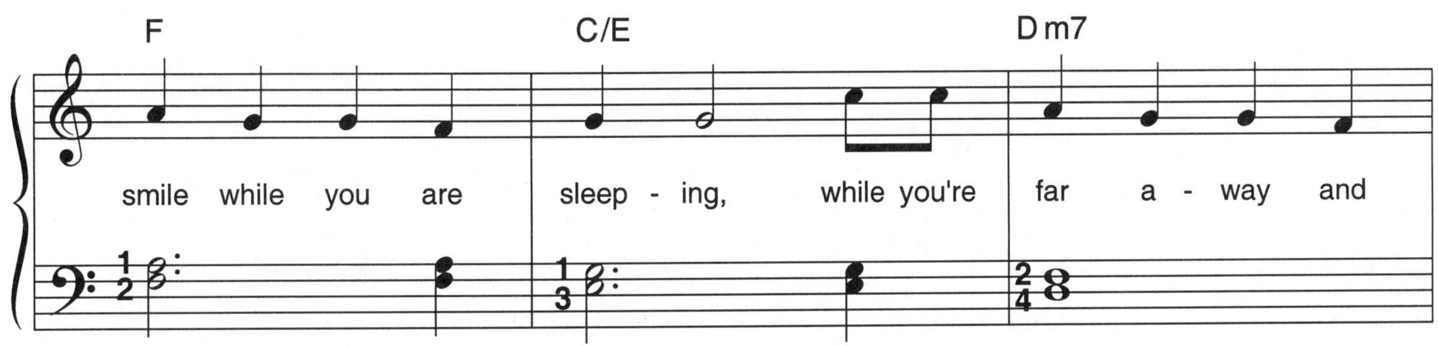

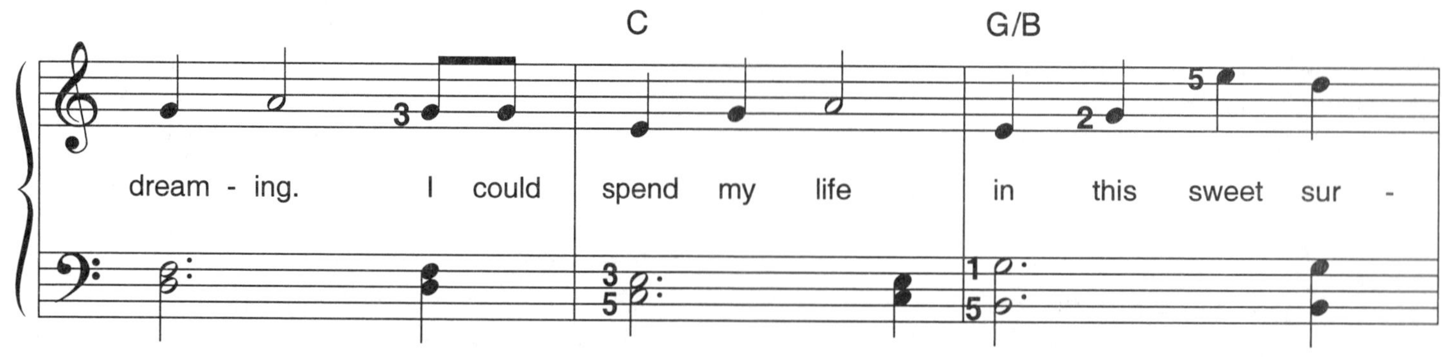
C
G/B
dream - ing. I could
spend my life
in this sweet sur -

Am7
1st time only
F
C/E
ren - der.
I could
stay lost in this
mo - ment for -

Dm7
Em7
ev - er.
Ev - 'ry mo - ment
spent with you

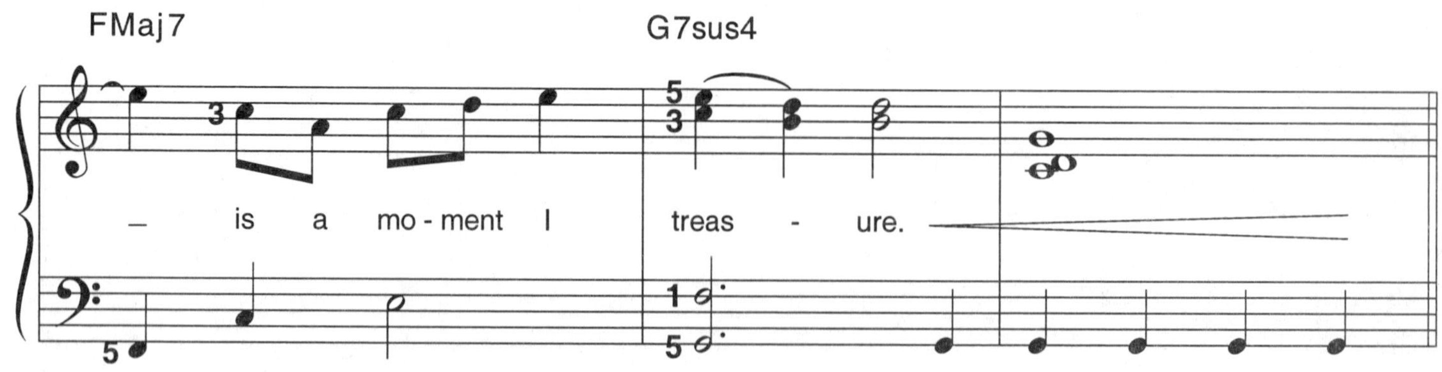
FMaj7
G7sus4
is a mo - ment I
treas - ure.

C
G/B
Dm7
mf
Don't wan - na
close my eyes,
don't wan - na
F
G
fall a - sleep 'coz I'd
miss you ba - by, and I
don't wan - na miss a thing.
C
G/B
Dm7
'Coz e - ven when I
dream of you,
the sweet - est dream would
To Coda
1. F
G7
nev - er do. I'd still
miss you, ba - by, and I
don't wan - na miss a thing.
C
G/B
Am7
mp
Lay - ing

2.
F
G7
C
miss you ba - by, and I
don't wan - na miss a thing.
I don't wan - na
B♭
F/A
miss one smile.
I don't wan - na
miss one kiss.
A♭
I just wan - na
be with you, right
here with you,
E♭/G
B♭
just like this.
I just wan - na
hold you close,
F/A
feel your heart so
close to mine,
and just

Verse 2:
Laying close to you, feeling your heart beating,
And I'm wondering what you're dreaming,
Wondering if it's me you're seeing.
Then I kiss your eyes and thank God we're together.
I just wanna stay with you in this moment together.

That's The Way It Is

Recorded by CELINE DION

Words and Music by
MAX MARTIN, KRISTIAN LUNDIN
and ANDREAS CARLSSON
Arranged by Richard Bradley

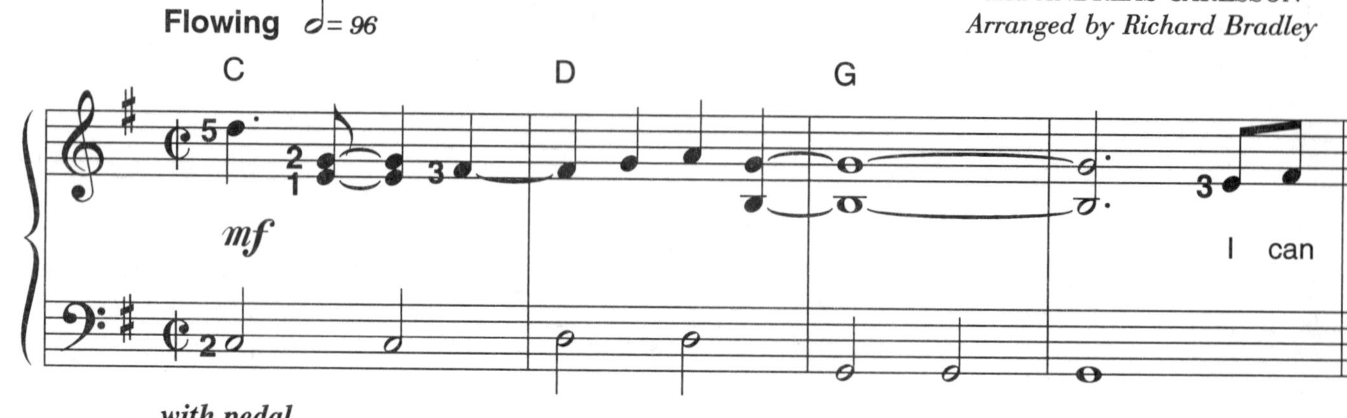

Em
D
G
know it will come to you, yeah. Don't sur -

Am
C
D
ren - der, 'cause you can win in this

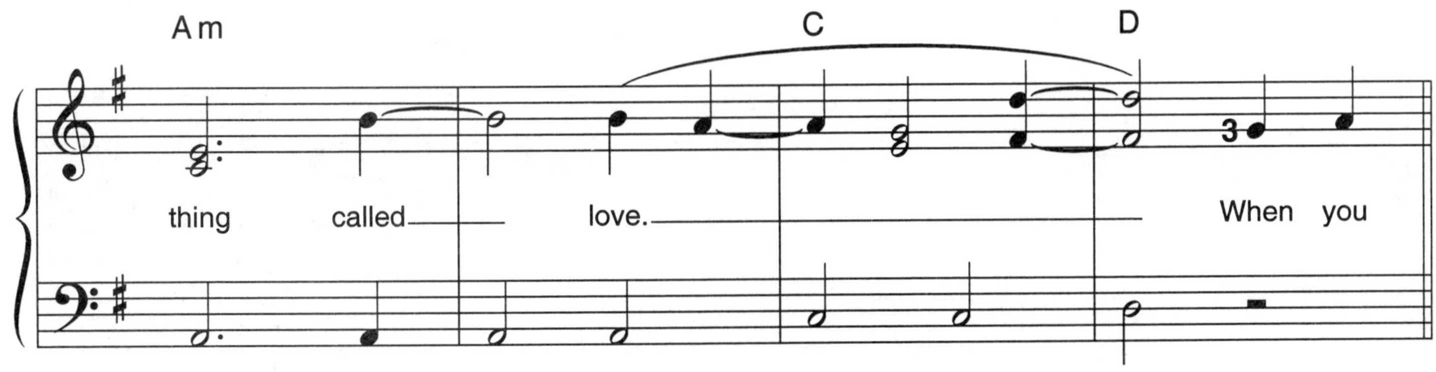
Am
C
D
thing called love. When you

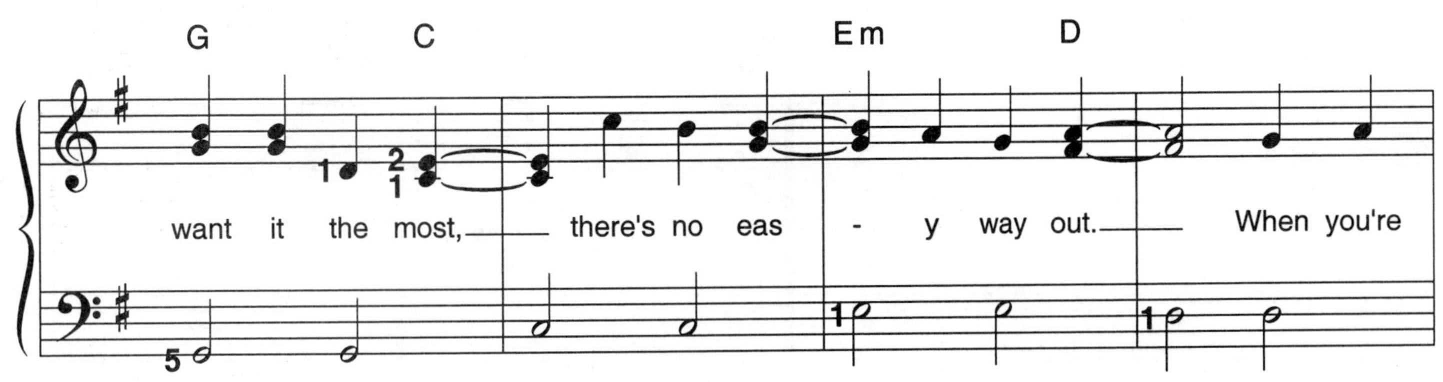
G
C
Em
D
want it the most, there's no eas - y way out. When you're

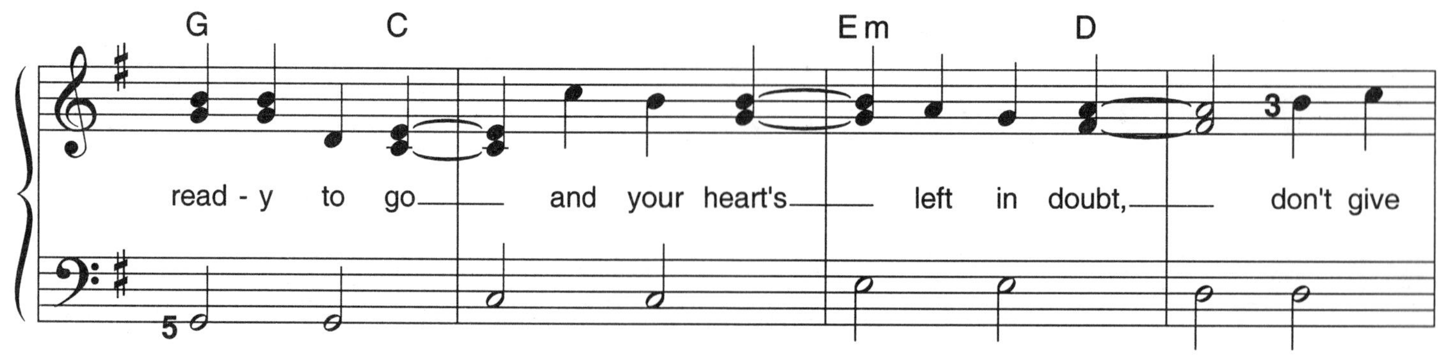
G C Em D
3
read - y to go and your heart's left in doubt, don't give
5

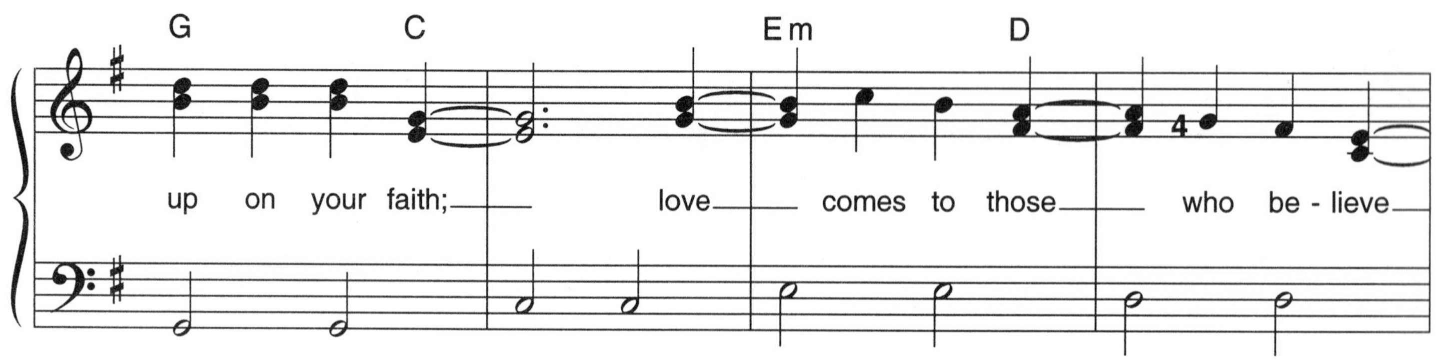
G C Em D
4
up on your faith; love comes to those who be - lieve

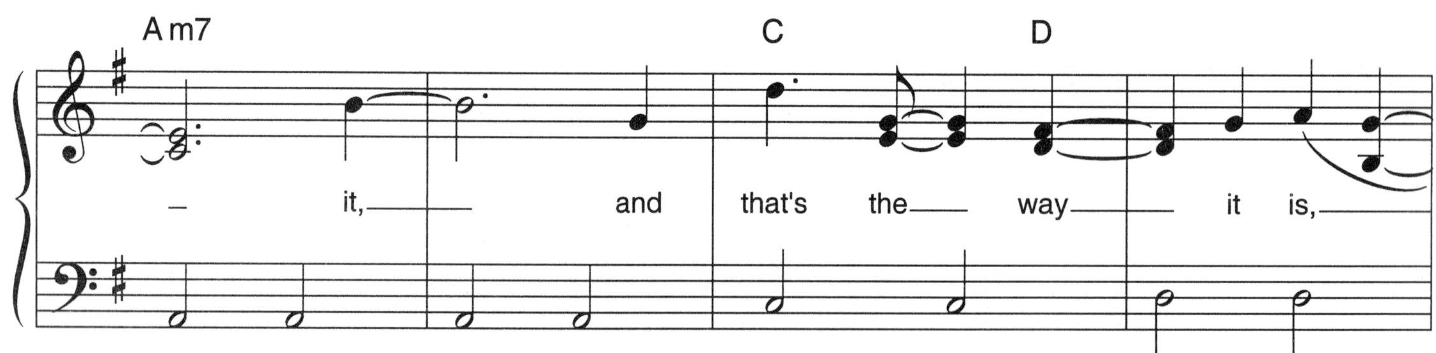
Am7 C D
it, and that's the way it is,

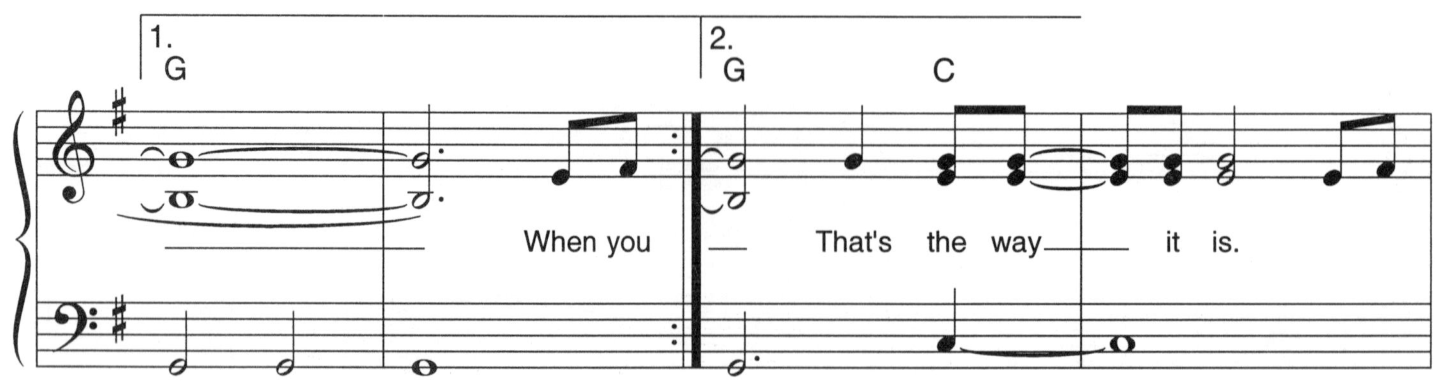
1.
G
2.
G C
When you
That's the way it is.

Em
D
Am

C
D
Gm
When life is - emp - ty, with

Gm7/F
E♭
no to - mor - row, and lon - li - ness starts to

B♭
F/A
Gm7
call, ba - by, don't wor - ry, for -

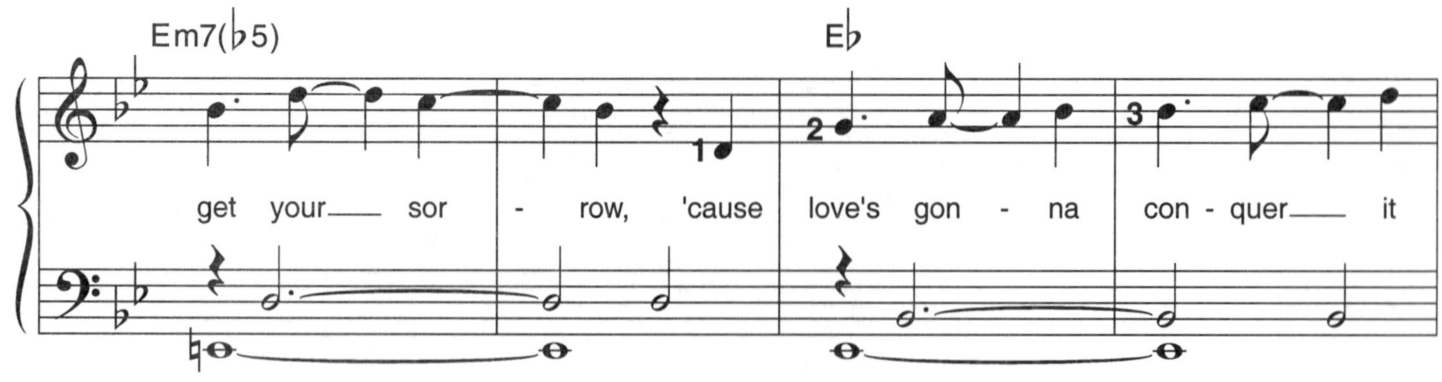
Em7(♭5)
E♭
get your sor - row, 'cause love's gon - na con - quer it

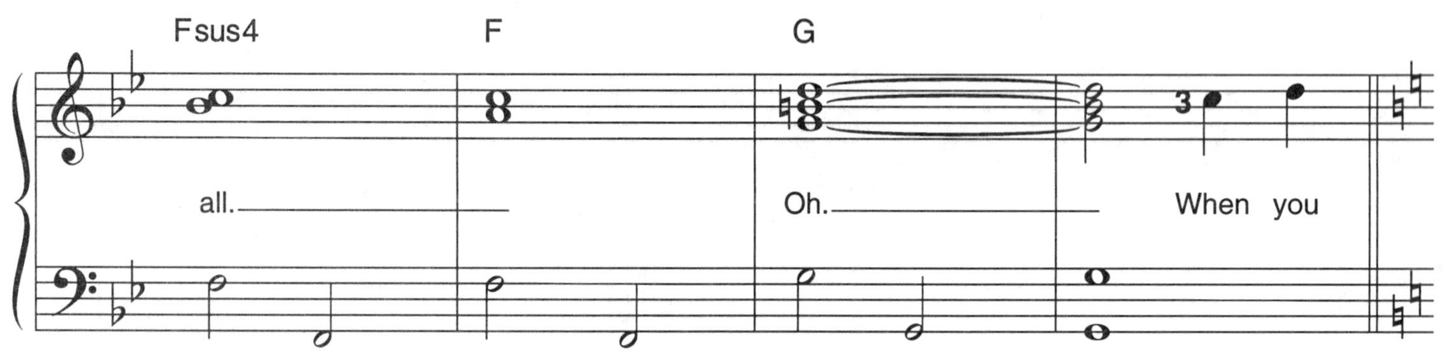
Fsus4
F
G
all. Oh. When you

C
F
Am
G
want it the most, there's no eas - y way out. When you're

C
F
Am
G
read - y to go and your heart's left in doubt, don't give

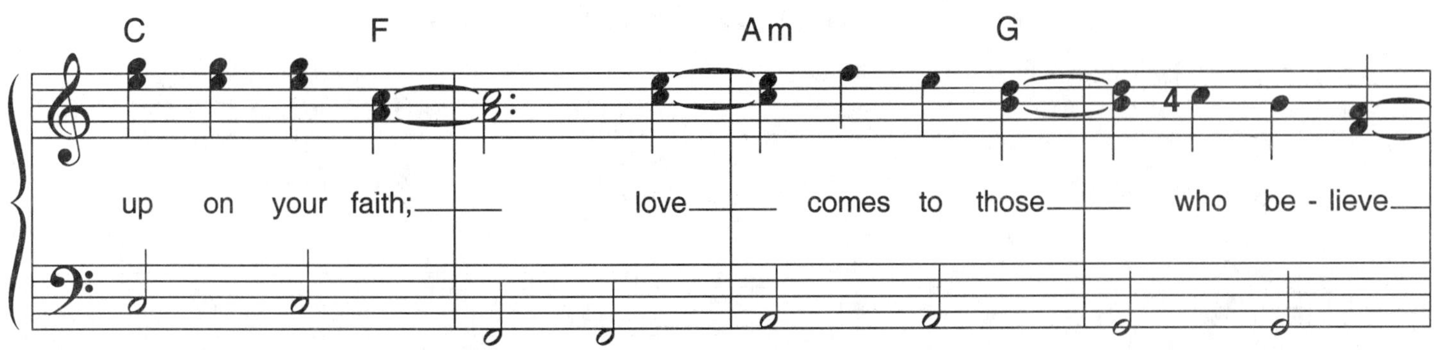

Verse 2:
When you question me for a simple answer,
I don't know what to say, no.
But it's plain to see, if you stick together,
You're gonna find the way, yeah.

I Will Remember You

From the Fox Searchlight Film *The Brothers McMullen*
Recorded by SARAH McLACHLAN

Words and Music by
SARAH McLACHLAN, SEAMUS EGAN
and DAVE MERENDA
Arranged by Richard Bradley

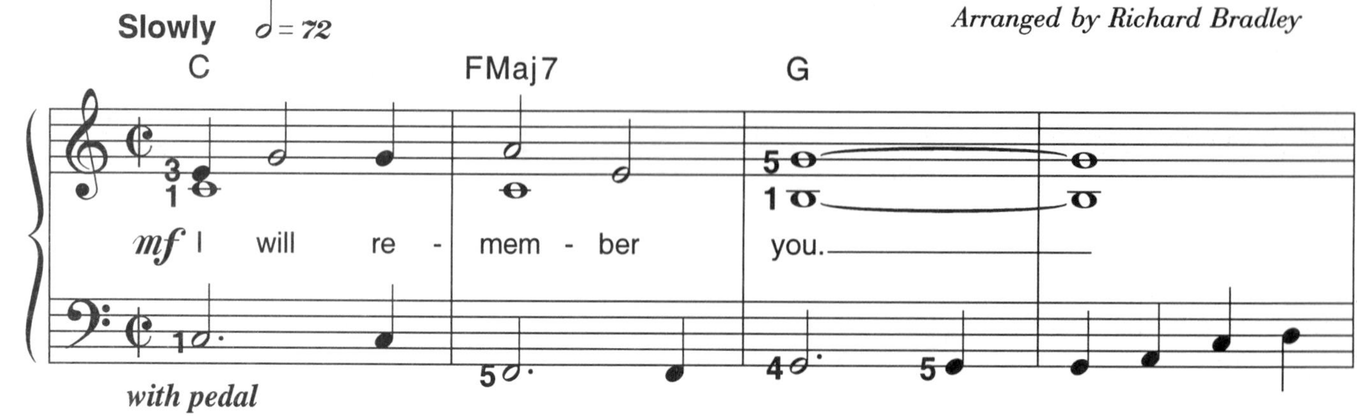

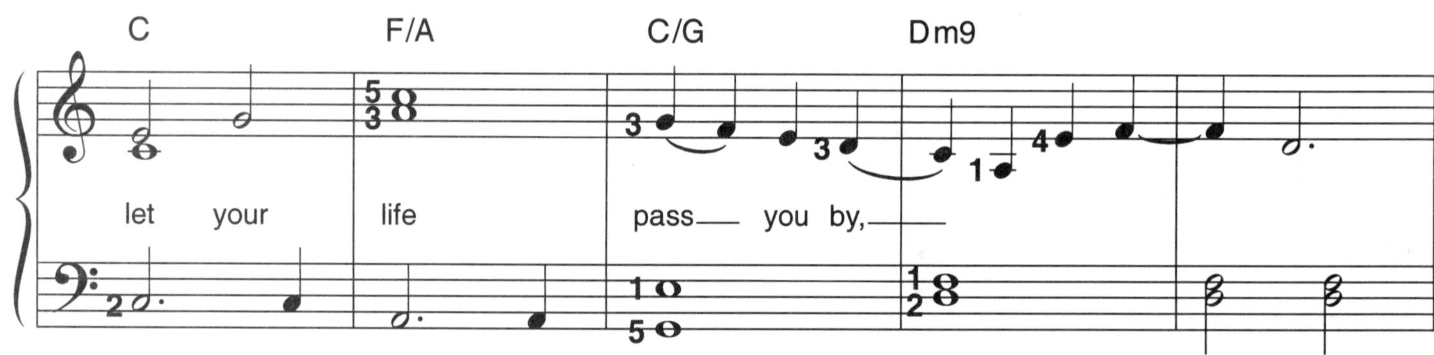

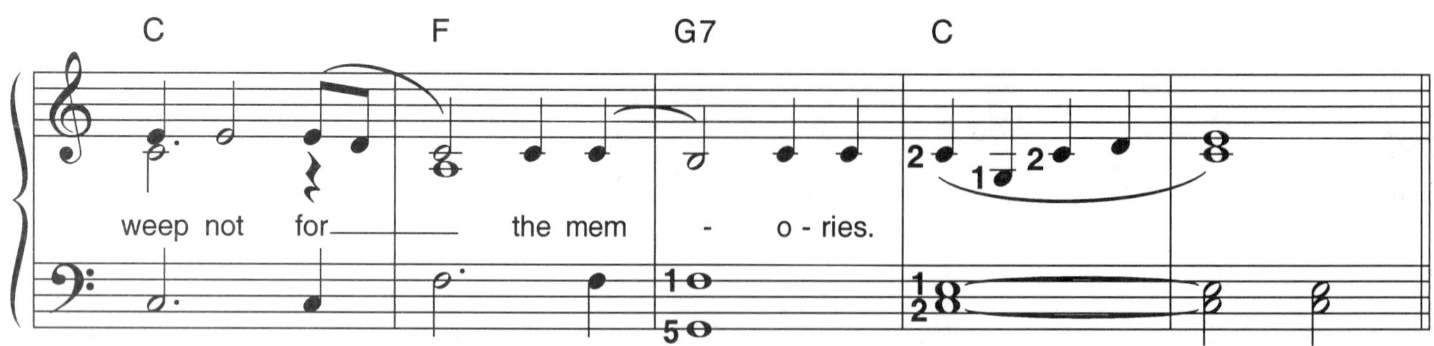

C
F
G7
I'm so tired,
I can't sleep,
C
F
G7
stand - in' on the
edge of some - thing
much too
Am
C
FMaj7
deep. It's
fun - ny how we
feel so much but we
G7
C
can - not say a
word. We are
scream - ing in - side,
F
G7
C
oh, we
can't be heard.

C
FMaj7
G
I will re - mem - ber you.
C
FMaj7
G7
Will you re - mem - ber me?
Don't
C
F/A
C/G
Dm9
let your life pass you by,
C
F
G7
To Coda
weep not for the mem - o - ries.
1.
C
FMaj7

Verse 2:
So afraid to love you,
More afraid to lose.
I'm clinging to a past
That doesn't let me choose.
Where once there was a darkness,
A deep and endless night.
You gave me everything you had,
Oh, you gave me life.
(To Chorus:)

(Optional Verse, Album version)
Remember the good times that we had,
I let them slip away from us when things got bad.
Now clearly I first saw you smiling in the sun.
I wanna feel your warmth upon me,
I wanna be the one.
(To Chorus:)

Smooth

Recorded by SANTANA featuring ROB THOMAS

Music by ITAAL SHUR
and ROB THOMAS
Lyrics by ROB THOMAS
Arranged by Richard Bradley

Dm
B♭
A7
Dm
B♭
qui-ta,
my Span-ish Har-lem Mo-na
Lis-a.

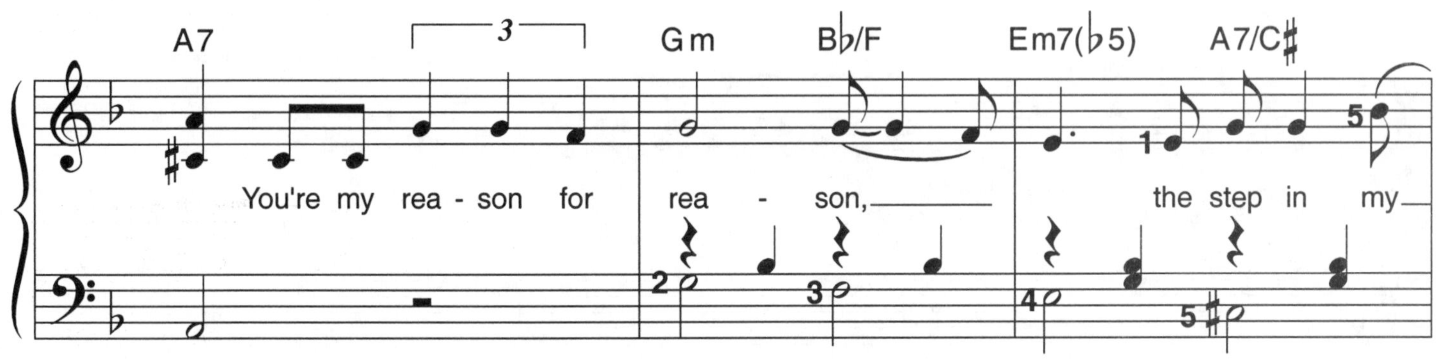
A7
3
Gm
B♭/F
Em7(♭5)
A7/C♯
You're my rea-son for
rea - son,
the step in my

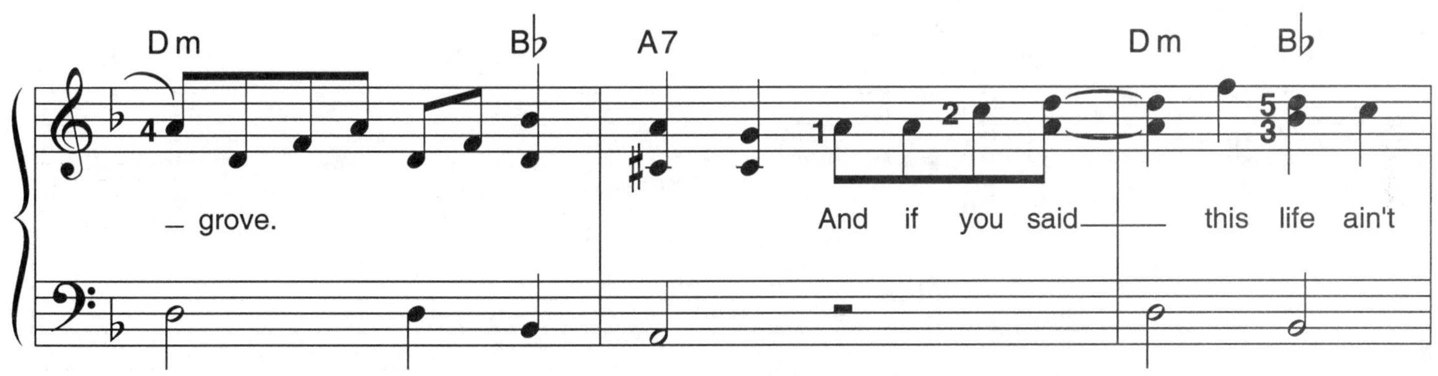
Dm
B♭
A7
Dm
B♭
grove.
And if you said
this life ain't

A7
Dm
B♭
A7
good e-nough, I would
give my world to
lift you up. I could

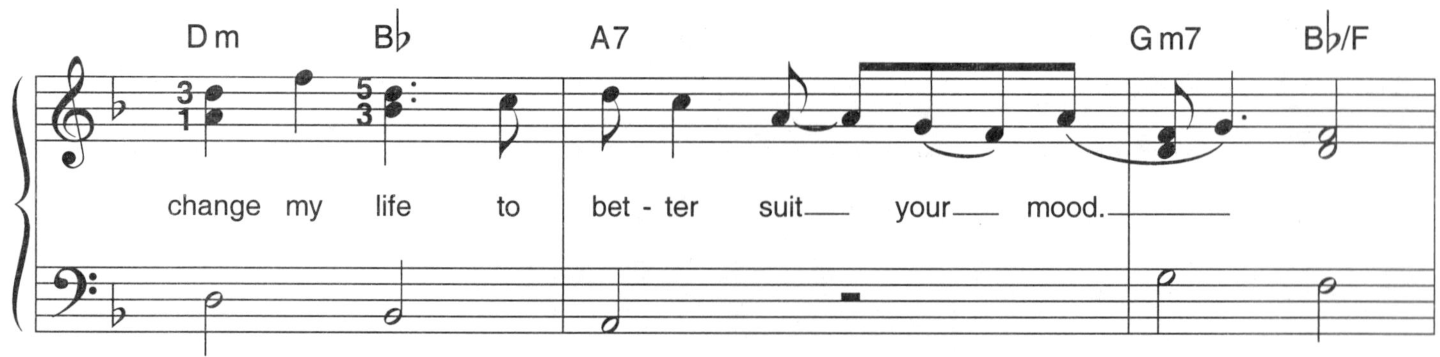
Dm
B♭
A7
Gm7
B♭/F
change my life to bet - ter suit___ your___ mood.___

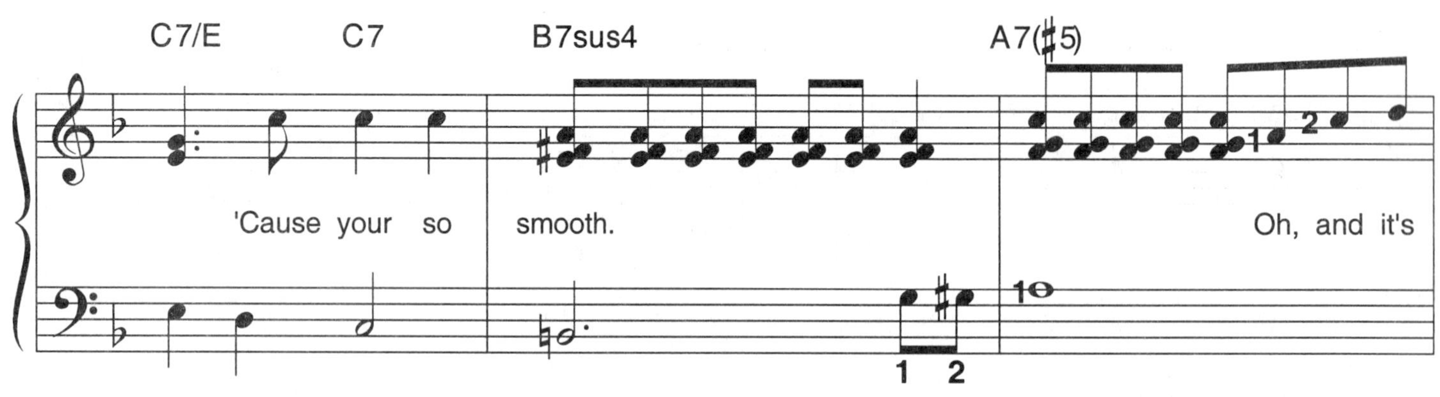
C7/E
C7
B7sus4
A7(♯5)
'Cause your so smooth. Oh, and it's

Dm
B♭
A7
Dm
B♭
just like the o - cean un - der the moon.___ Well, it's the same as the e - mo - tion that I

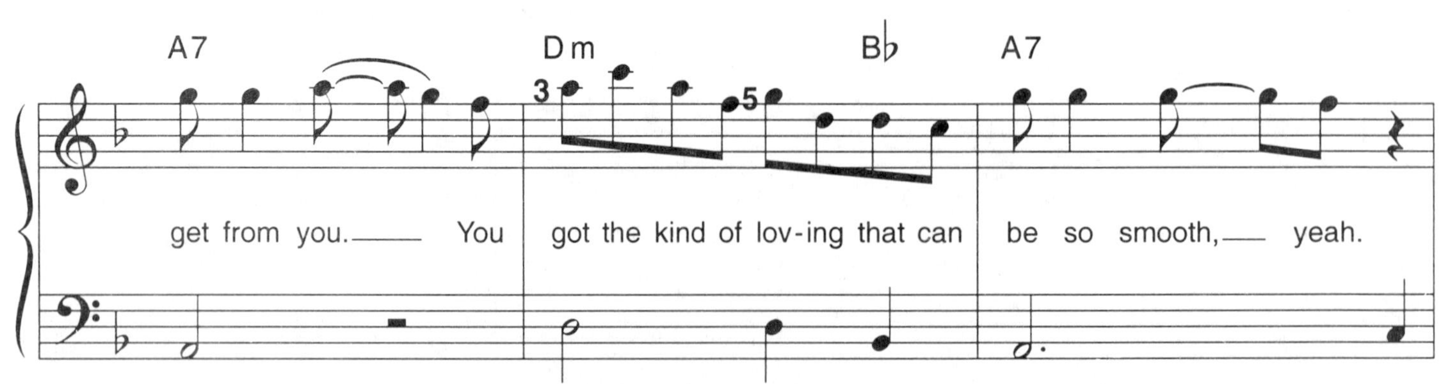
A7
Dm
B♭
A7
get from you.___ You got the kind of lov - ing that can be so smooth,___ yeah.

Verse 2:
Well, I'll tell you one thing,
If you would leave, it be a crying shame.
In every breath and every word.
I hear your name calling me out, yeah.
Well, out from the barrio,
You hear my rhythm on your radio.
You feel the tugging of the world,
So soft and slow, turning you 'round and 'round.

I Do (Cherish You)

Recorded by 98°

Words and Music by
KEITH STEGALL and DAN HILL
Arranged by Richard Bradley

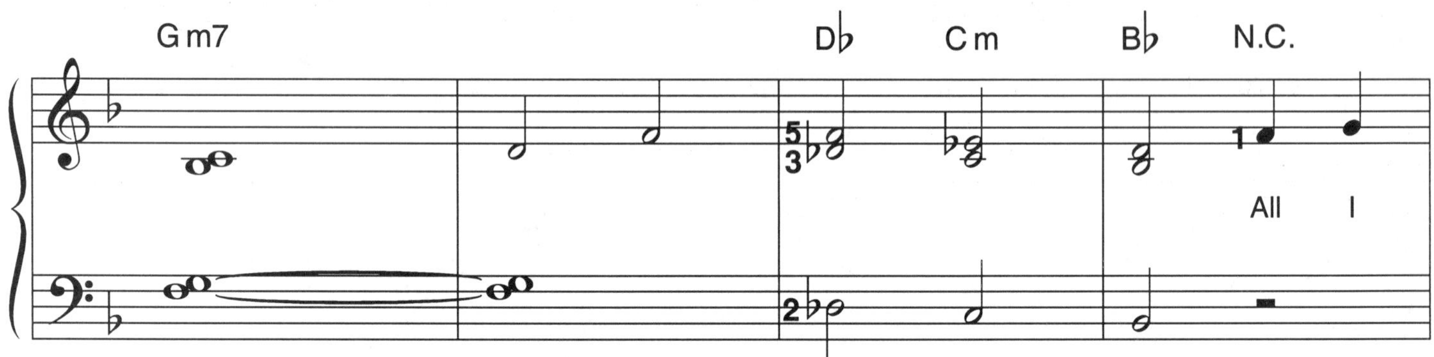

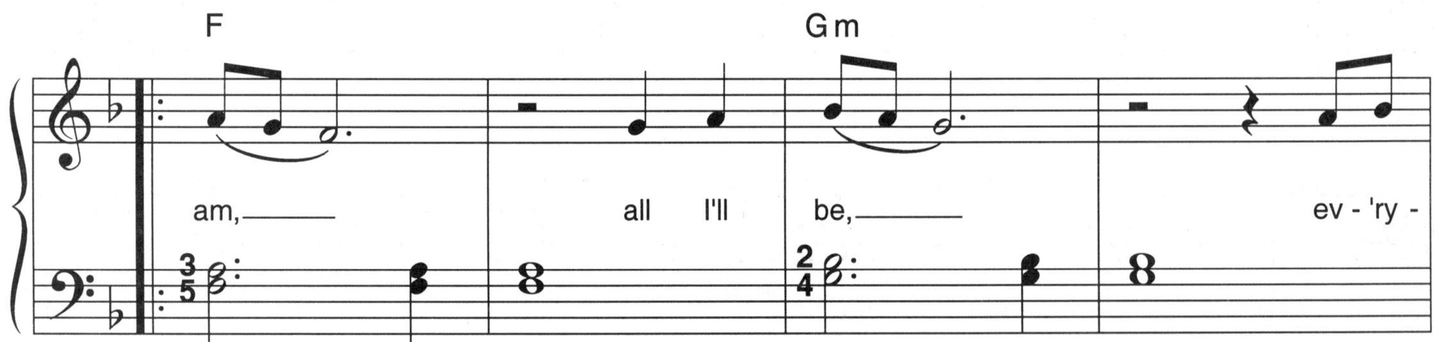

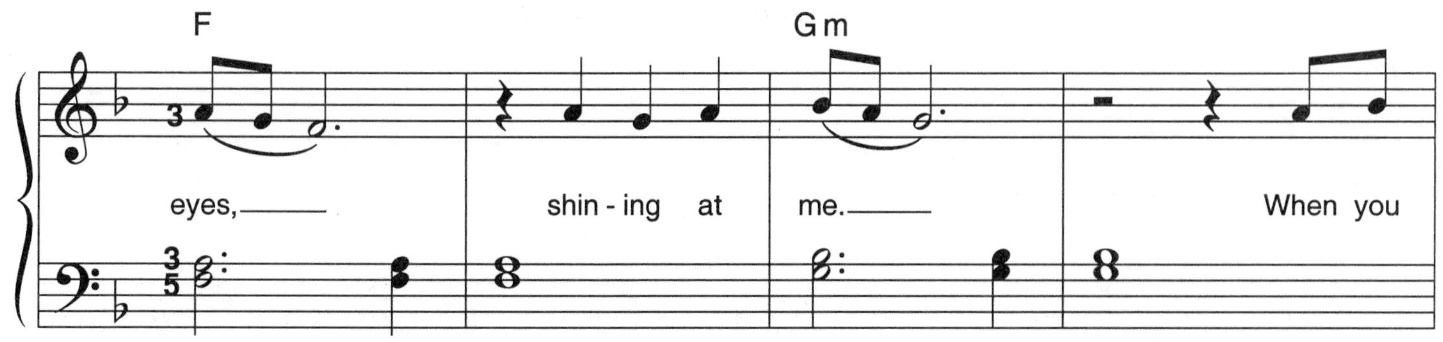
F
Gm
eyes,
shin - ing at
me.
When you

F/A
C7/G
smile, I can feel
all my
pas - sion un - fold
- ing.

B♭
F/A
Your
hand brush - es mine,
and a

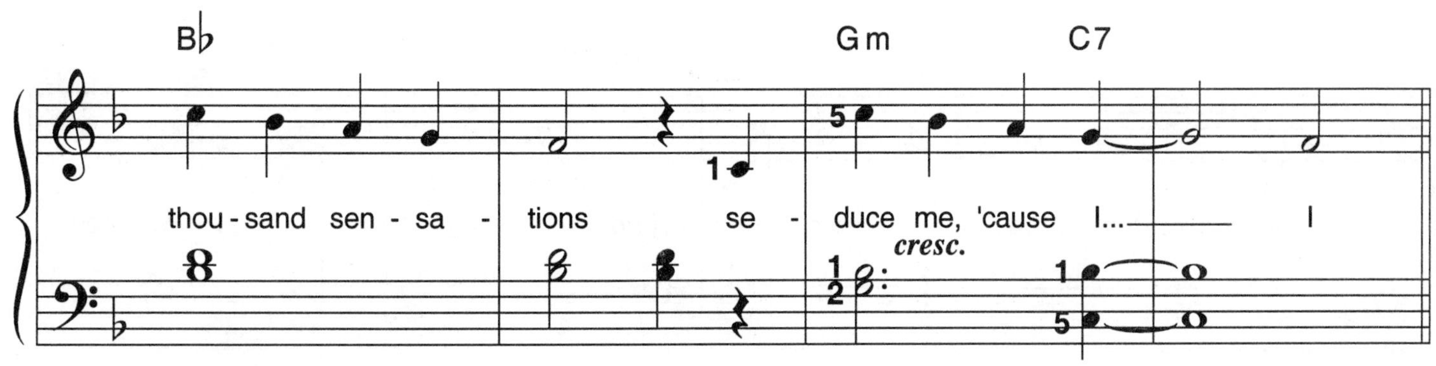
B♭
Gm
C7
thou - sand sen - sa -
tions se -
duce me, 'cause I...
I
cresc.

F2
D m7
do
cher - ish
you,
for the
mf

G m
C7
rest of my life.
You don't
have to think twice;
I

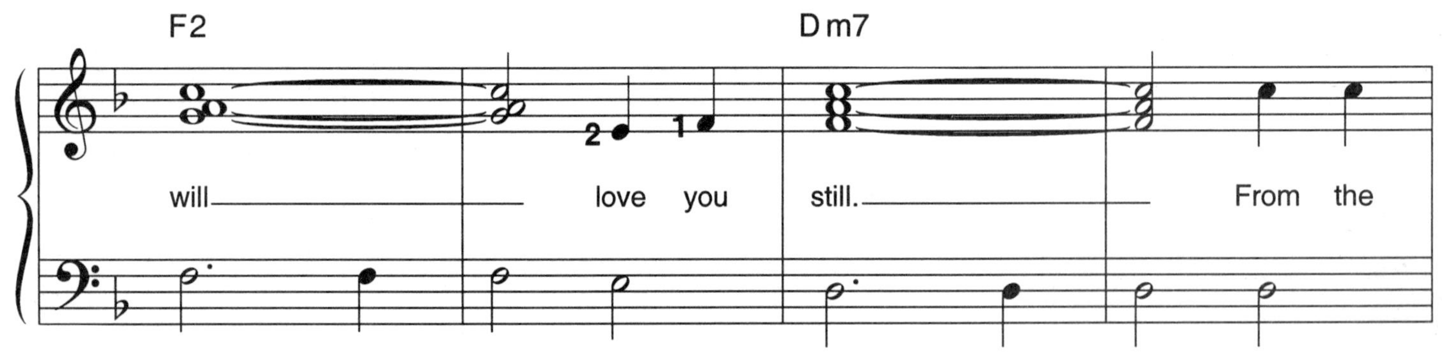
F2
D m7
will
love you
still.
From the

G m7
A7sus4
A7
depths of my soul,
it's be - yond my con - trol.
I've wait - ed

Dm
Dm7/C
Bm7(♭5)
so long to say this to you.
If you're
Gm7
1. C7
ask - ing do I love you this much,
I
F/G
F
Dm7
do.
mp
Oh, - ba -
Gm7
A♭
E♭/G
B♭/D
N.C.
by.
2. In my
2. C7
A♭Maj7
A♭7
much,
cresc.
yes, I
do.

Gm7
F♯7(♯5)
Fm7
If you're
ask - ing do I
love you this
Gm7
C/D
G2
much,
ba - by, I
do
cher - ish
f
Em7
Am
you.
From the
depths of my soul,
it's be -
B7
Em
Em7/D
yond my con - trol.
I've wait - ed
so long to
say this to you.
C♯m7(♭5)
Am7
dim. poco a poco
If you're
ask - ing do I
love you this

Verse 2:
In my world before you,
I lived outside my emotions.
Didn't know where I was going
Till that day I found you.
How you opened my life
To a new paradise.
In a world torn by change,
Still with all of my heart,
Till my dying day . . .
(To Chorus:)

Back At One

Recorded by BRIAN McKNIGHT

Words and Music by
BRIAN McKNIGHT
Arranged by Richard Bradley

Slowly ♩ = 144

C Am7

mp It's un - de - ni - a - ble that we should be to -

F

geth - er. It's un - be - liev - a - ble how I

Dm7 Em7 F G C9

used to say that I'd fall nev - er. The ba - sis is I

Am7

need to know. If you don't know just how I feel, then

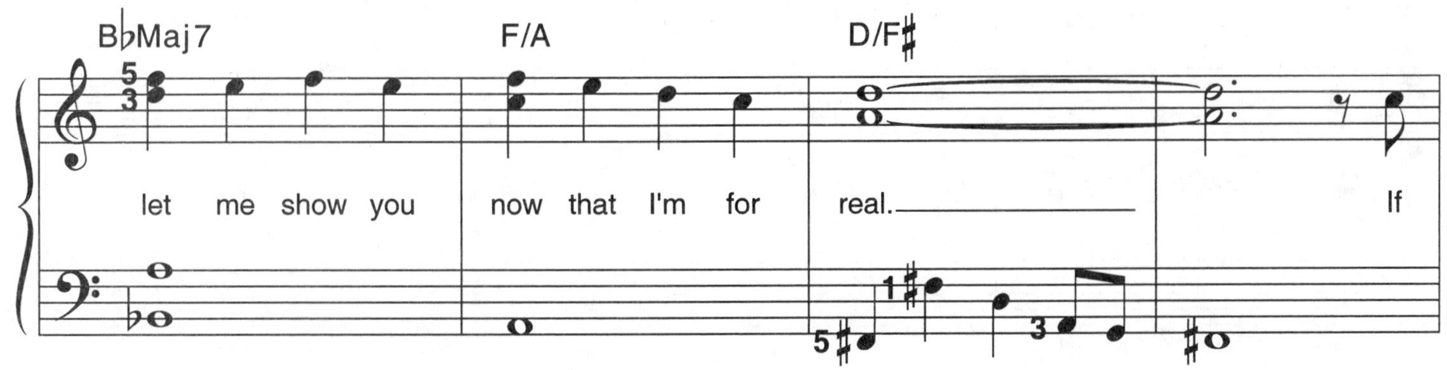

B♭Maj7
F/A
D/F♯
let me show you
now that I'm for
real.
If

B♭Maj7
F/A
Dm7/G G7
all things
in
time, time will re -
veal.
Yeah.

C
C/B
Am7
One,
you're like a
dream come true.
Two,
just wan - na

G
F
C/E
Dm7
be with you.
Three,
girl, it's
plain to see
that
you're the on - ly

Em7 F G C C/B
one for me. And four, re - peat steps one through three.
Am7 G F F/E
Five, make you fall in love with me. If ev - er I be - lieve my work is
Dm7 G9 To Coda 1. C
done, then I'll start back at one.
2. F C/E F
one.
Say fare-well to the dark of night; I see the com-ing of the sun.
C/E A
I feel like a lit - tle child whose life has just be - gun. You

Verse 2:
It's so incredible, the way things work themselves out.
And all emotional, once you know what it's all about, hey.
And undesirable, for us to be apart.
I never would have made it very far,
'Cause you know you've got the keys to my heart.
'Cause one, you're like a dream come true.

Then The Morning Comes

Recorded by SMASHMOUTH

Words and Music by
GREG CAMP
Arranged by Richard Bradley

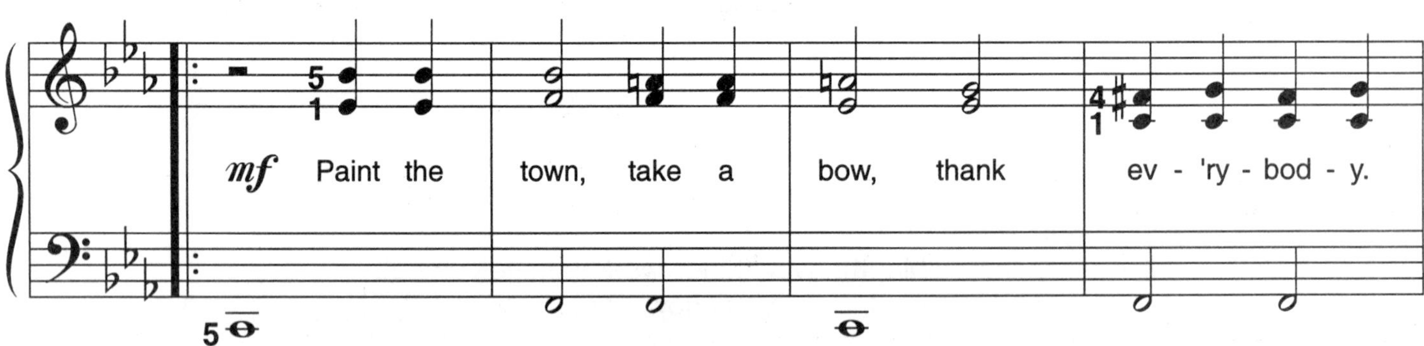

You are the few, the proud, you are the an - ti - bod - y;
mind, soul, and Zen.
And the world's a stage. And the world's a phase.
And the end is near.
To Coda
So push re - wind, just in time, thank an - y - bod - y.

N.C.
You're gon - na
do it a - gain.
The
way that you
E♭
A♭
B♭
A♭
walk,
it's just the
way that you talk,
E♭
A♭
B♭
Fm
like it
ain't no
thing.
And
ev - 'ry sin - gle
E♭
A♭
1.
G7
N.C.
day is
just a
fling,
then the morn - ing
comes.

2.
C
C/E
And when it comes, it moves so
F
C
C/E
slow, kind of like it's say - ing, "I told you
F
F/G
C
C/E
so." Look - ing back be - fore she
F
E7
Am
D
Am
goes, to - mor - row's gon - na hurt.

D
Am
D
Am
D
4
Cm
F
Cm
F
Cm
F
Cm
F
2
1 2
Cm
F
Cm
F
1
Cm
F
Cm
D.S. 𝄋 al Coda 𝄌

Verse 2:
Take your knocks, shake them off, duck everybody.
You're gonna take them again.
You are your foe, your friend,
You are the paparazzi.
You are the tragedian.

Music Of My Heart

From the Miramax Picture *Music of the Heart*
Recorded by GLORIA ESTEFAN and *NSYNC

Words and Music by
DIANE WARREN
Arranged by Richard Bradley

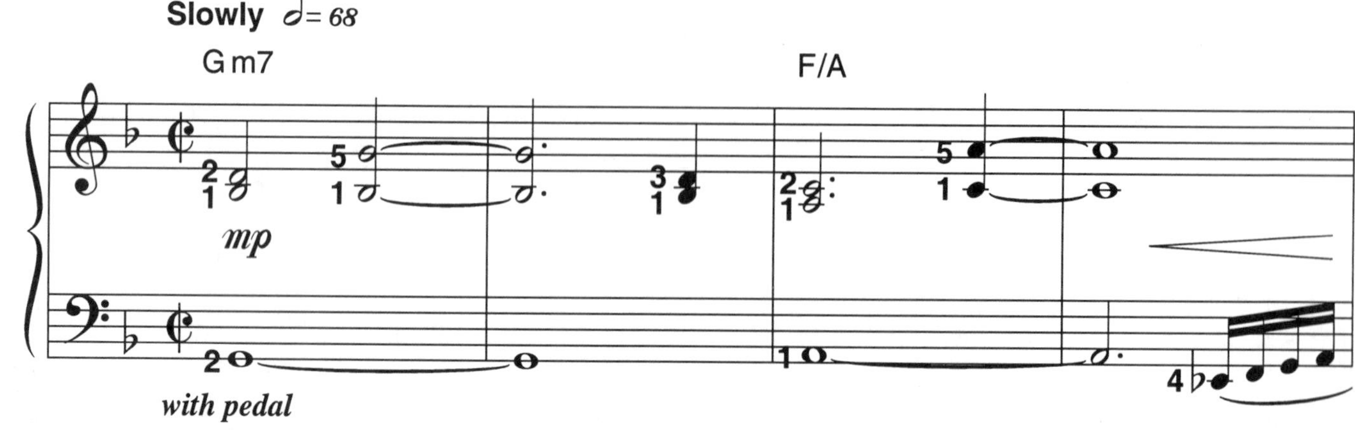

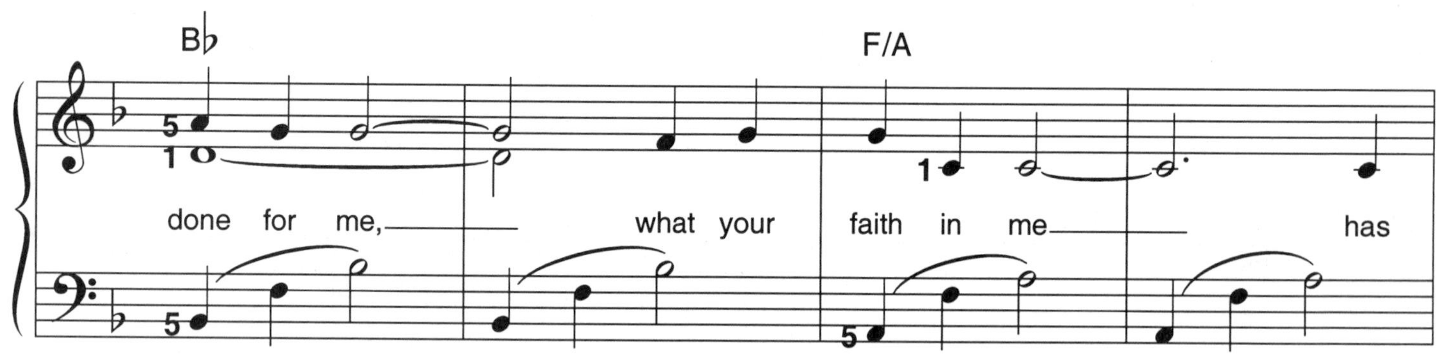

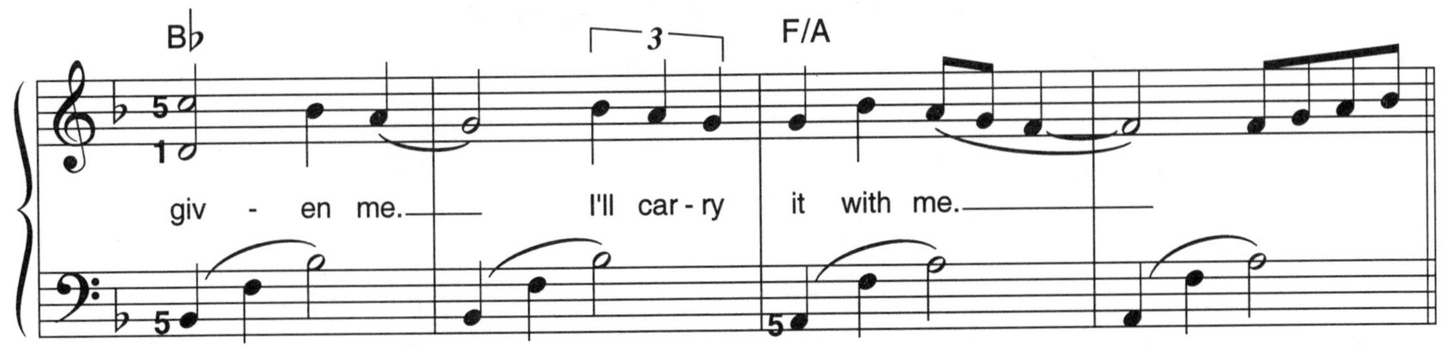
B♭
3
F/A
giv - en me.
I'll car - ry
it with me.

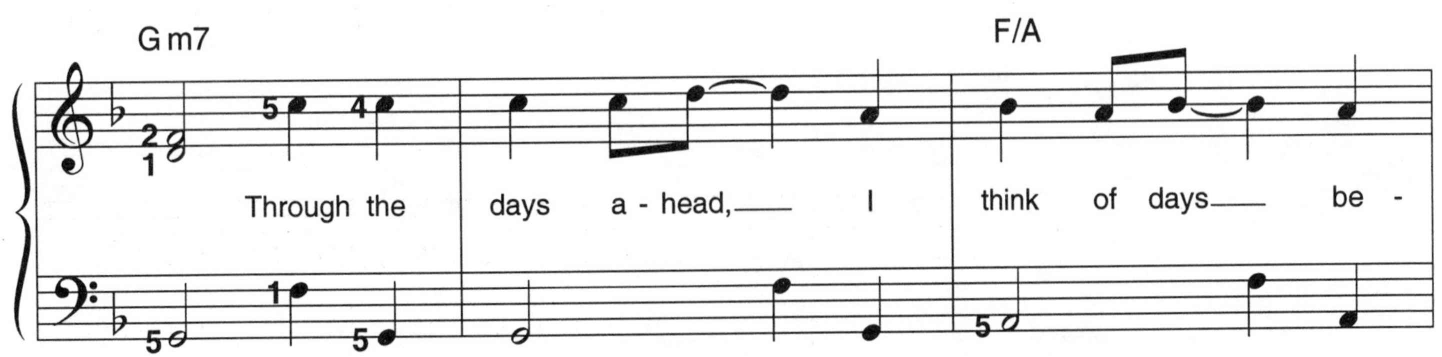
Gm7
F/A
Through the
days a - head,
I
think of days
be -

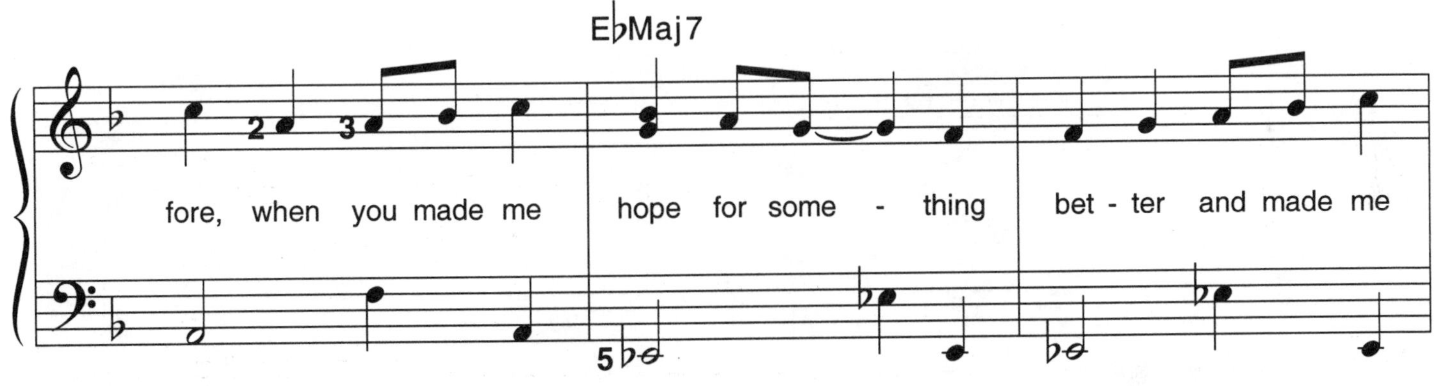
E♭Maj7
fore, when you made me
hope for some - thing
bet - ter and made me

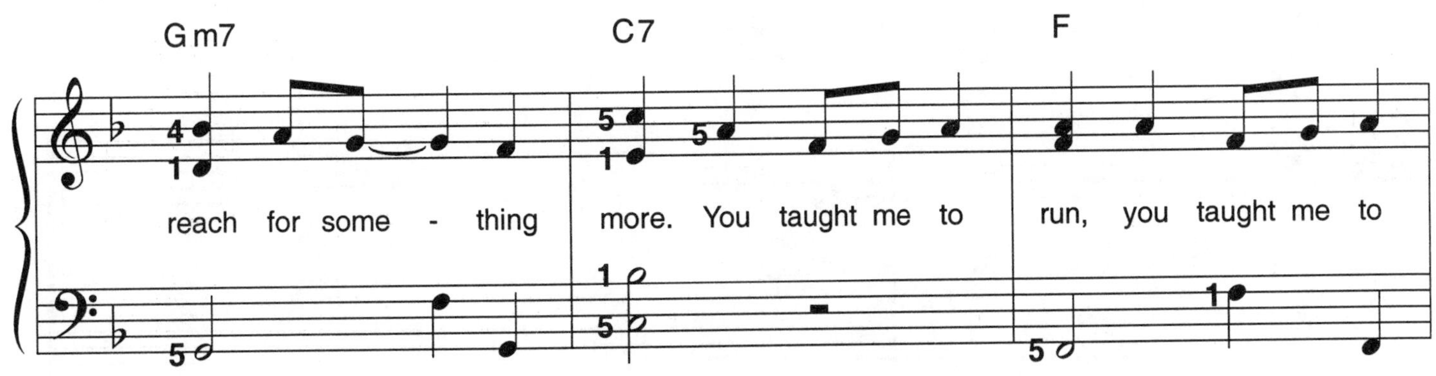
Gm7
C7
F
reach for some - thing
more. You taught me to
run, you taught me to

C/E
Gm7
fly, helped me to free the me— in-side. Helped me hear the
B♭
F/A
Gm7
mu-sic of— my heart. Helped me hear the mu-sic of— my
C7
F
C/E
heart. You o-pened my eyes, you o-pened the door to some-thing I've
E♭Maj9
1.
Gm9
nev-er-known— be-fore. And your love is the
C7
E♭9
mu-sic of my heart.

2.
Gm9
C7
B♭
C
love is the mu - sic of my heart. What you taught me, on - ly
B♭/D
C/E
your love could ev - er teach me. You got through where no one could reach
F
B♭
Gm7
me be - fore. Coz you al - ways saw in
F/A
E♭Maj9
me all the best that I could be. It was you who set me
C11
F
C/E
free. You taught me to run, you taught me to fly, helped me to

Gm7
Bb
free the me___ in-side. Helped me hear the mu-sic___ of my
F/A
Gm7
F/A
C7
D7
heart. Helped me hear the mu-sic___ of my heart. You taught me to
G
D/F#
Am7
run, you taught me to fly, helped me to free the me___ in-side.
C
G/B
Helped me hear the mu-sic___ of my heart. Helped me hear the
Am7
D7
G
mu-sic___ of my heart. You o-pened my eyes, you o-pened the

Verse 2:
You were the one always on my side,
Always standing by, seeing me through.
You were the song that always made me sing.
I'm singing this for you.
Everywhere I go, I think of where I've been
And of the one who knew me better
Than anyone ever will again.

I Want It That Way

Recorded by BACKSTREET BOYS

Words and Music by
MAX MARTIN and
ANDREAS CARLSSON
Arranged by Richard Bradley

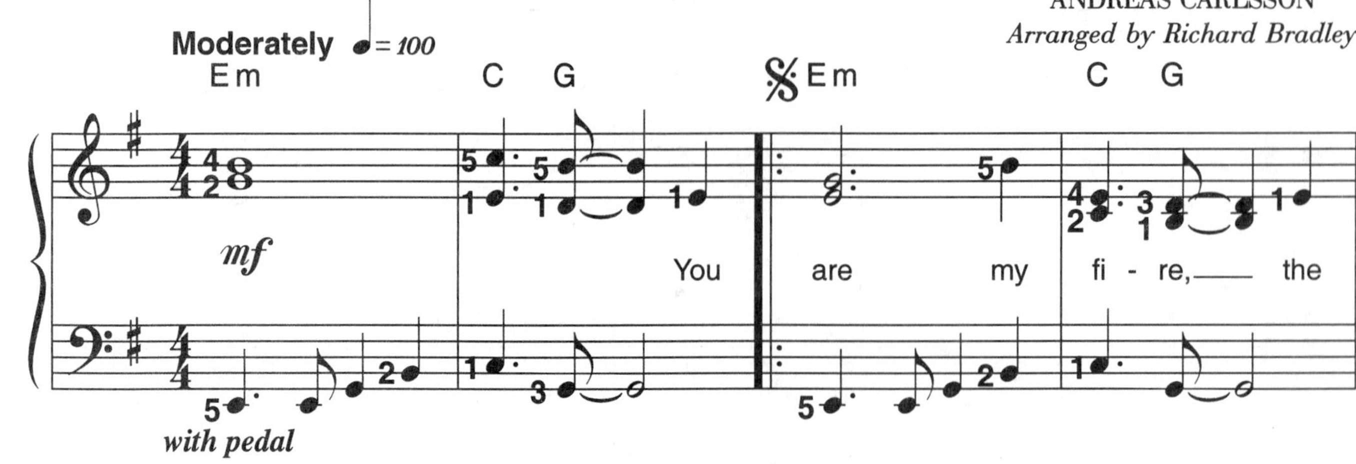

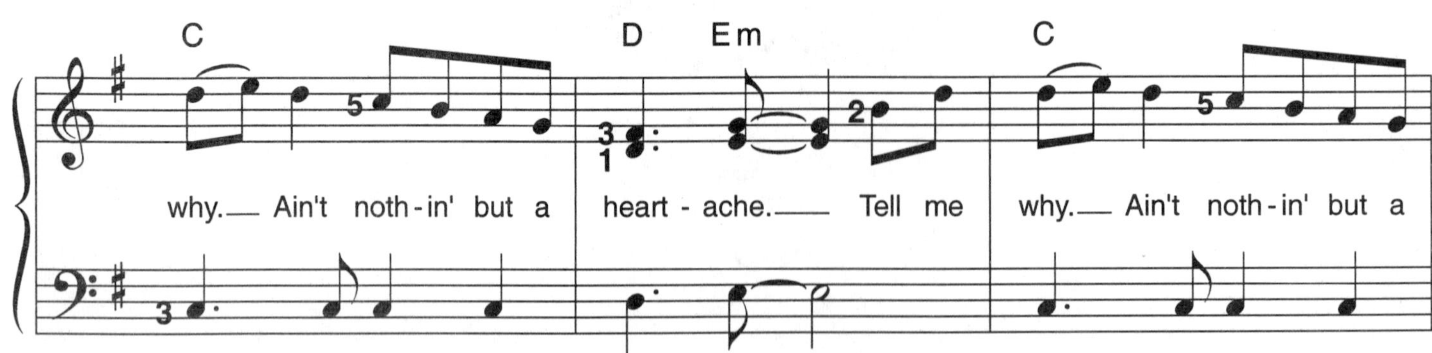

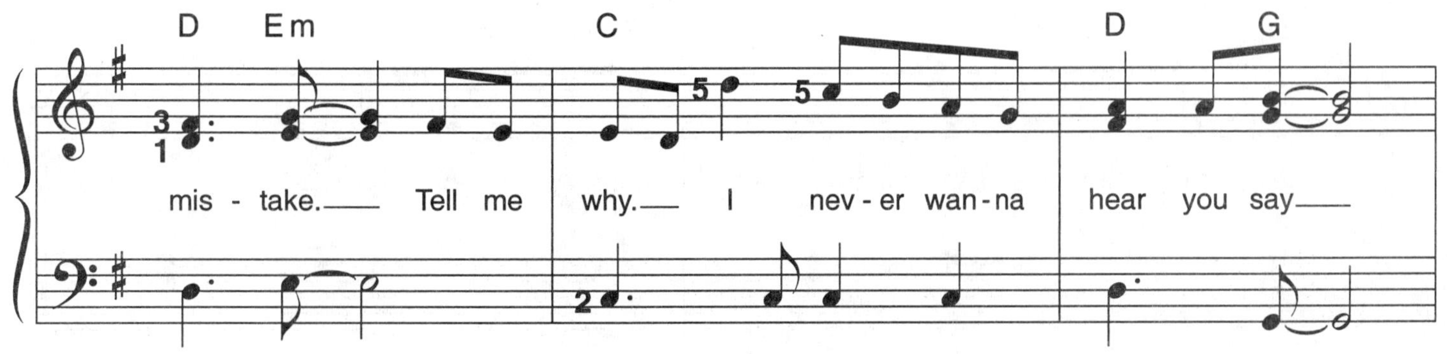
D Em C D G
mis - take. Tell me why. I nev - er wan - na hear you say

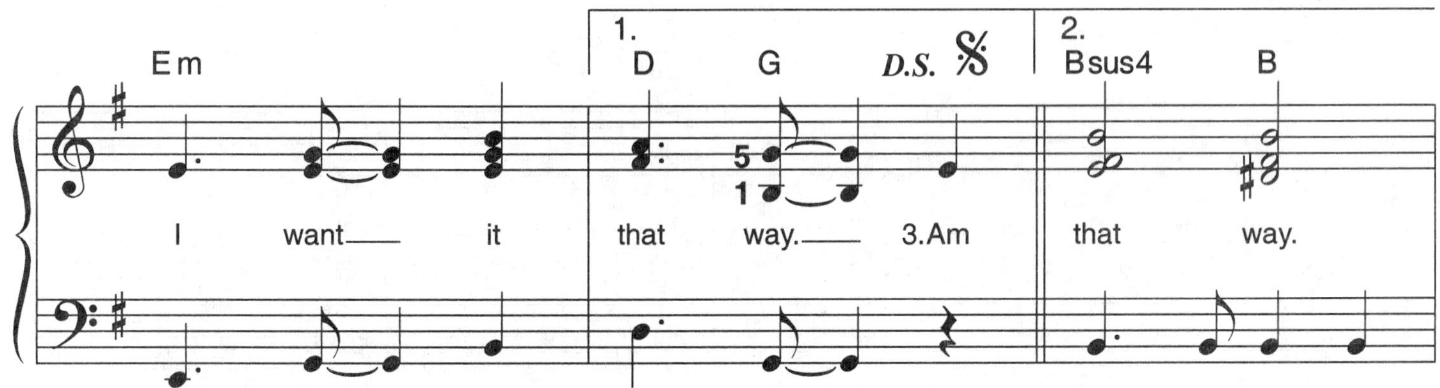
Em 1. D G D.S. 2. Bsus4 B
I want it that way. 3.Am that way.

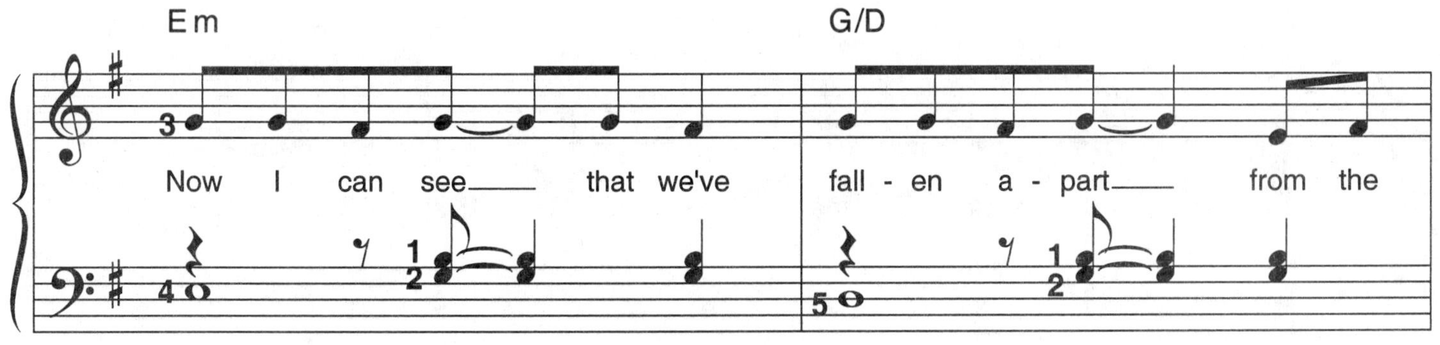
Em G/D
Now I can see that we've fall - en a - part from the

C Am D
way that it used to be, yeah. No

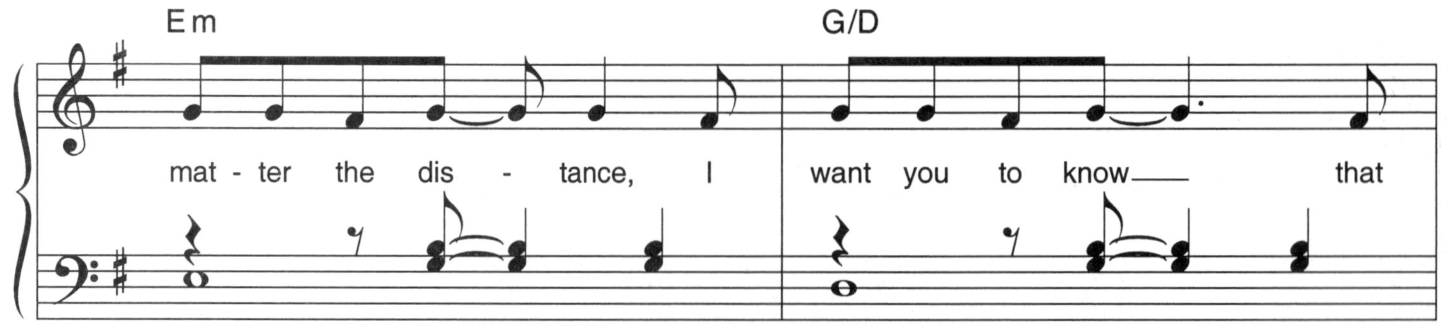
Em
G/D
mat - ter the dis - tance, I
want you to know that

C
Dsus4
D
C
5
1
3
deep down in - side of
me you
are my

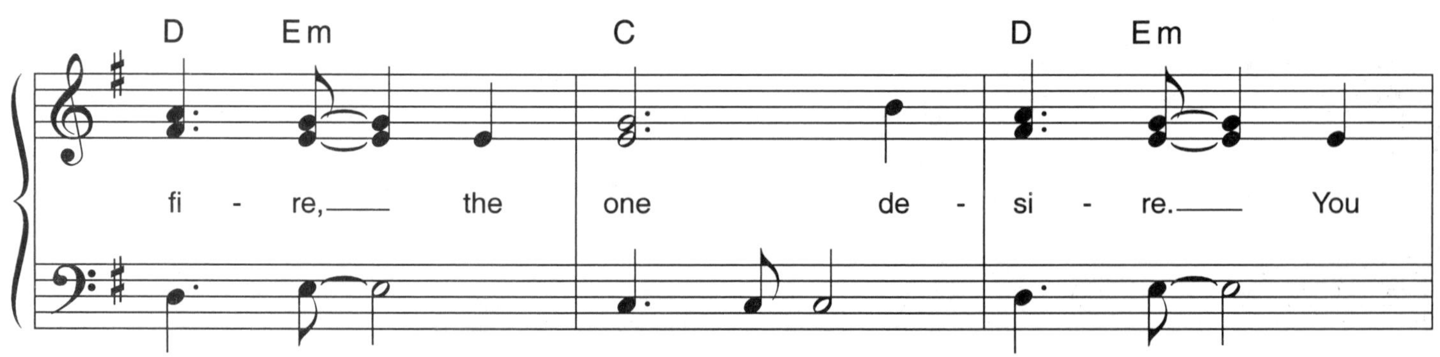
D
Em
C
D
Em
fi - re, the
one de -
si - re. You

C
D
G
Em
5
2
1
8
are, you are, you
are, you are.

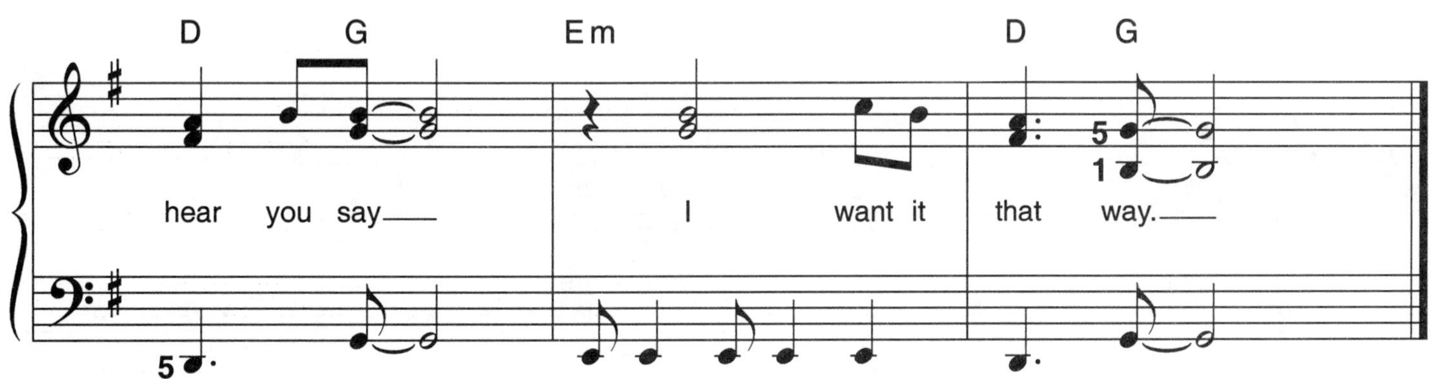

Verse 2:
But we are two worlds apart.
Can't reach to your heart
When you say
I want it that way.

Verse 3:
Am I your fire, your one desire?
Yes, I know it's too late,
But I want it that way.

From This Moment On

Recorded by SHANIA TWAIN

Words and Music by
SHANIA TWAIN and R.J. LANGE
Arranged by Richard Bradley

Slowly 𝅗𝅥 = 72

F/C Bb/D C/E F C7

mf

From this

with pedal

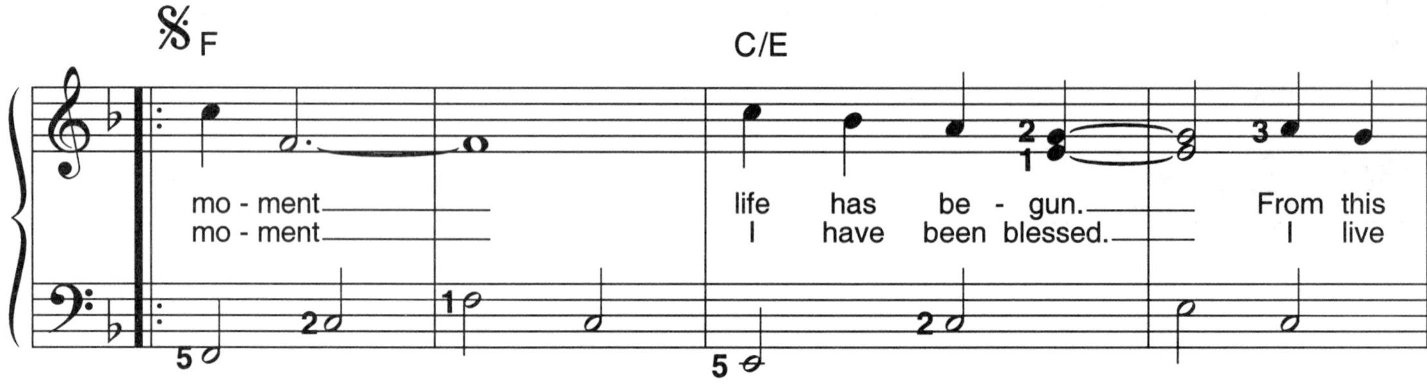

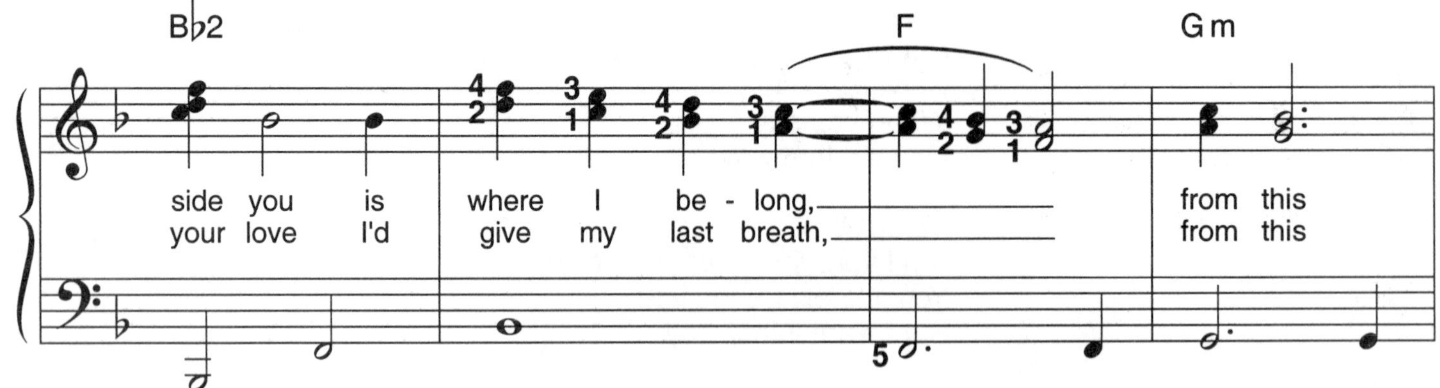

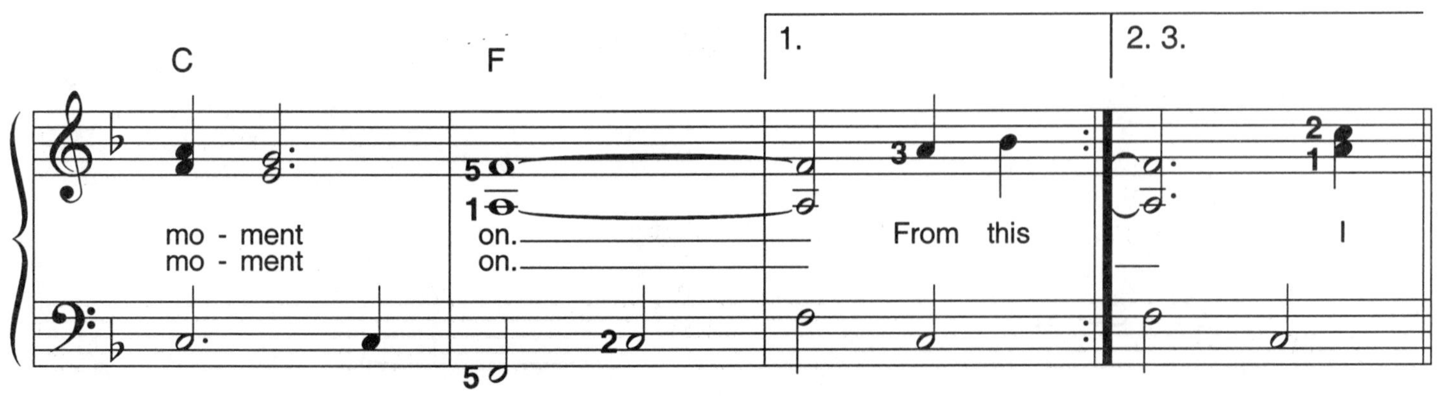
C
F
1.
2. 3.
mo - ment
mo - ment
on.
on.
From this
I

F
B♭2
B♭
give my hand to
you with all my
heart.
Can't

C
F
wait to live my
life with you, can't
wait to start.

B♭2
B♭
You and I will
nev - er be a -
part.
My

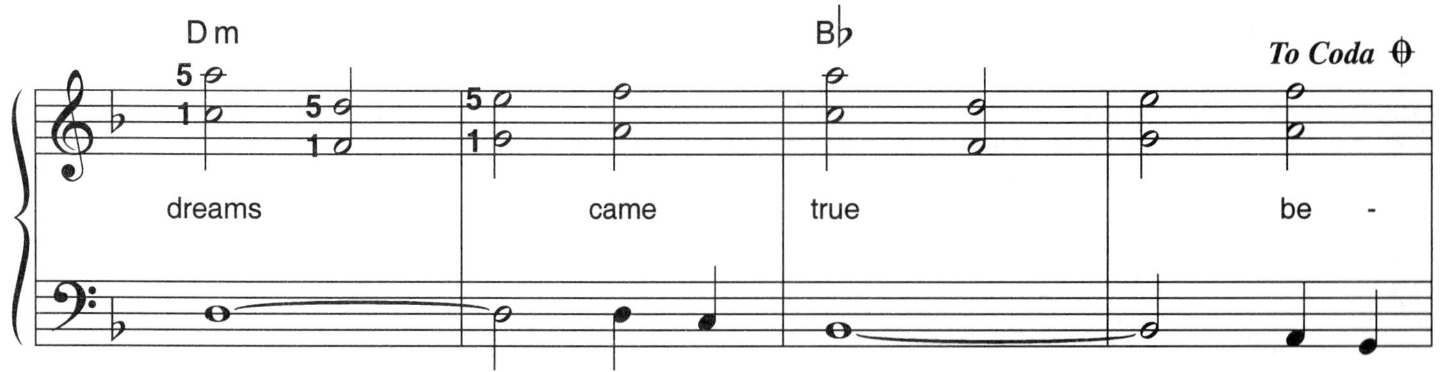
Dm
B♭
To Coda
dreams
came
true
be -

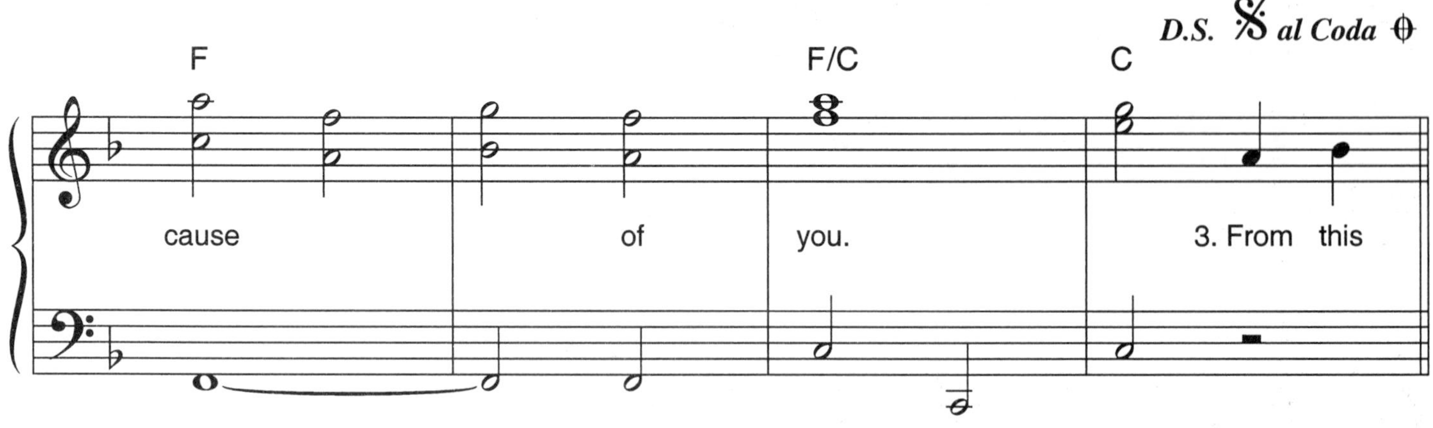
D.S. al Coda
F
F/C
C
cause
of
you.
3. From this

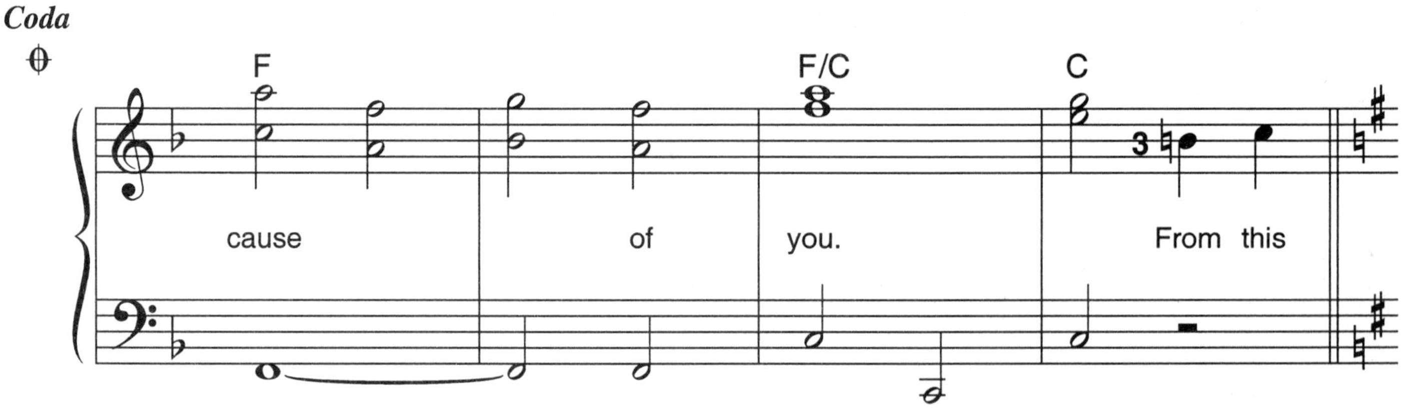
Coda
F
F/C
C
cause
of
you.
From this

G
D/F♯
mo - ment,
as
long as I live,
I will

Verse 3:
From this moment, as long as I live,
I will love you, I promise you this.
There is nothing I wouldn't give,
From this moment on.

Chorus 2:
You're the reason I believe in love.
And you're the answer to my prayers from up above.
All we need is just the two of us.
My dreams came true because of you.

. . . Baby One More Time

Recorded by BRITNEY SPEARS

Words and Music by
MAX MARTIN
Arranged by Richard Bradley

E♭
Fm
G
Cm
And
now you're out of
sight, yeah.

Cm
G7/B
G7
Show me
how you want it
to be.
Tell me,

E♭
Fm
G
Cm
ba - by,
'cause I need to
know now.
Oh, be - cause

Cm
G7/B
G7
my lone - li -
ness is
kill - ing me,
and I,

E♭
Fm
Gsus4
G
must con - fess I still be - lieve (still be - lieve)
Cm
G7/B
A♭
B♭
that when I'm not with you I lose my mind. Give me a sign.
E♭
1. 3.
Fm
G
Cm
Fine
Hit me, ba - by, one more time.
2.
Fm7
G
Cm
N.C.
Hit me, ba - by, one more time. Oh, ba - by, ba - by.
Oh, ba - by, ba - by.

Cm
Oh, ba - by, ba - by, how
G7/B
E♭
was I sup - posed to know?
Fm
Gsus4
G
A♭Maj7
Oh, pret - ty ba - by, I
B♭
Fm7
should - n't have let you go.
A♭
B♭
Cm
I must con - fess that my lone - li - ness

Verse 2:
Oh, baby, baby, the reason I breathe is you.
Boy, you've got me blinded.
Oh, pretty baby, there's nothing that I wouldn't do.
It's not the way I planned it.

(God Must Have Spent) A Little More Time On You

Recorded by *NSYNC

Words and Music by
CARL STURKEN and EVAN ROGERS
Arranged by Richard Bradley

E♭
B♭
Why do I feel like I'm los - ing con - trol? Nev - er
E♭
B♭
thought that love could feel like this. And you
E♭
B♭
changed my world with just one kiss.
E♭
D
How can it be that right here with me there's an
E♭
Fsus4
F
an - gel? It's a mir - a - cle. Your

Chorus:
B♭
E♭
F
G m7
mf love is like a riv - er, peace - ful and deep. Your
soul is like a se - cret that I could nev - er keep.
When I look in - to your eyes I know that it's true,
A♭
B♭/D
God must have spent a lit - tle more time on you.
1

B♭/D
E♭
F
Gm7
2. 3.
To Coda Φ
On you, on you, on you,
you.
B♭/D
E♭
F
B♭/D
On you, on you, on you,
you.
B♭/D
E♭
F
Gm7
On you, on you, on you,
you.
D.S. % al Coda Φ
B♭/D
E♭
F
B♭/D
On you, on you, on you,
you.
Nev-er

Verse 2:
In all of creation,
All things great and small,
You are the one that surpasses them all.
More precious than any diamond or pearl;
They broke the mold when you came in this world.
And I'm trying hard to figure it out,
Just how I ever did without the warmth of your smile.
The heart of a child that's deep inside,
Leaves me purified.
(Chorus:)

To Love You More

Recorded by CELINE DION

Words and Music by
JUNIOR MILES and DAVID FOSTER
Arranged by Richard Bradley

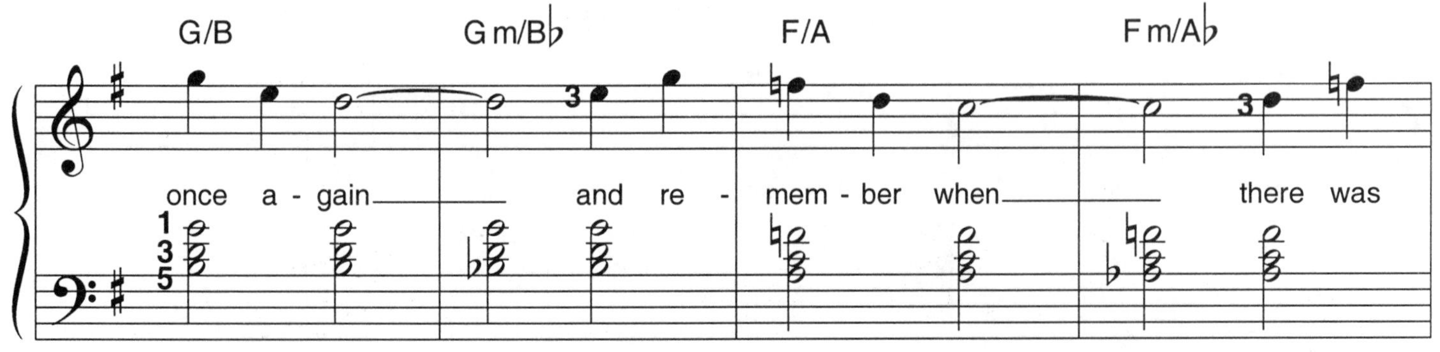
G/B
Gm/B♭
F/A
Fm/A♭
once a - gain and re - mem - ber when there was

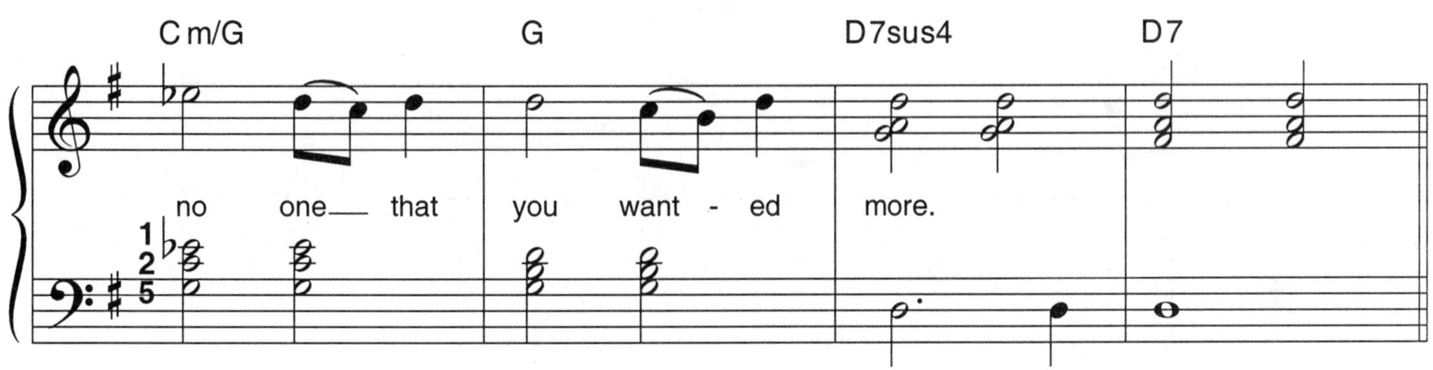
Cm/G
G
D7sus4
D7
no one that you want - ed more.

G
D/F♯
Don't go, you know you will break my heart.

Em
C/E
C/G
D7/C
She won't love you like I will. I'm the

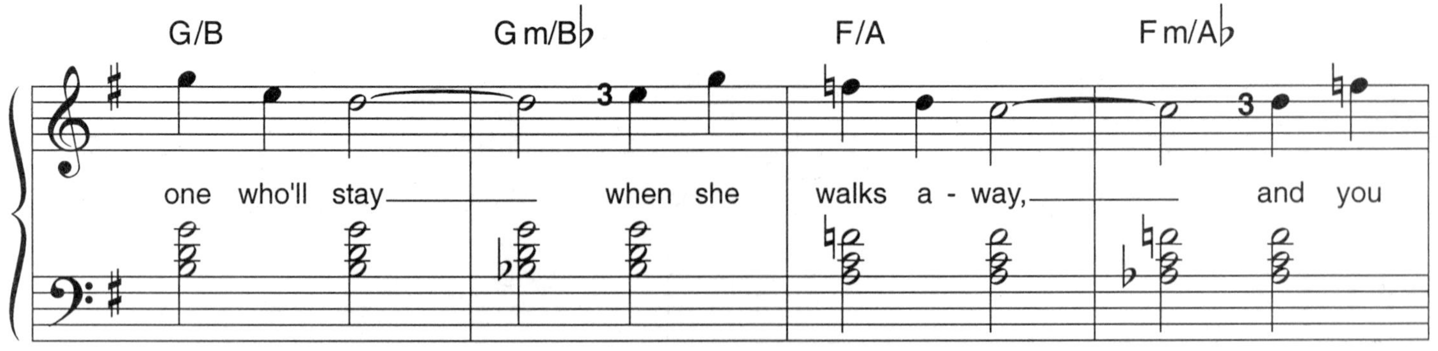
G/B
Gm/B♭
F/A
Fm/A♭
one who'll stay when she walks a - way, and you

Cm/G
G
Dsus4
D
N.C.
know I'll be stand - ing here still. I'll be

G
D
Em
Bm
wait - ing for you, here in - side my heart. I'm the

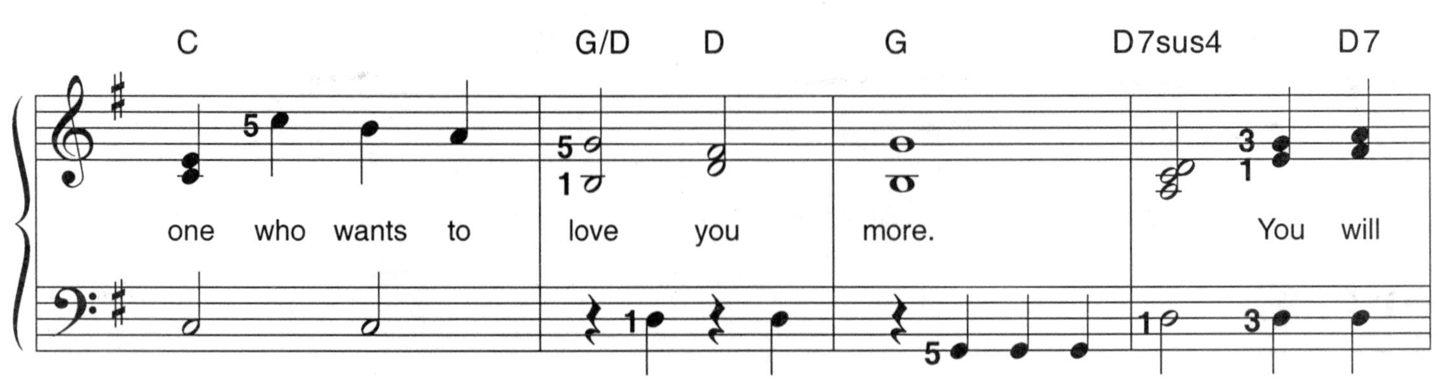
C
G/D
D
G
D7sus4
D7
one who wants to love you more. You will

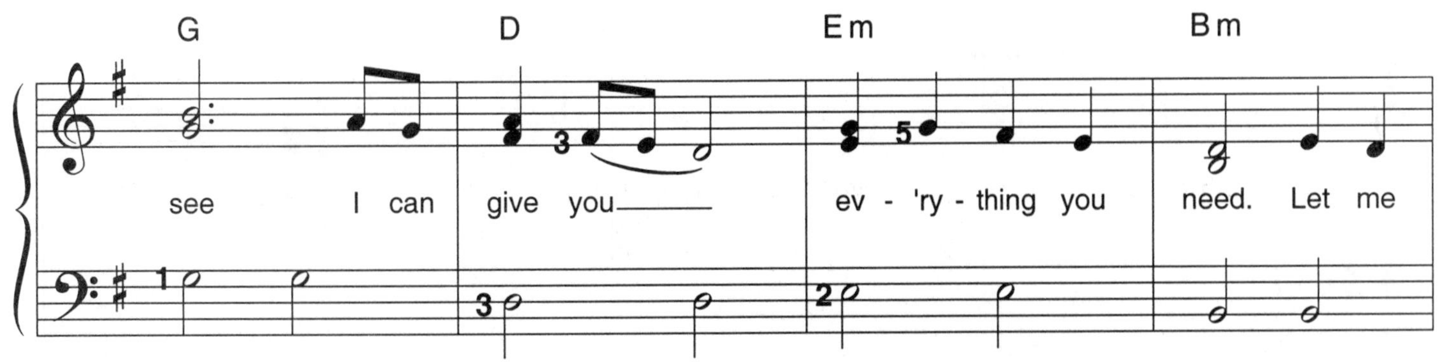
G
D
Em
Bm
see I can give you
ev - 'ry - thing you
need. Let me

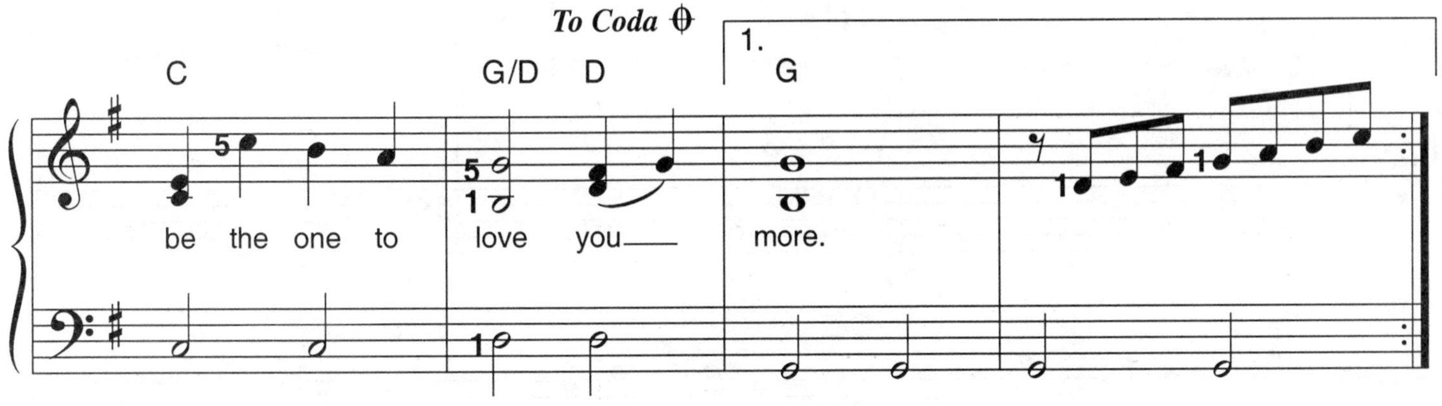
To Coda
1.
C
G/D D
G
be the one to
love you
more.

2.
G
E♭
more.
And
some way

Cm
G
all the love that we
had can be
saved.

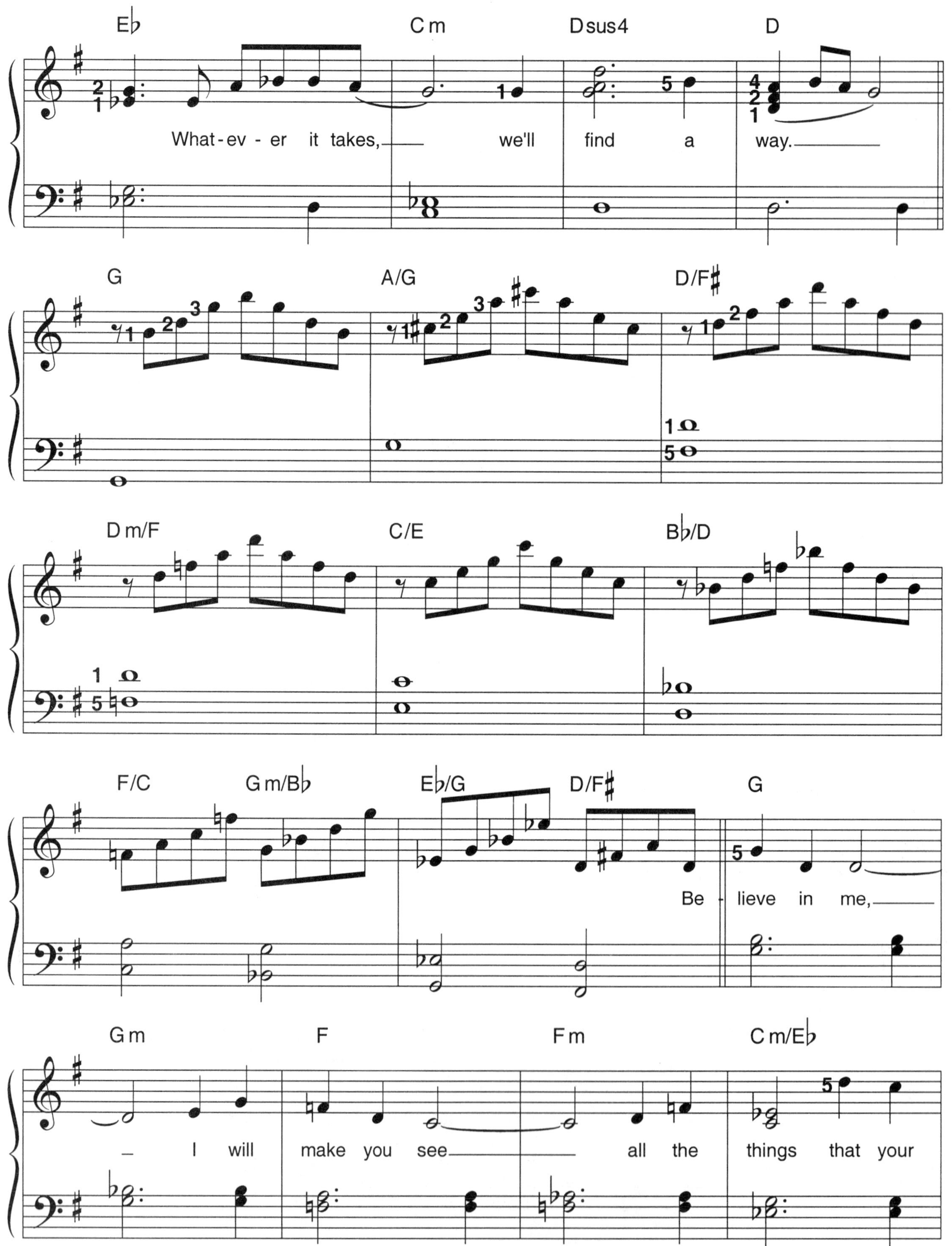

E♭
Cm
Dsus4
D
What-ev - er it takes,
we'll
find
a
way.
G
A/G
D/F♯
Dm/F
C/E
B♭/D
F/C
Gm/B♭
E♭/G
D/F♯
G
Be - lieve in me,
Gm
F
Fm
Cm/E♭
I will
make you see
all the
things that your

Verse 2:
See me as if you never knew.
Hold me so you can't let go.
Just believe in me,
I will make you see all the things
That your heart needs to know.

Over The Rainbow

When this standard from *The Wizard of Oz* won the Best Song Oscar in 1939, its singer, Judy Garland, won a special Oscar for her outstanding performance as a screen juvenile.

Lyric by E.Y. HARBURG
Music by HAROLD ARLEN
Arranged by Richard Bradley

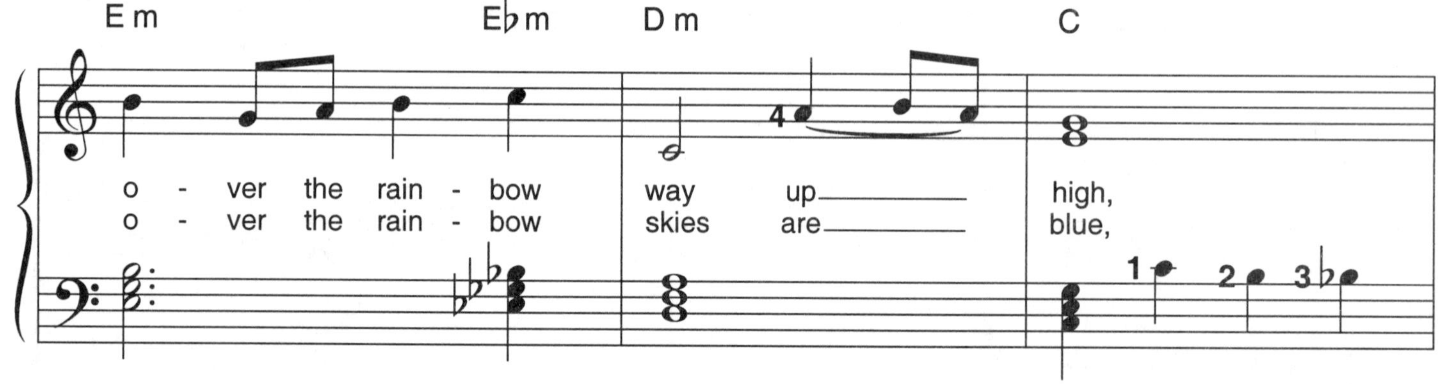

1.
C
2.
C
by.
true.
Some - day I'll wish up - on a star and

D m
E m
D m
wake up where the clouds are far be - hind me.
Where

C
Cdim
troub - les melt like lem - on drops, a - way, a - bove the chim - ney tops, that's

D m
Dm7
G7
C
D m
where you'll find me.
Some - - - where
mf

Em
E♭m
Dm
C
o - ver the rain - bow,
blue - birds
fly,
F
C
B♭7
C
C♯dim
birds
fly
o - ver the rain - bow,
Dm7
G7
C
B♭7
why then, oh why can't
I?
C
B♭7
C
mp
p

What A Wonderful World

Louis Armstrong's recording of this stanadrd is still heard today.

Words and Music by
GEORGE DAVID WEISS and BOB THIELE
Arranged by Richard Bradley

A7
Dm
D♭
C7
3
dark sac-red night, and I think to my-self what a won-der-ful

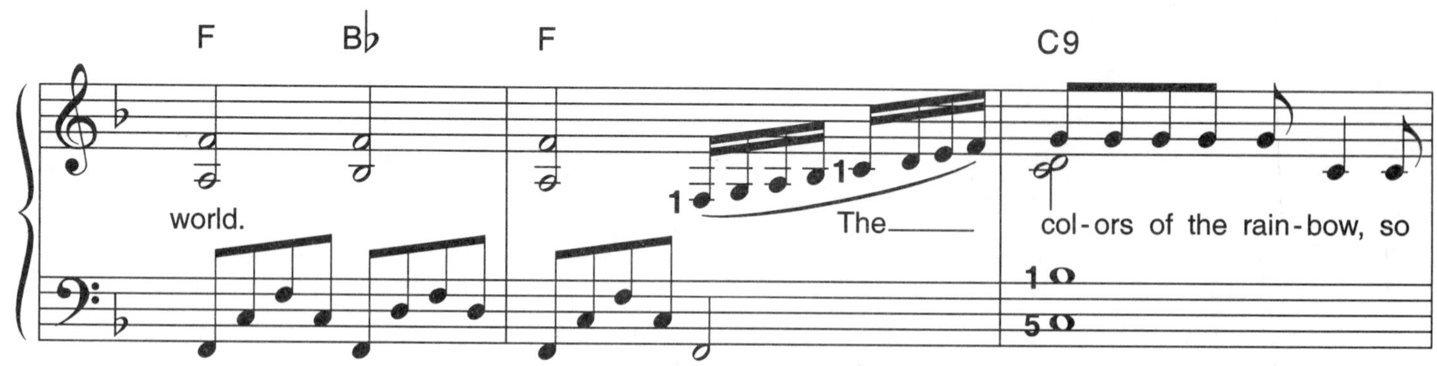
F
B♭
F
C9
world. The___ col-ors of the rain-bow, so

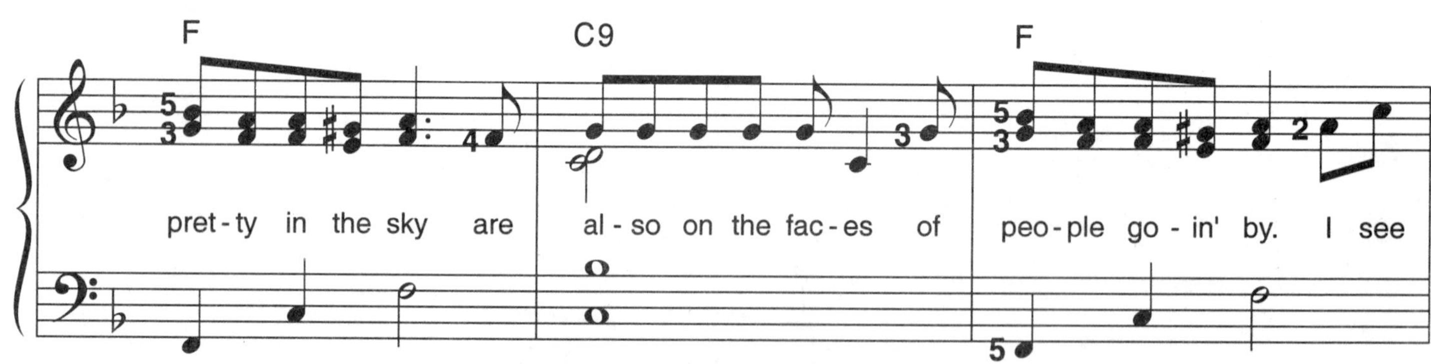
F
C9
F
pret-ty in the sky are al-so on the fac-es of peo-ple go-in' by. I see

Dm
C/E
Dm/F
C/E
Dm
E♭dim
friends shak-in' hands, say-in', "How do you do!" they're real-ly say-in'

Gm Ebdim C7/E C7 F Am Bb Am
"I love you." I hear ba - bies cry, I watch them grow,
Gm7 F A7 Dm Db
they'll learn much more than I'll ev - er know and I think to my - self
C7 F Am7(b5) D7
what a won - der - ful world. Yes, I
Gm9 G7 Gm7 C7 F Bb/F F
think to my - self what a won - der - ful world.

As Time Goes By

Best remembered as the "Play it again, Sam" song from the movie *Casablanca*, this standard has been recorded by Perry Como, Petula Clark and many others.

Words and Music by
HERMAN HUPFELD
Arranged by Richard Bradley

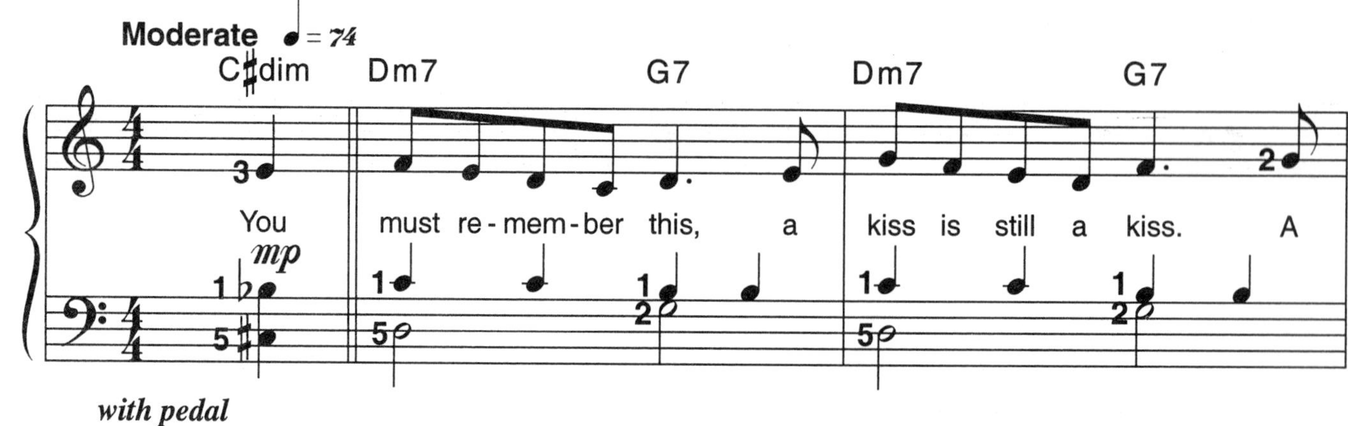

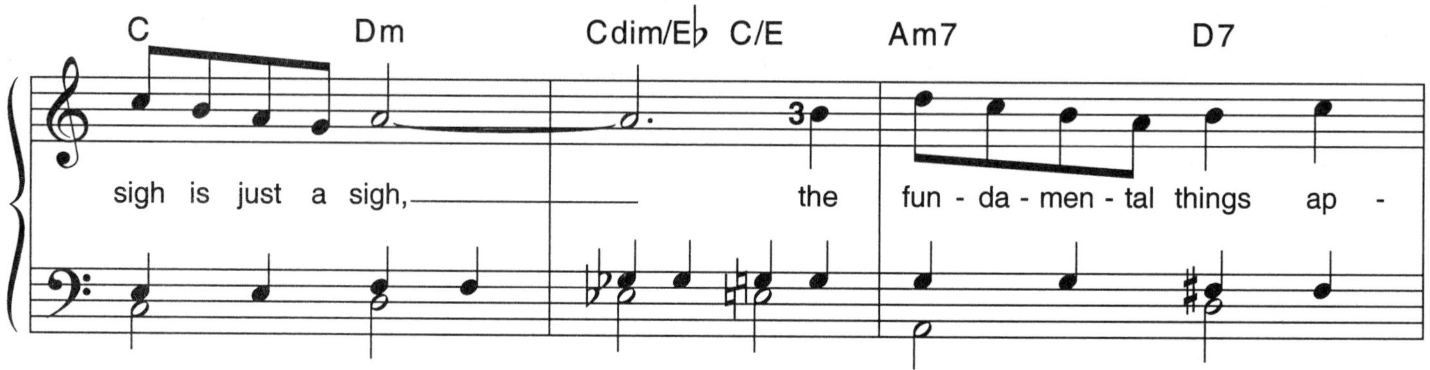

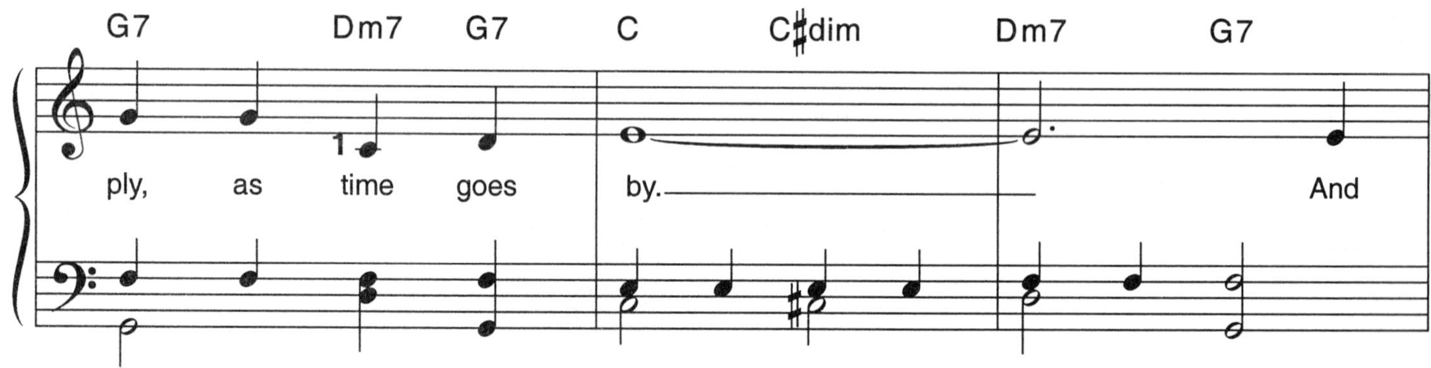

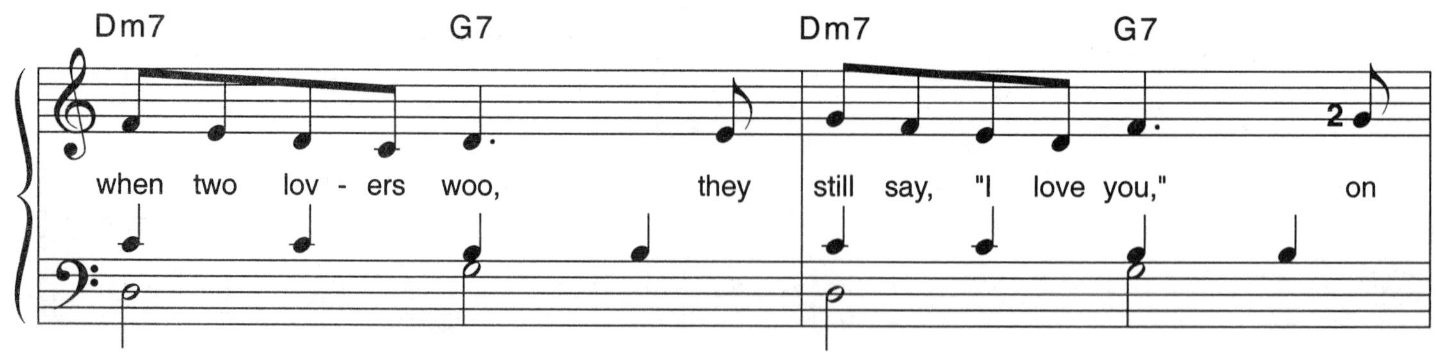

C Dm Cdim/E♭ C/E Am7 D7
that you can re - ly; No mat - ter what the fu - ture

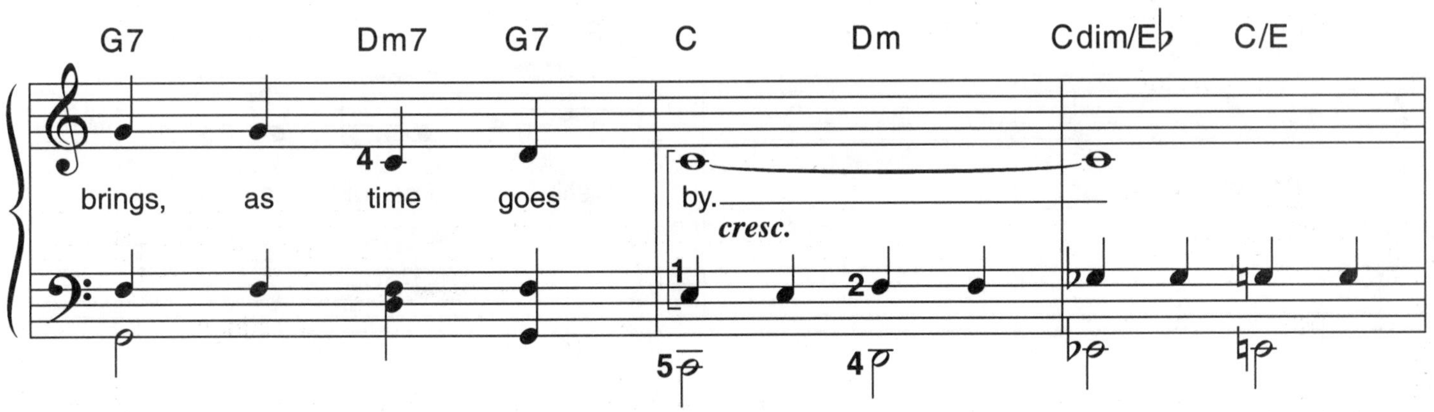
G7 Dm7 G7 C Dm Cdim/E♭ C/E
brings, as time goes by.
cresc.

F F+
Moon - light and love songs nev - er out of date.
mf

F6 F♯dim
Hearts full of pas - sion, jeal - ous - y and hate;

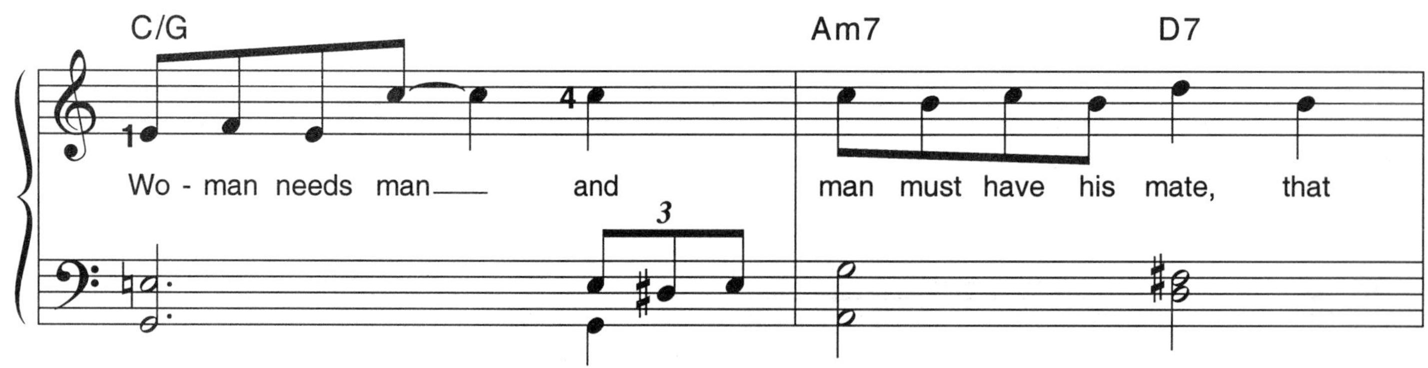
C/G
Am7
D7
Wo - man needs man___ and man must have his mate, that

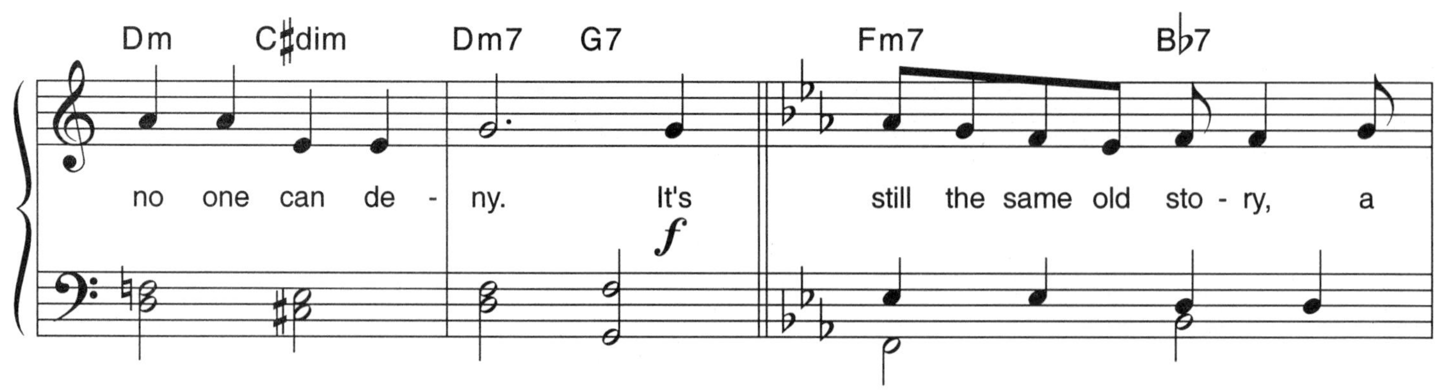
Dm
C♯dim
Dm7
G7
Fm7
B♭7
no one can de - ny. It's still the same old sto - ry, a
f

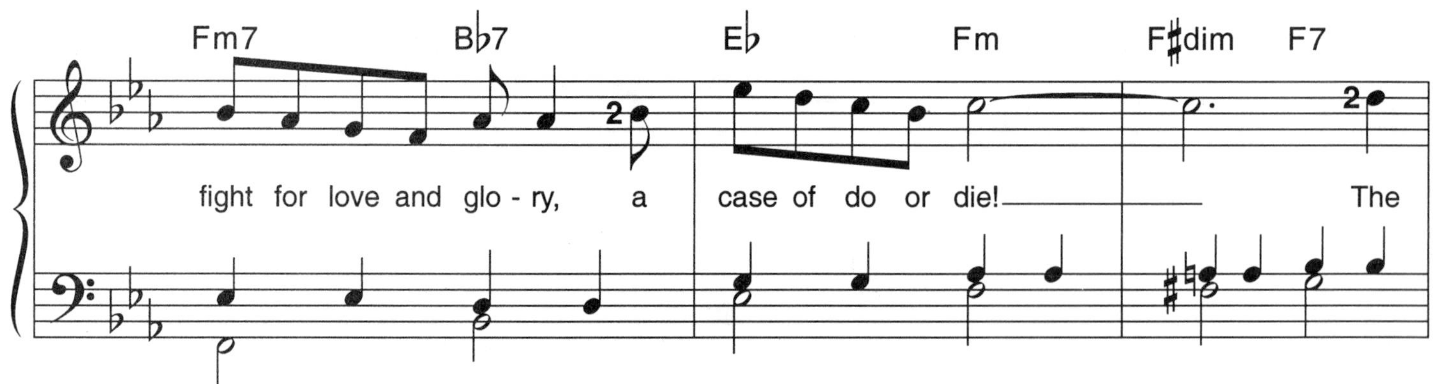
Fm7
B♭7
E♭
Fm
F♯dim
F7
fight for love and glo - ry, a case of do or die!_____ The

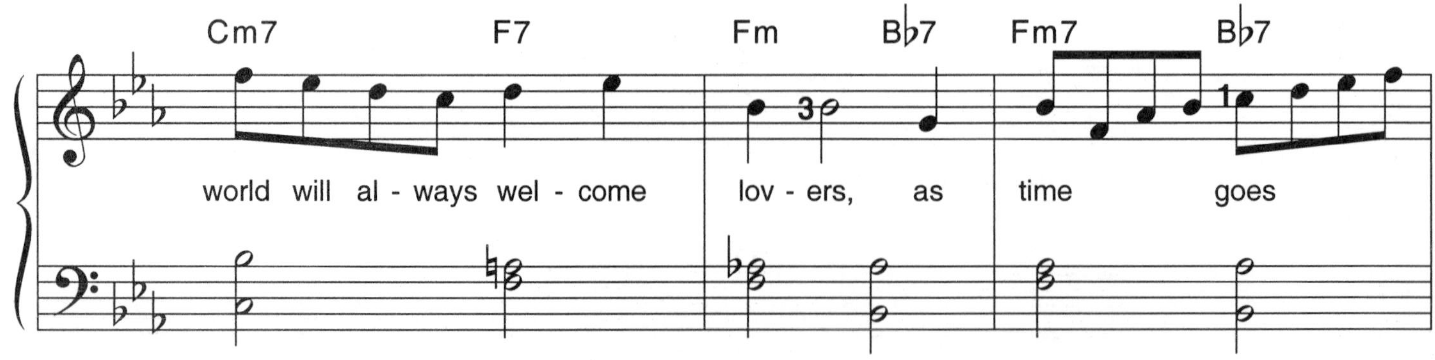
Cm7
F7
Fm
B♭7
Fm7
B♭7
world will al - ways wel - come lov - ers, as time goes

Dm7
G7
C♯dim
Dm7
G7
Dm7
G7
by.
mp
C
Dm
Cdim/E♭
C/E
Am7
D7
Dm7
G7
Dm7
E
G7
C
p
8vb

My Funny Valentine

Kim Novak sang this frequently recorded standard in the film *Pal Joey*.

Words by LORENZ HART
Music by RICHARD RODGERS
Arranged by Richard Bradley

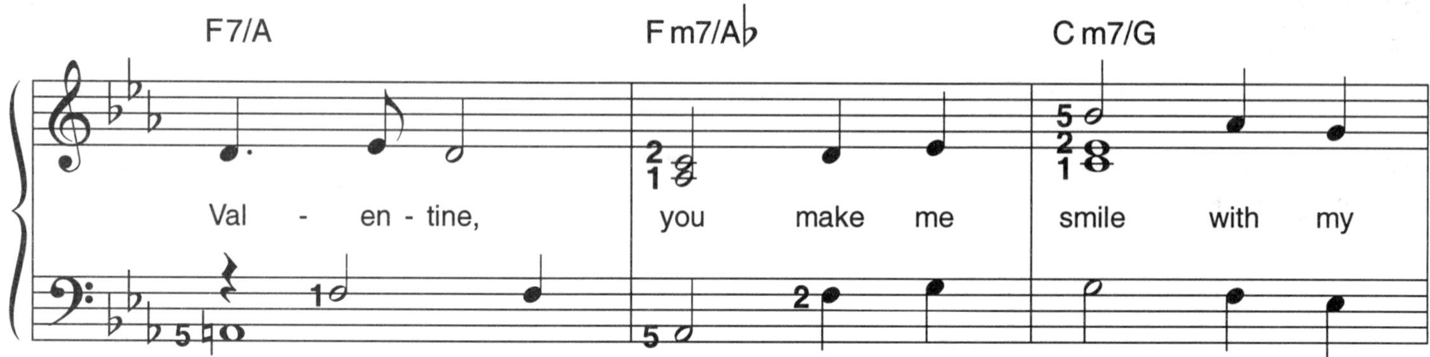

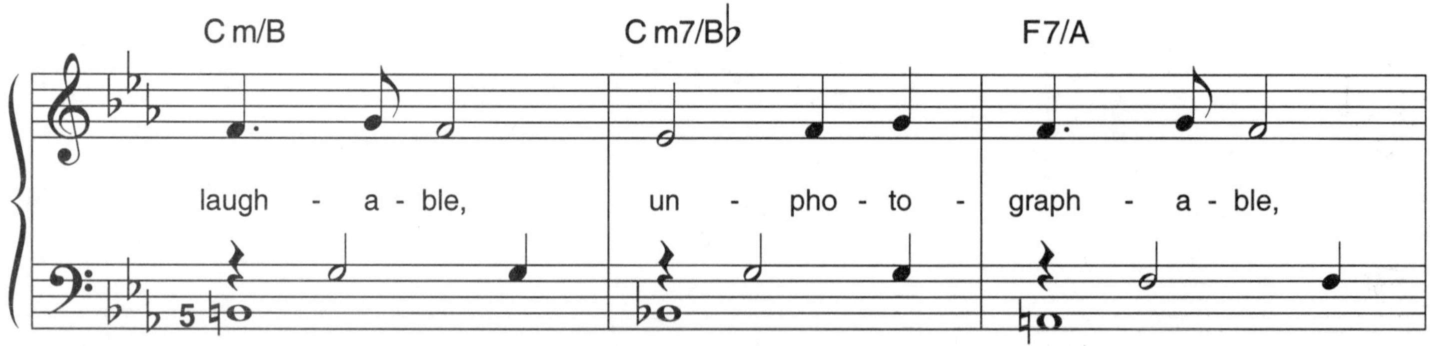

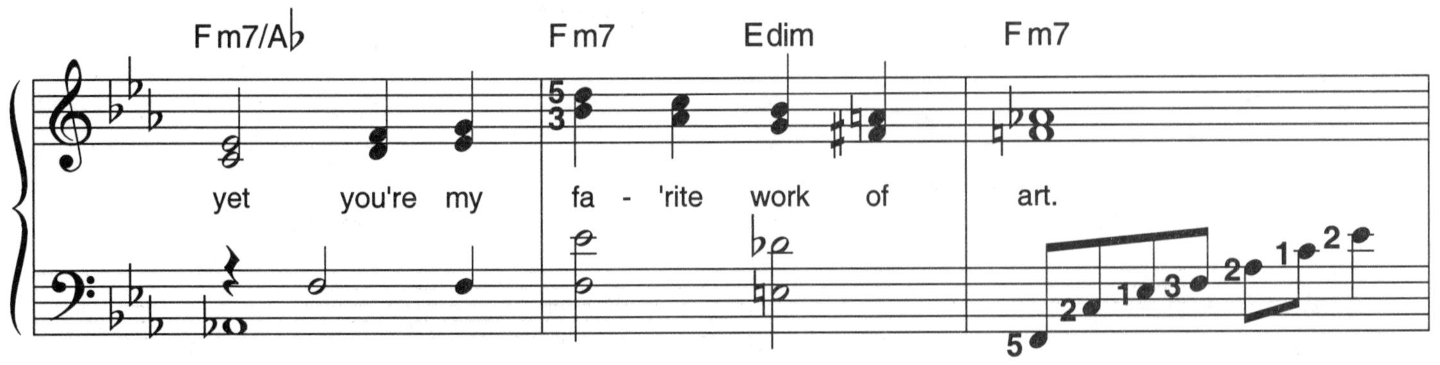
Fm7/A♭
Fm7
Edim
Fm7
yet you're my fa - 'rite work of art.

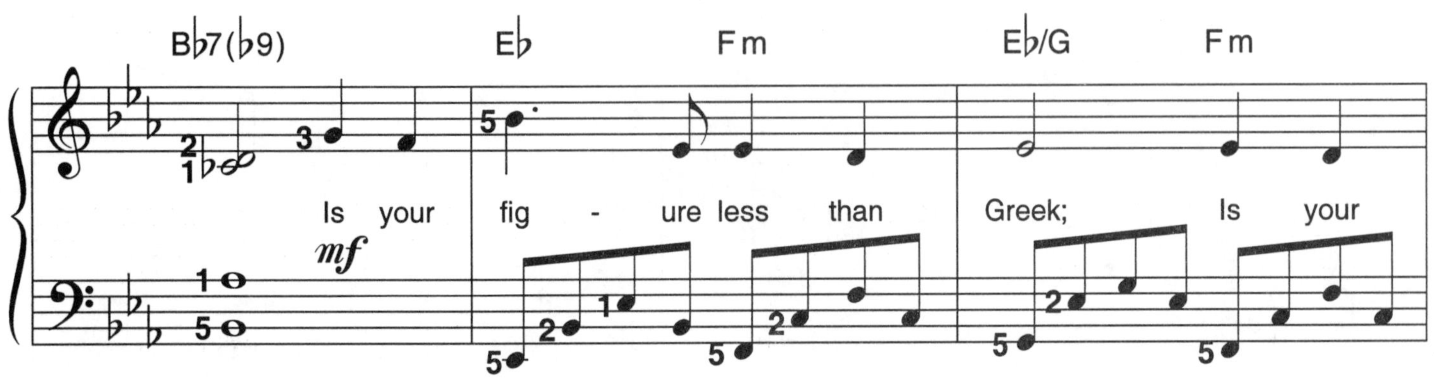
B♭7(♭9)
E♭
Fm
E♭/G
Fm
Is your fig - ure less than Greek; Is your
mf

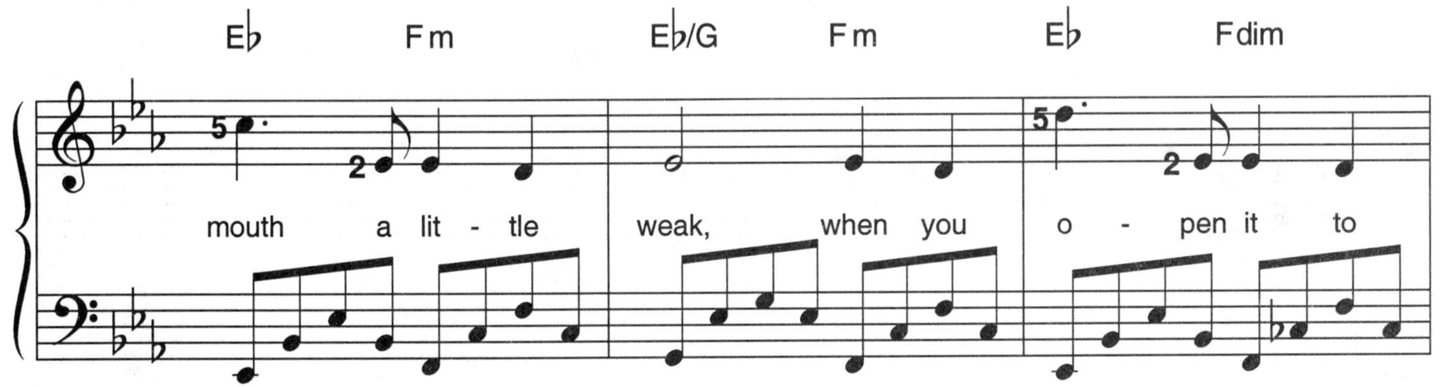
E♭
Fm
E♭/G
Fm
E♭
Fdim
mouth a lit - tle weak, when you o - pen it to

Cm7
B♭7
A♭
speak, are you smart?

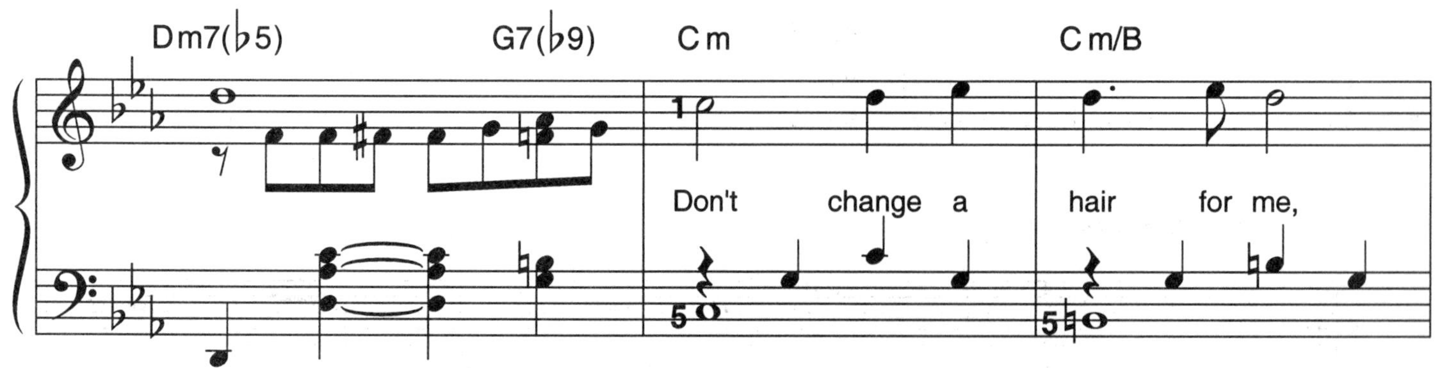
Dm7(♭5)
G7(♭9)
Cm
Cm/B
Don't change a hair for me,

Cm7/B♭
F7/A
Fm7/A♭
D7/A
G7/B
not if you care for me, stay, lit - tle Val - en - tine,

Cm
B♭m7
E♭7
A♭Maj7
Fm
B♭7
stay!
Each day is Val - en - tine's
f
mf

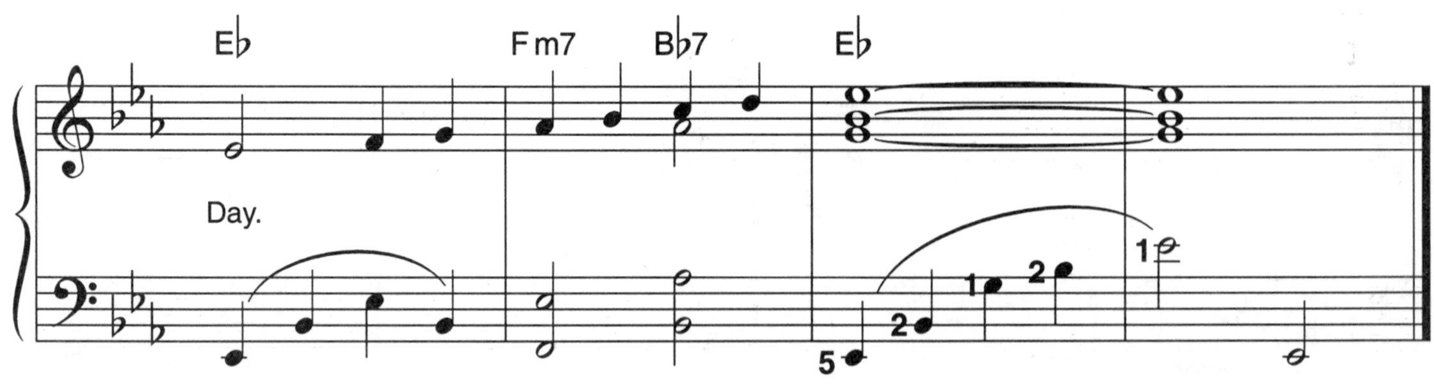
E♭
Fm7
B♭7
E♭
Day.

Ebb Tide

Frank Chacksfield & his Orchestra and Stanley Black & his Orchestra had popular recordings of this standard.

Lyric by CARL SIGMAN
Music by ROBERT MAXWELL
Arranged by Richard Bradley

Ebb Tide - 3 - 1

L.H.
Dm
E
R.H.
wide? At last we're face to face, and as we
mf
cresc.

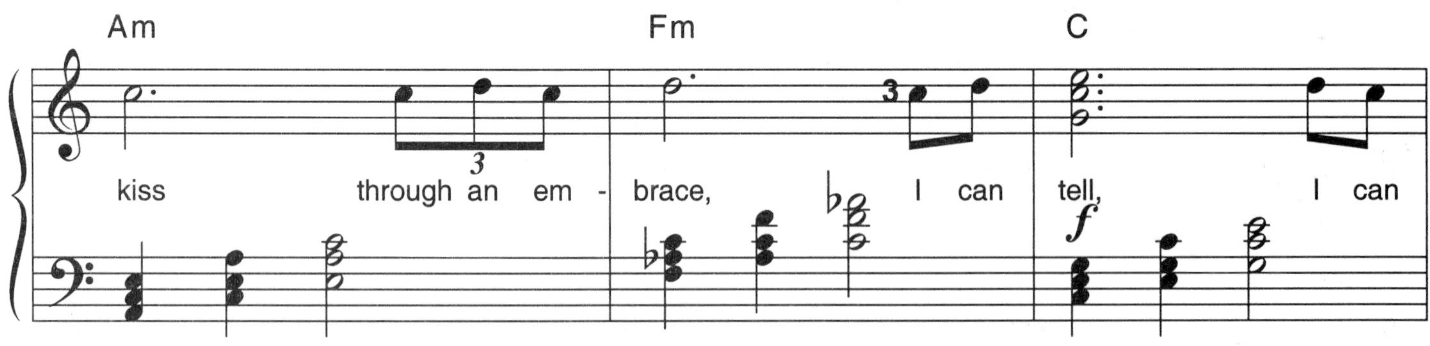
Am
Fm
C
kiss through an em - brace, I can tell, I can
f

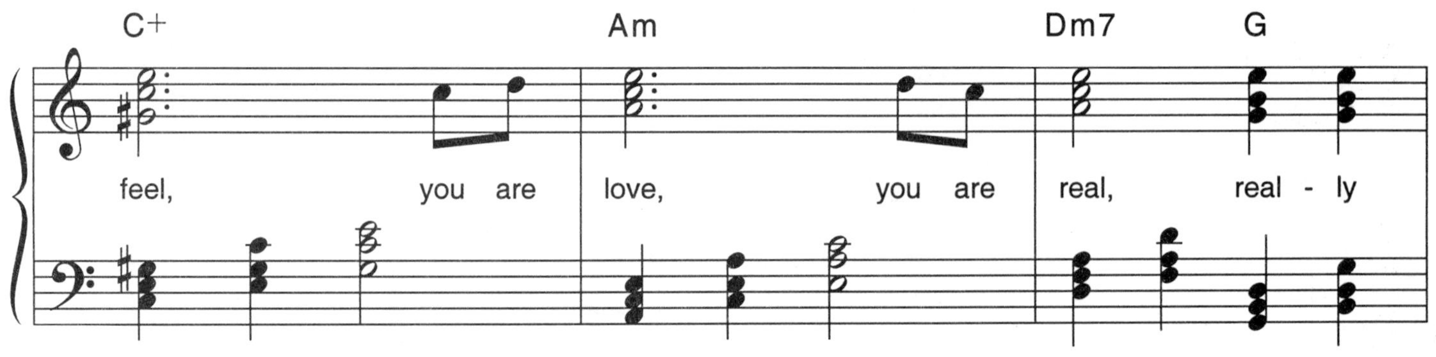
C+
Am
Dm7
G
feel, you are love, you are real, real - ly

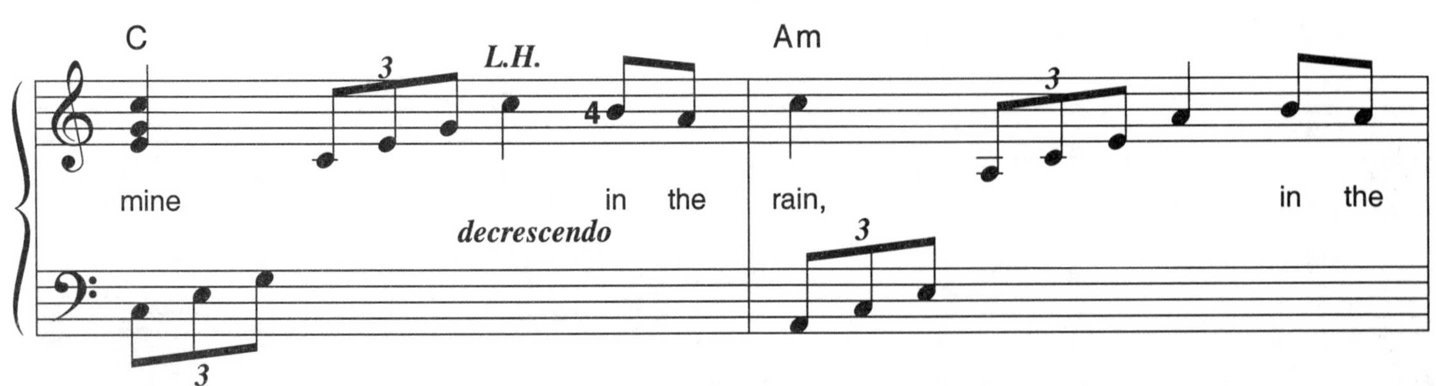
C
L.H.
Am
mine in the rain, in the
decrescendo

Fm
Dm
G7
dark, in the sun. Like the
C
Am
tide at it's ebb, I'm at
Dm
Fm
peace in the web of your
C
arms.
R.H.
L.H.

You Light Up My Life

This Oscar winning standard from the movie *You Light Up My Life* was a pop hit for Debby Boone in the seventies, and a hit again for LeAnn Rimes in the nineties.

Words and Music by
JOE BROOKS
Arranged by Richard Bradley

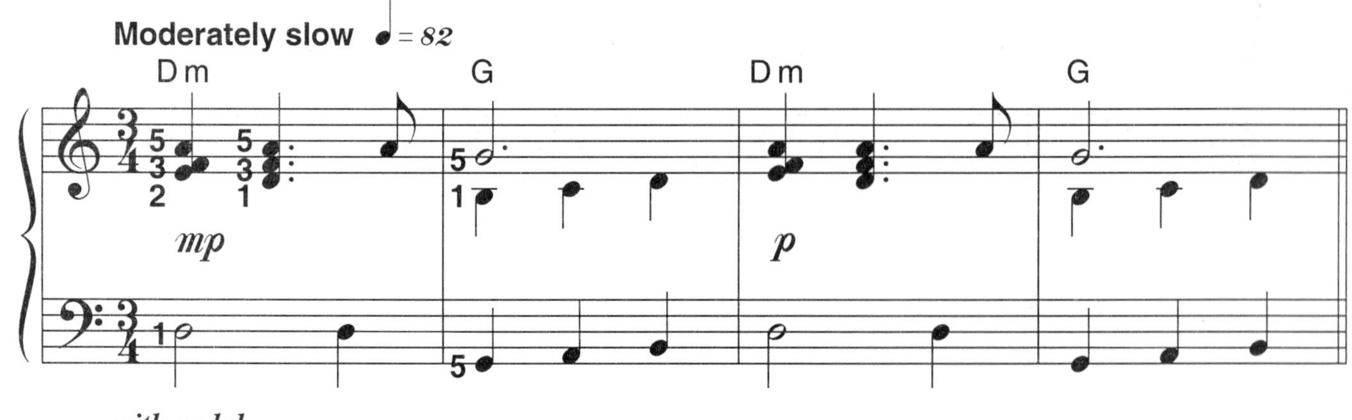

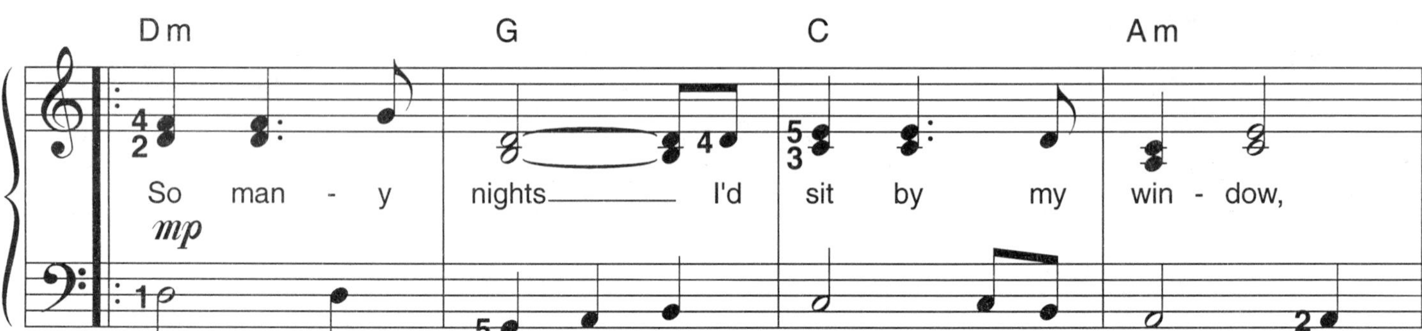

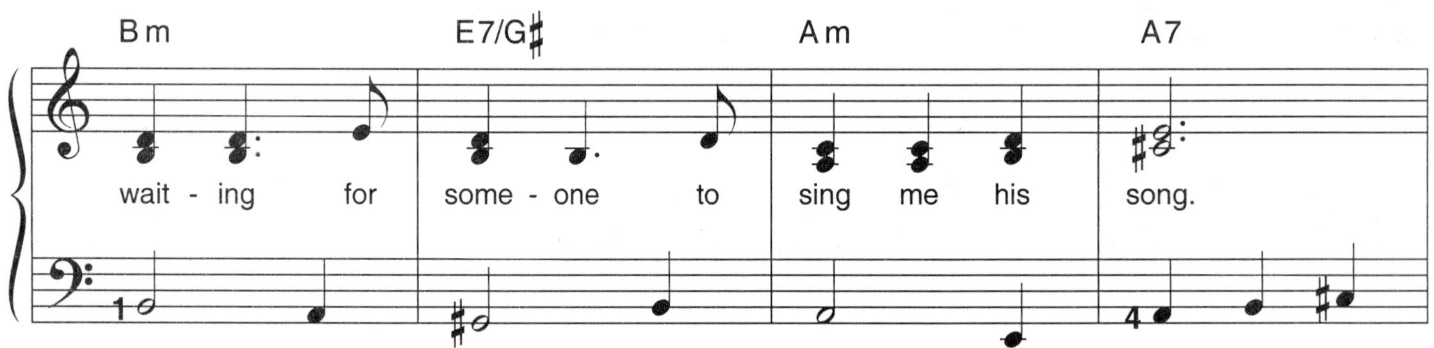

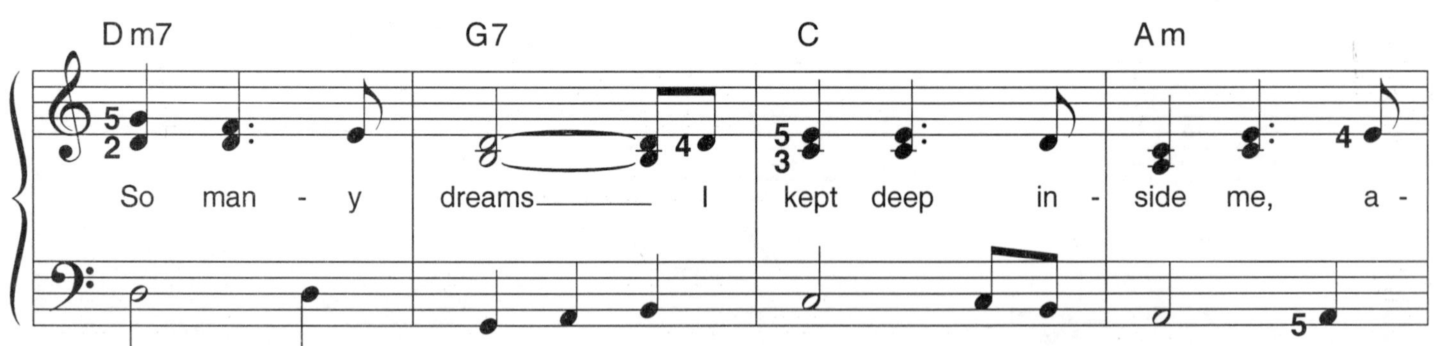

B
D
lone in the dark, but now you've come a -

G
GMaj7/F♯
long. And you light up my

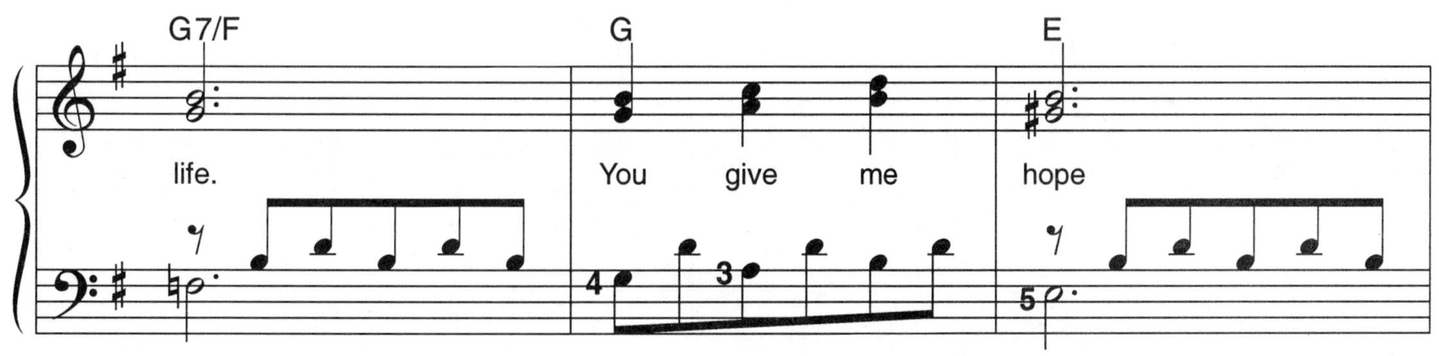
G7/F
G
E
life. You give me hope

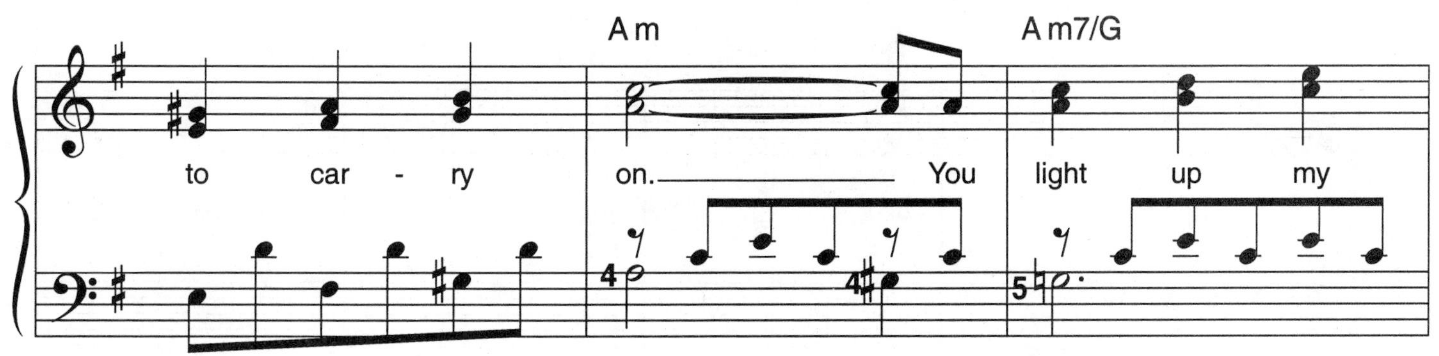
Am
Am7/G
to car - ry on. You light up my

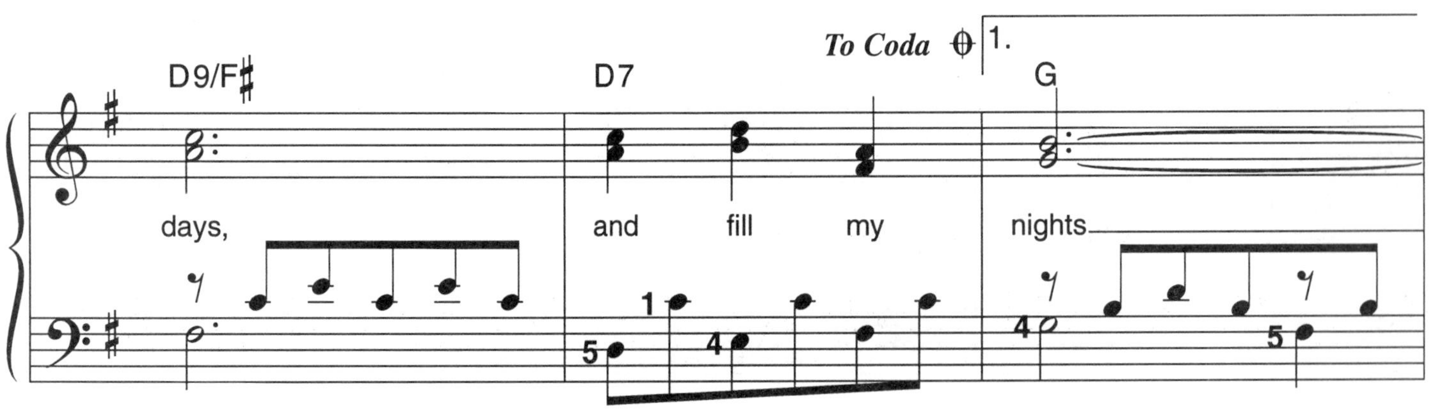
To Coda
1.
D9/F♯
D7
G
days,
and fill my
nights

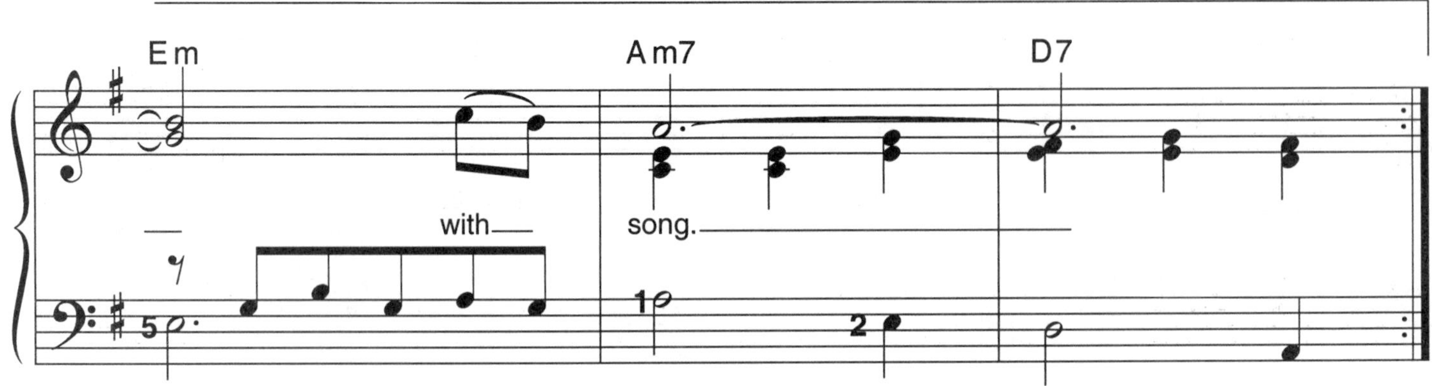
Em
Am7
D7
with
song.

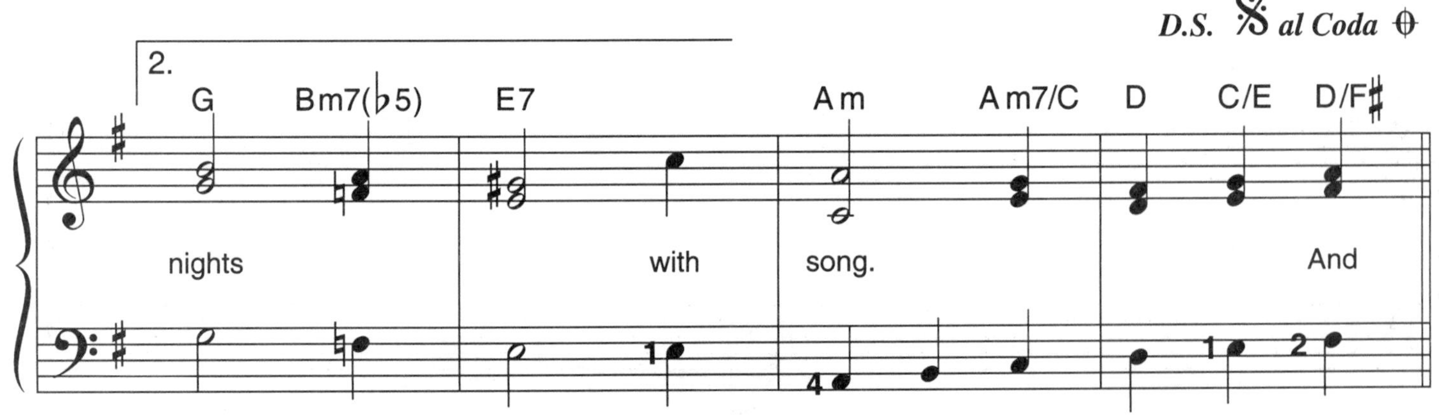
D.S. al Coda
2.
G
Bm7(♭5)
E7
Am
Am7/C
D
C/E
D/F♯
nights
with
song.
And

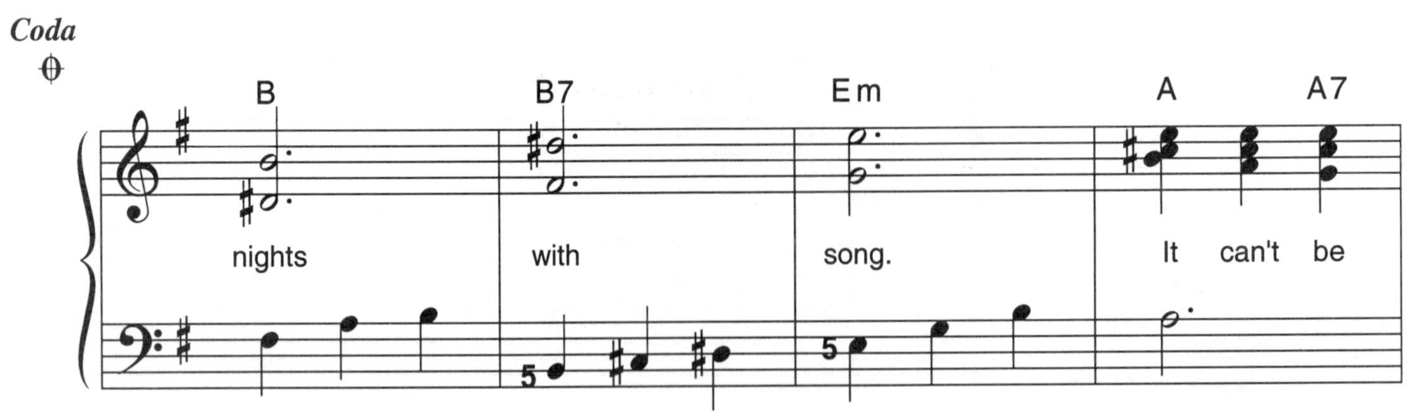
Coda
B
B7
Em
A
A7
nights
with
song.
It can't be

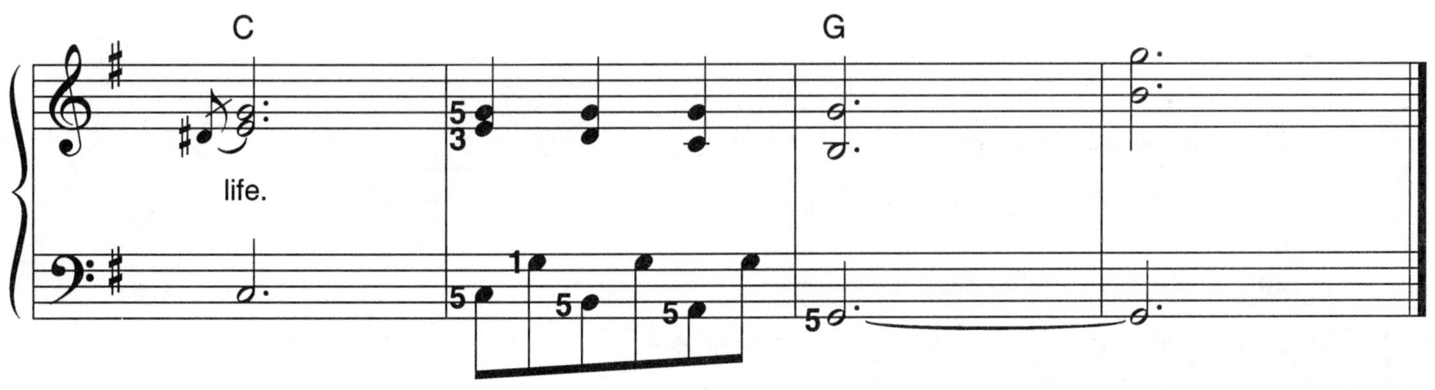

Verse 2:
Rollin' at sea, adrift on the waters,
Could it be finally I'm turning for home?
Finally a chance to say, "Hey! I love you."
Never again to be all alone.
Chorus:

Where Or When

Early recordings of this standard from the Browdway musical *Babes in Arms* include those by Al Hibbler, Lena Horne and Dinah Shore.

Words by LORENZ HART
Music by RICHARD RODGERS
Arranged by Richard Bradley

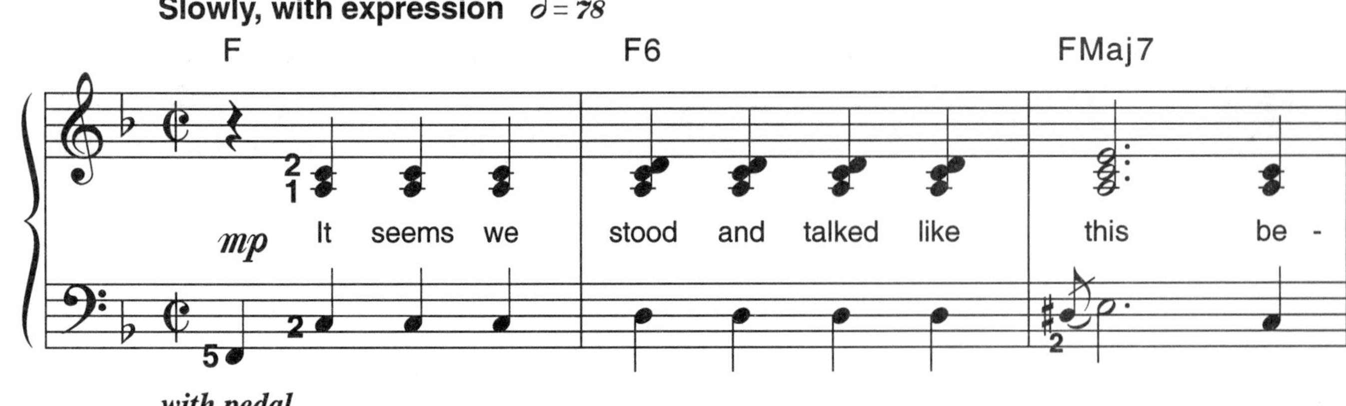

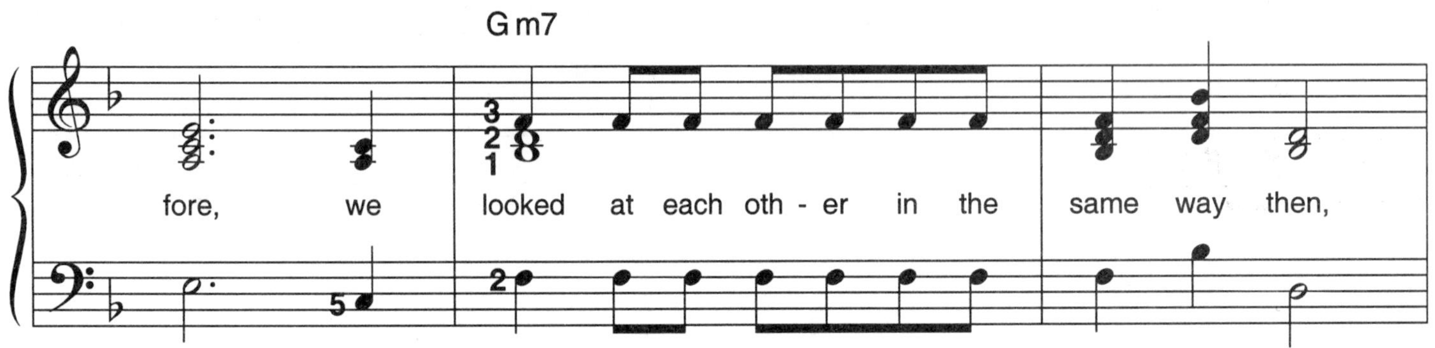

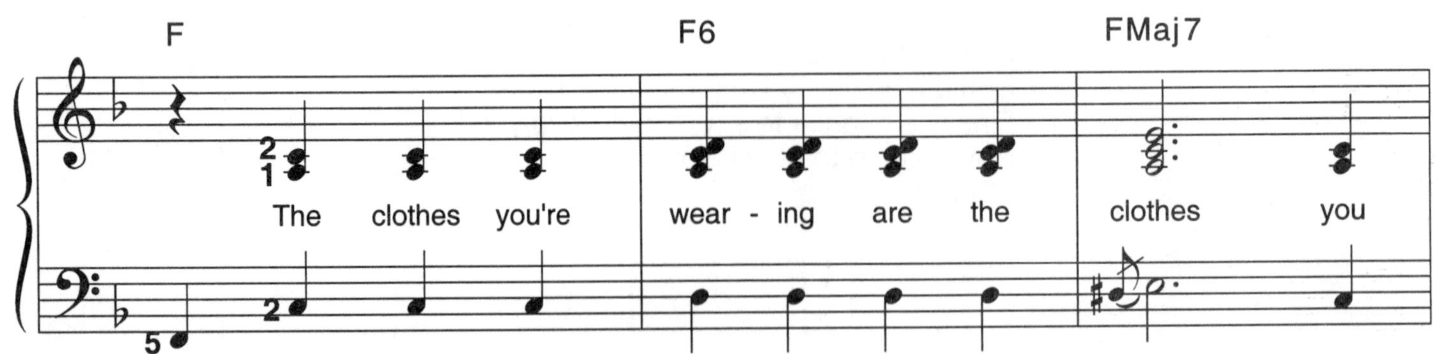

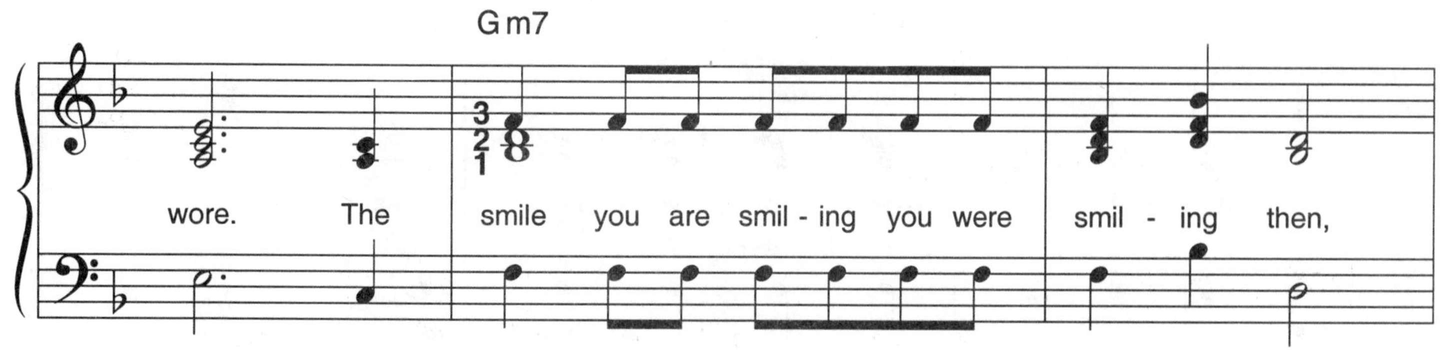
Gm7
wore. The smile you are smil - ing you were smil - ing then,

FMaj7 F6 Gm7 C7
but I can't re - mem - ber where or when.

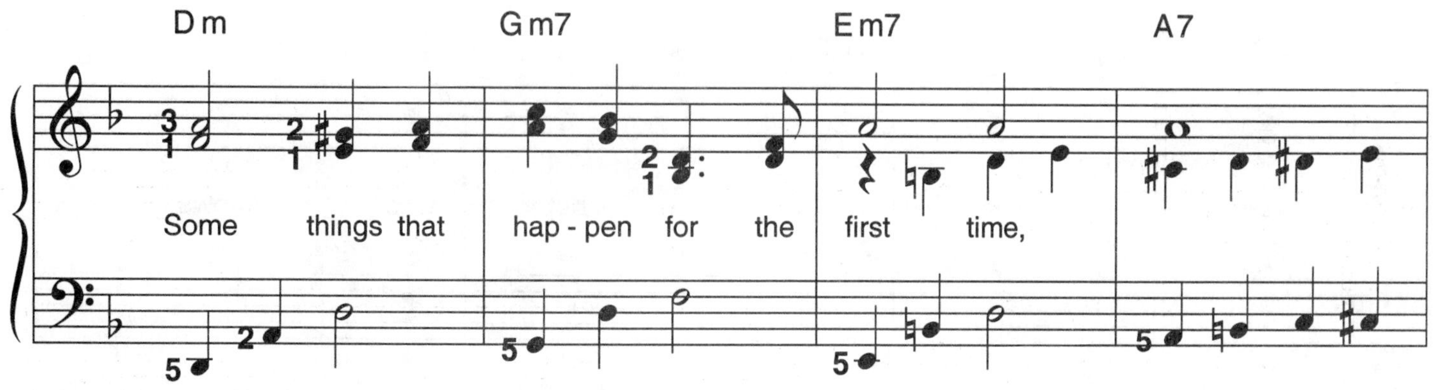
Dm Gm7 Em7 A7
Some things that hap - pen for the first time,

Dm Gm7 Dm7 G7 C9 C7(♭9)
seem to be hap - pen - ing a - gain.

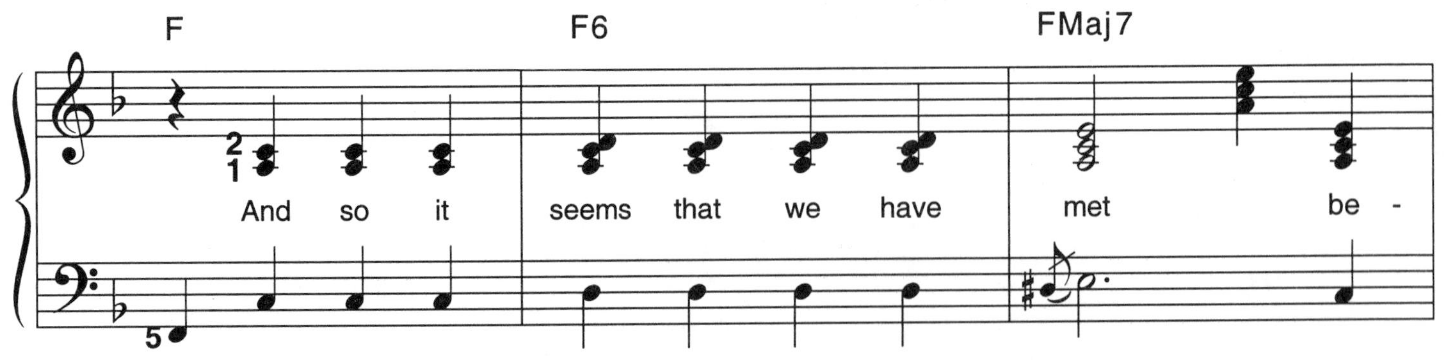
F
F6
FMaj7
And so it seems that we have met be -

F+
Gm
Am
fore, and laughed be - fore, and
cresc

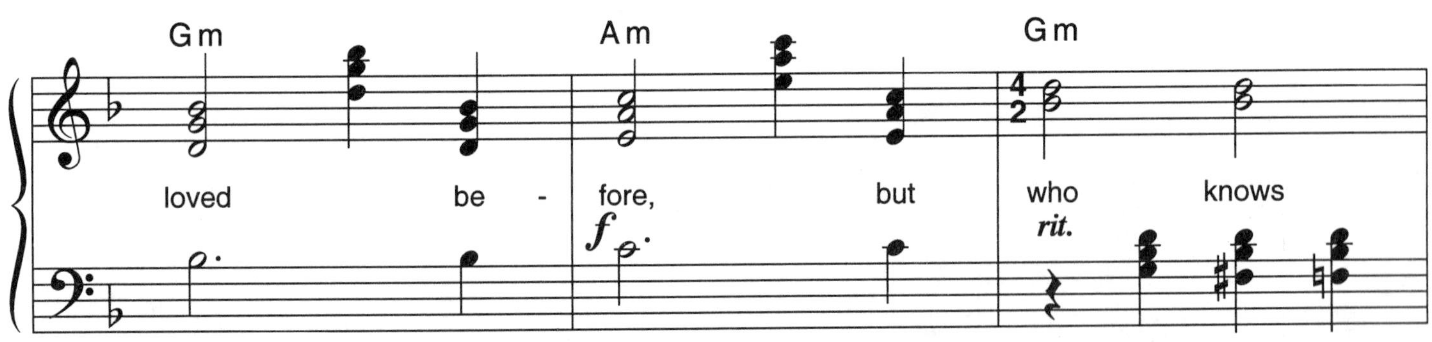
Gm
Am
Gm
loved be - fore, but who knows
f
rit.

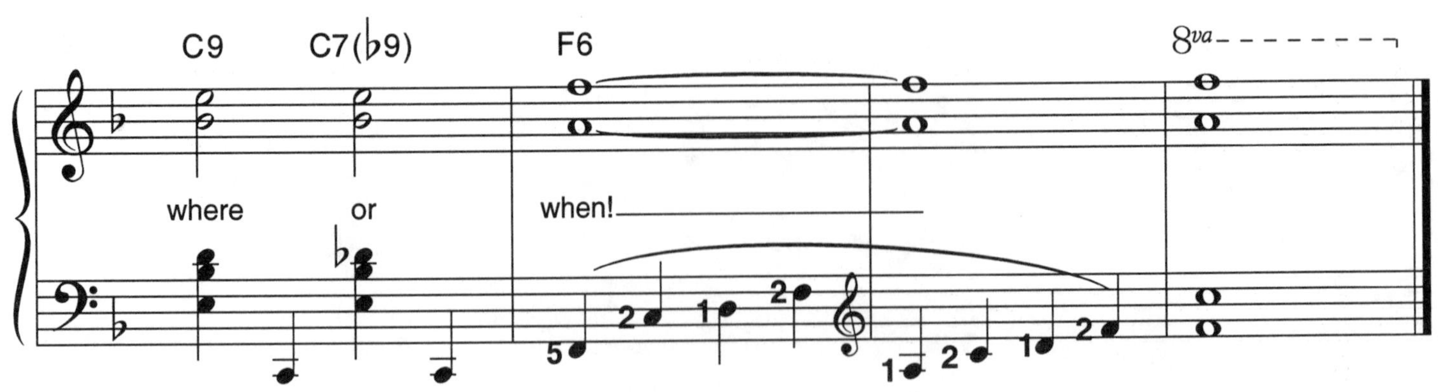
C9
C7(♭9)
F6
8va
where or when!

Someone To Watch Over Me

This standard from the Broadway musical *Oh Kay* has been recorded by Frank Sinatra, Gogi Grant and many others.

Music and Lyrics by
GEORGE GERSHWIN and IRA GERSHWIN
Arranged by Richard Bradley

Moderate ♩ = 74

C F/A Fdim/A♭

mp There's a some - bod - y I'm long-ing to see.

with pedal

C/G Cdim/G♭ G7/F Gdim/E Dm7

I hope that he turns out to be some - one who'll

G7(♭9) C C♯dim Dm7 G7(♭9)

watch o - ver me.

C F/A Fdim/A♭

I'm a lit - tle lamb who's lost in the wood.

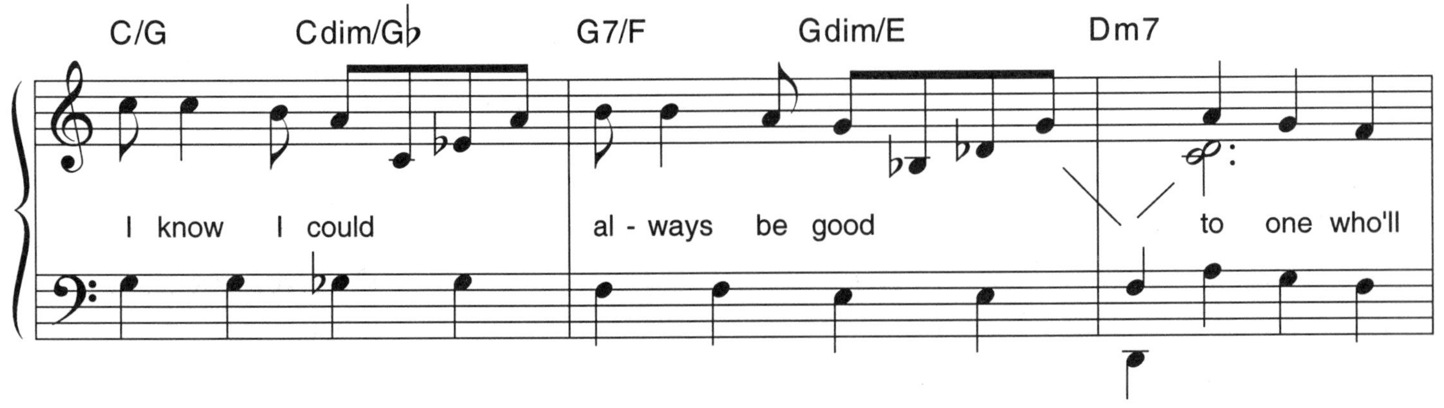
C/G
Cdim/G♭
G7/F
Gdim/E
Dm7
I know I could
al - ways be good
to one who'll

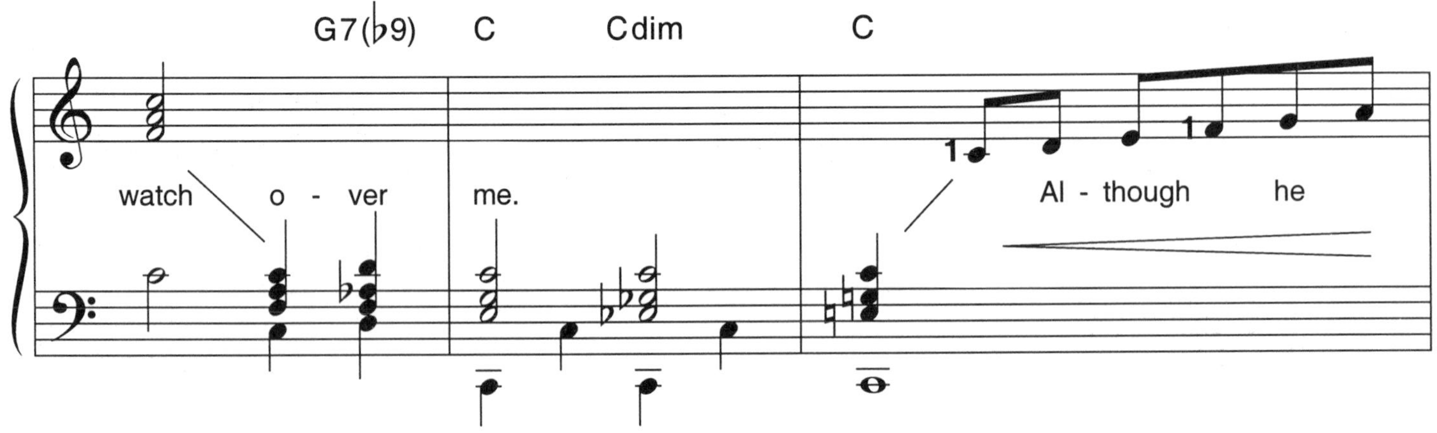
G7(♭9)
C
Cdim
C
watch o - ver
me.
Al - though he

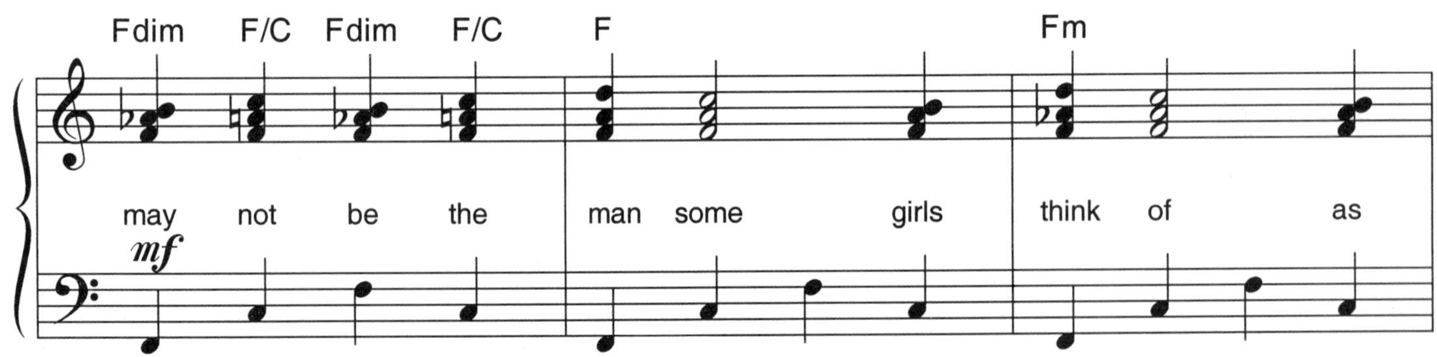
Fdim
F/C
Fdim
F/C
F
Fm
may not be the
man some girls
think of as
mf

C/E
F♯m7(♭5)
B7
E7
hand - some, to
my heart he
car - ries the

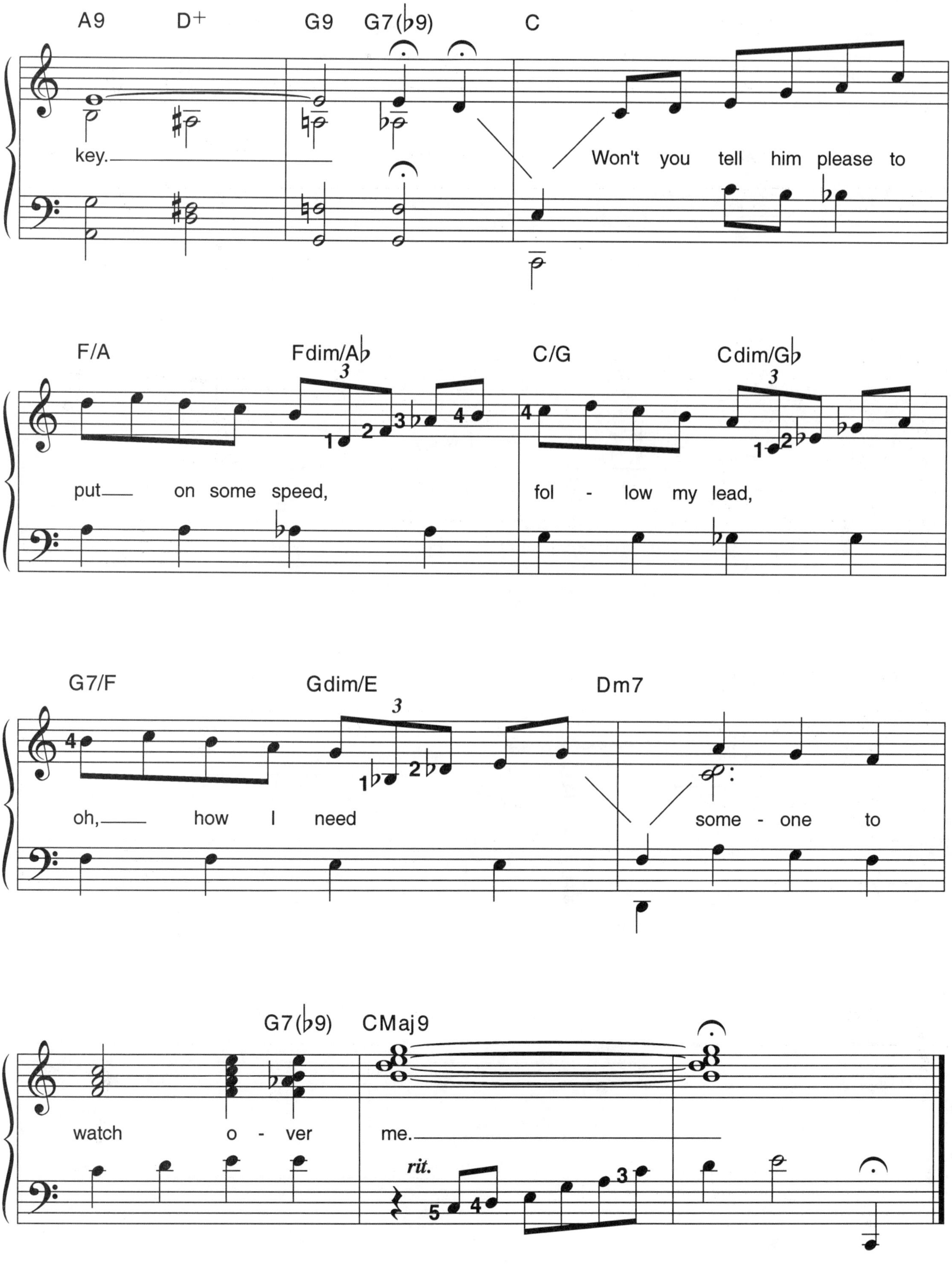

A9 D+ G9 G7(♭9) C

key. Won't you tell him please to

F/A Fdim/A♭ C/G Cdim/G♭

put on some speed, fol - low my lead,

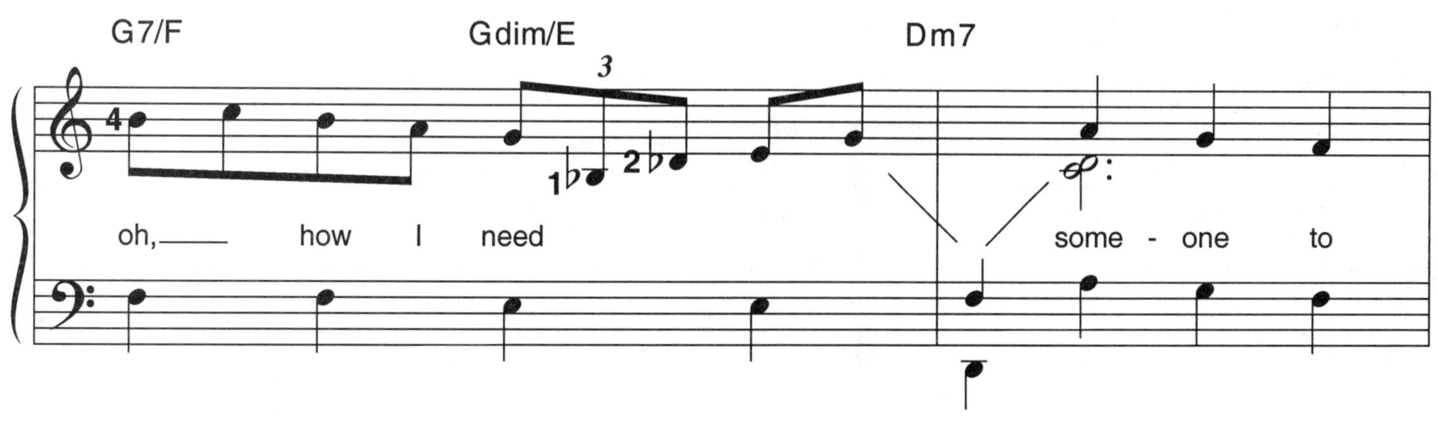

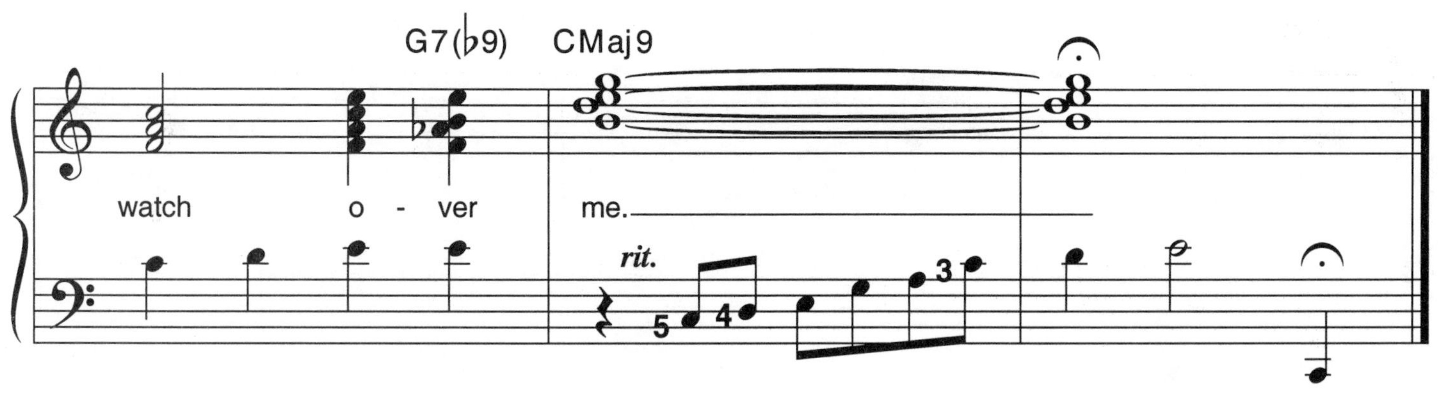

What Are You Doing The Rest Of Your Life?

This standard from the motion picture *The Happy Ending* was nominated for a Best Song Oscar in 1969.

Lyric by ALAN and MARILYN BERGMAN
Music by MICHEL LEGRAND
Arranged by Richard Bradley

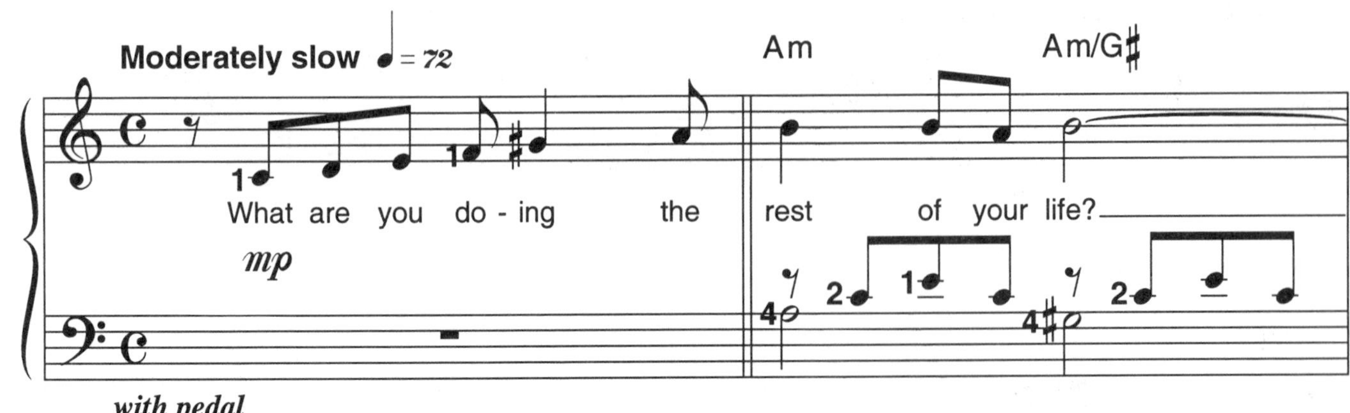

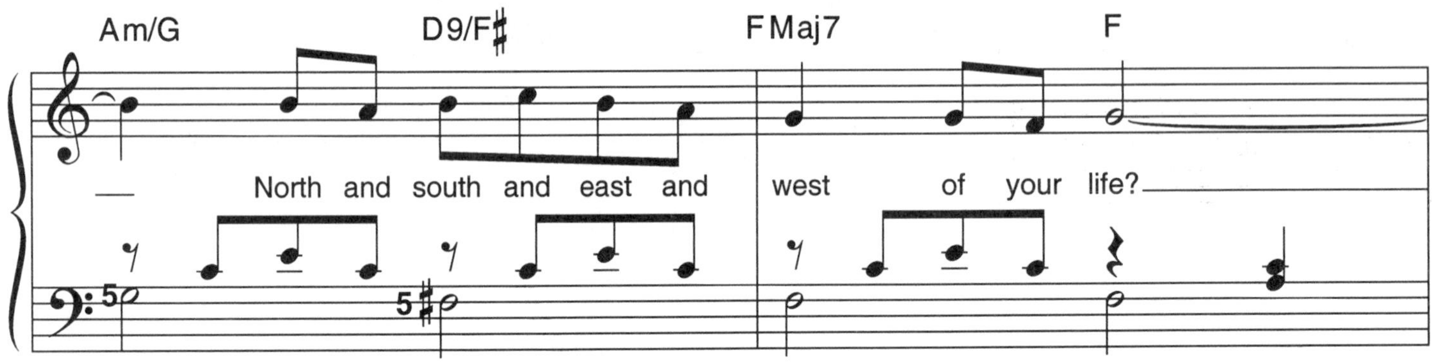

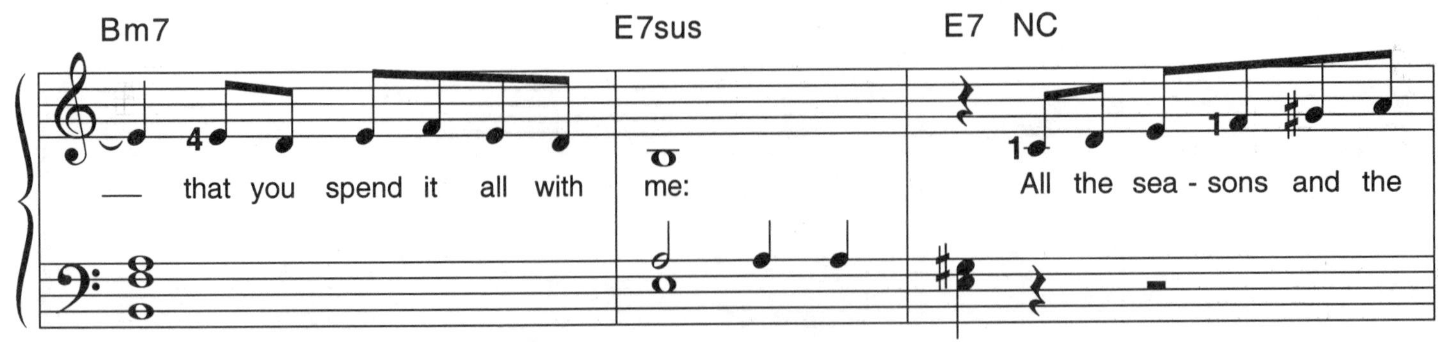

Am
Am/G♯
Am7/G
D9/F♯
times of your days, All the nick - els and the
FMaj7
F
Em
dimes of your days. Let the rea - sons and the
Dm
Dm7/C
Bm7
E7
rhymes of your days all be - gin and end with
AMaj7
A6
NC
Bm7
E7
me. I want to see your face in ev - 'ry kind of

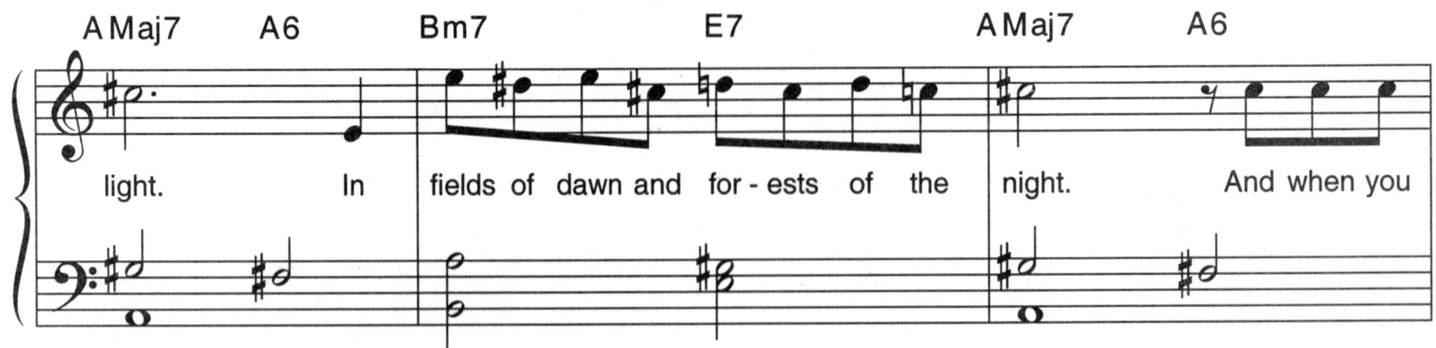
AMaj7
A6
Bm7
E7
AMaj7
A6
light. In fields of dawn and for - ests of the night. And when you

A♭Maj7
D♭7
G♭Maj7
NC
stand be - fore the can - dles on a cake, Oh, let me be the

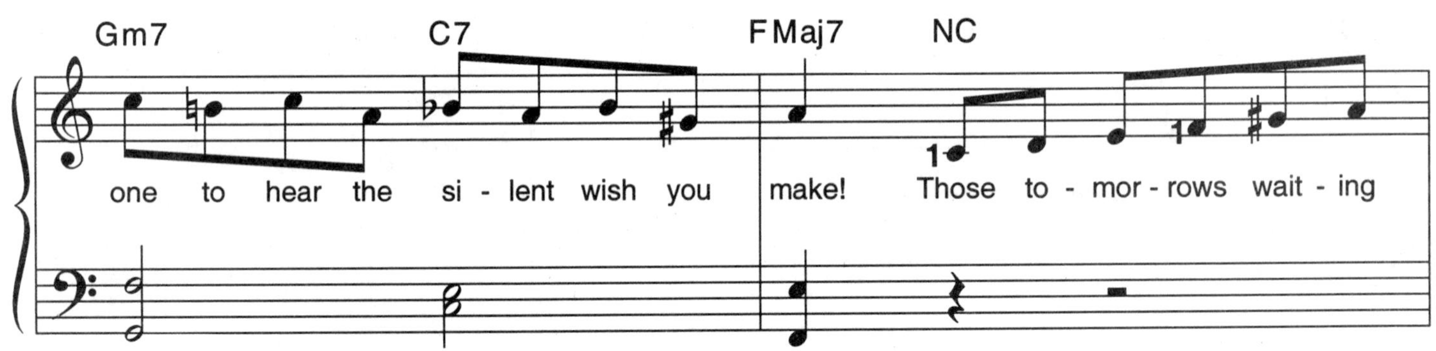
Gm7
C7
FMaj7
NC
one to hear the si - lent wish you make! Those to - mor - rows wait - ing

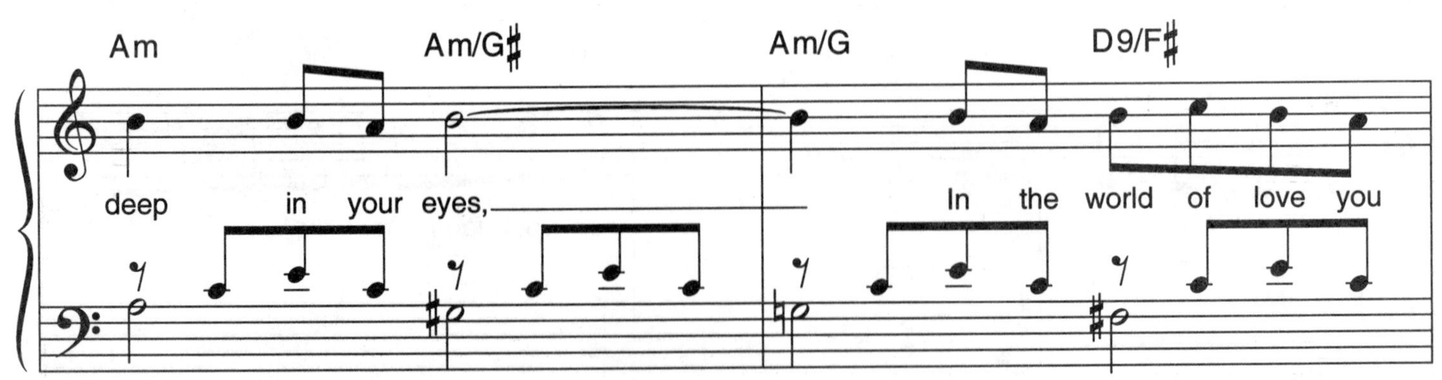
Am
Am/G♯
Am/G
D9/F♯
deep in your eyes, In the world of love you

FMaj7 F Em
keep in your eyes, I'll a - wak - en what's a -
Dm Dm7/C Bm7 E7sus
sleep in your eyes. It may take a kiss or two!
E7 F Em Dm Bm7 E7
Thru all of my life, sum - mer, win - ter, spring and
FMaj7 F7♭5 Am/E
fall of my life, All I ev - er will re - call of my life is
Bm7 E7 Am
all of my life with you!

Bewitched (Bothered And Bewildered)

Doris Day, Frank Sinatra, Ella Fitzgerald and many others have recorded this standard from the Broadway musical *Pal Joey*.

Words by LORENZ HART
Music by RICHARD RODGERS
Arranged by Richard Bradley

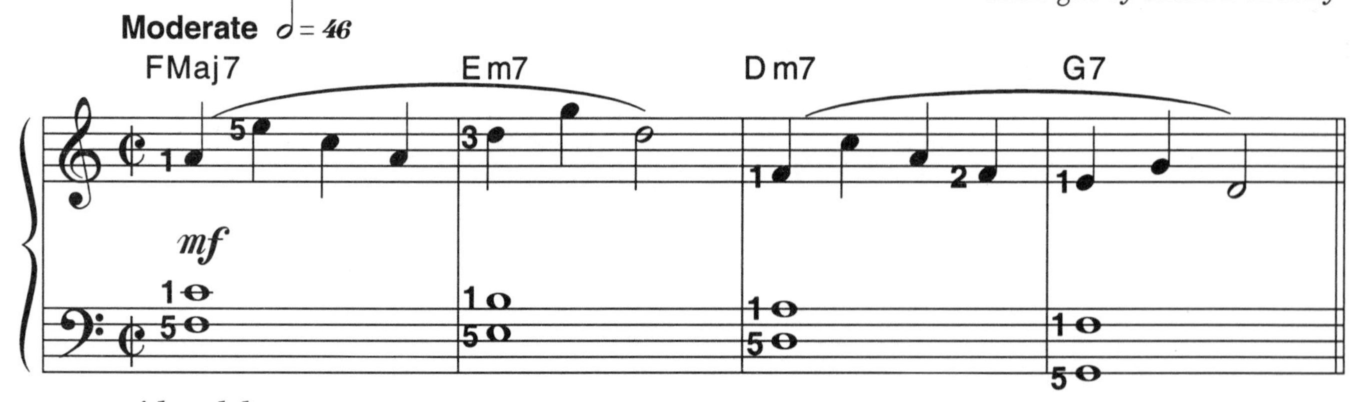

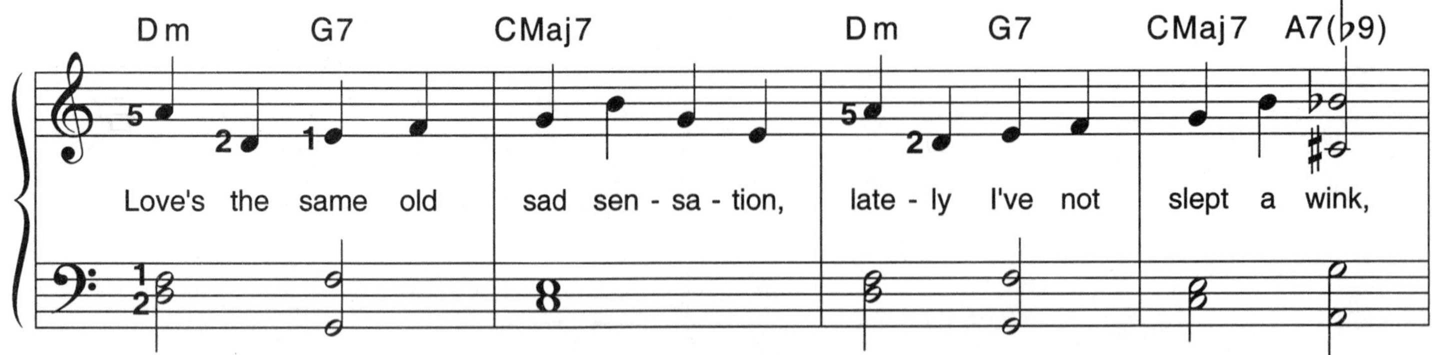

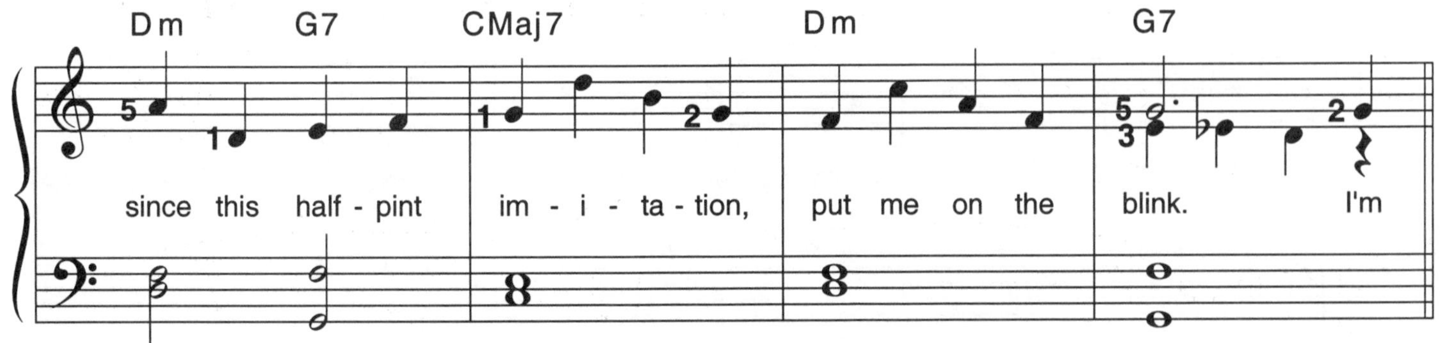
Dm G7 CMaj7 Dm G7
since this half - pint im - i - ta - tion, put me on the blink. I'm

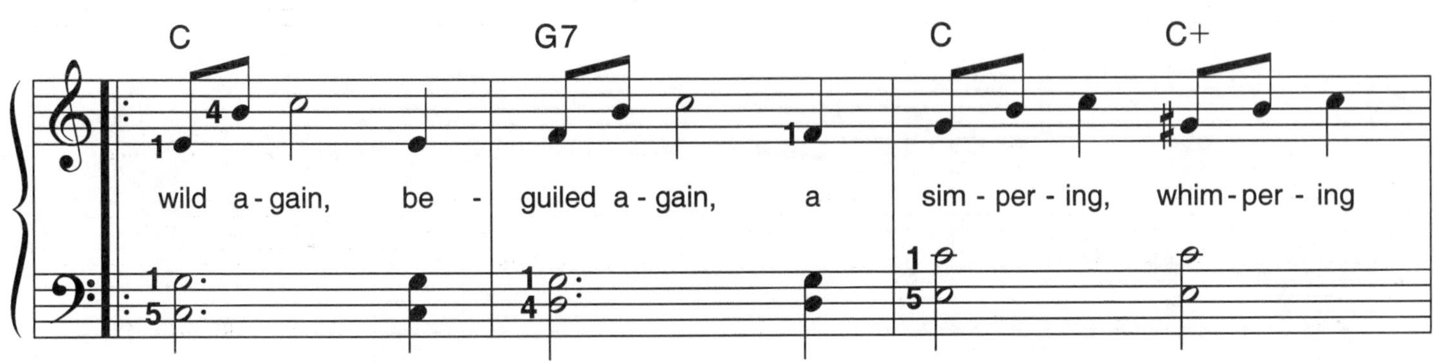
C G7 C C+
wild a - gain, be - guiled a - gain, a sim - per - ing, whim - per - ing

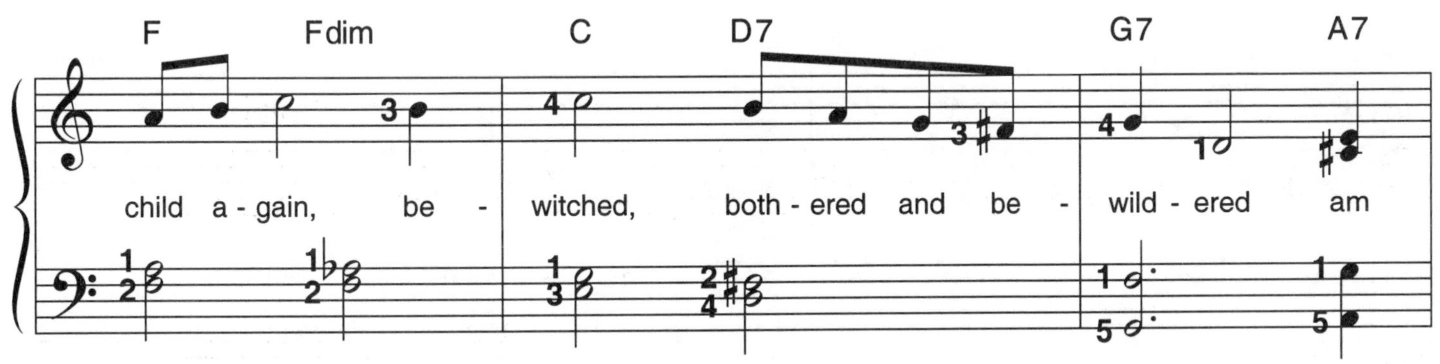
F Fdim C D7 G7 A7
child a - gain, be - witched, both - ered and be - wild - ered am

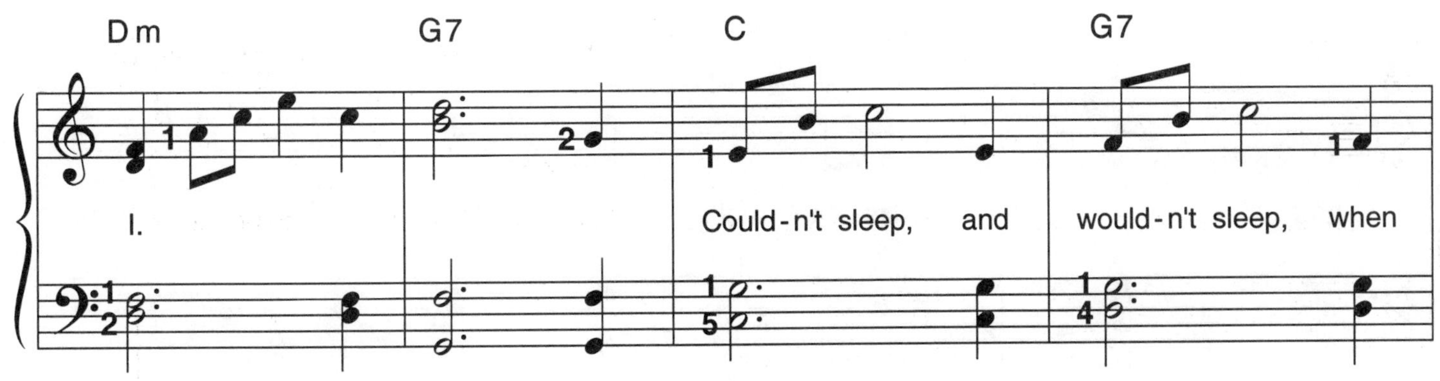
Dm G7 C G7
I. Could - n't sleep, and would - n't sleep, when

C
C+
F
Fdim
C
D7
love came and told me I should-n't sleep, be - witched, both-ered and be -

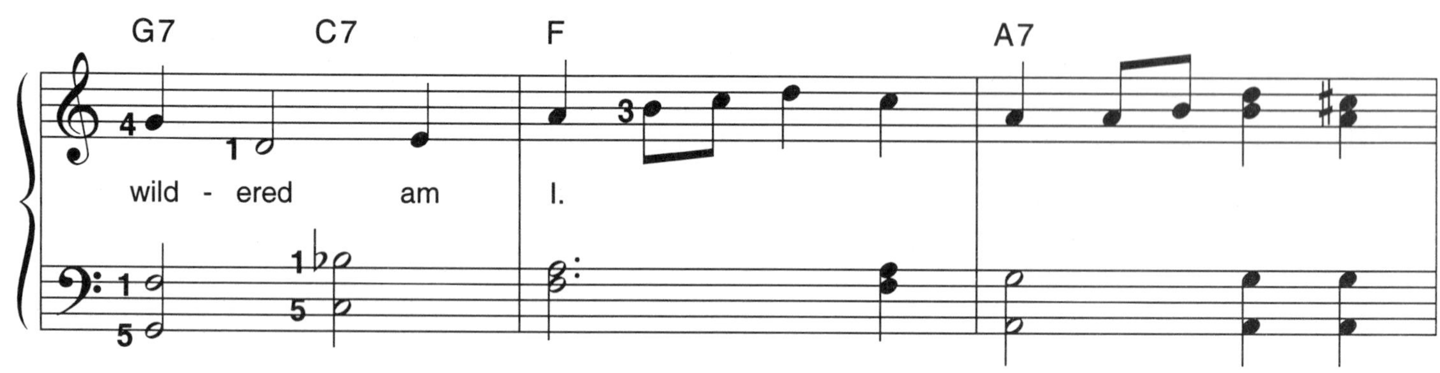
G7
C7
F
A7
wild - ered am I.

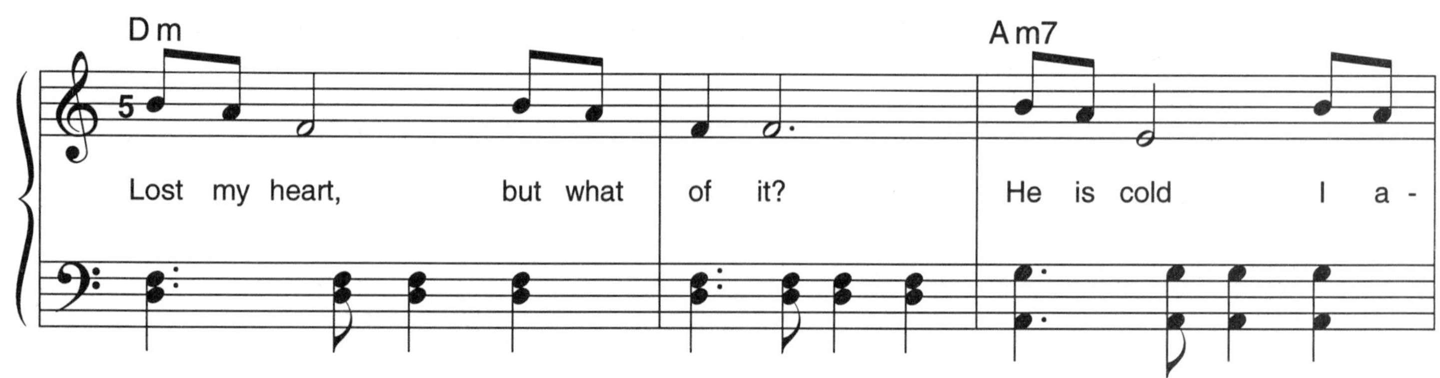
Dm
Am7
Lost my heart, but what of it? He is cold I a -

Dm
G7
Dm
G7
gree. He can laugh, but I love it, al-though the

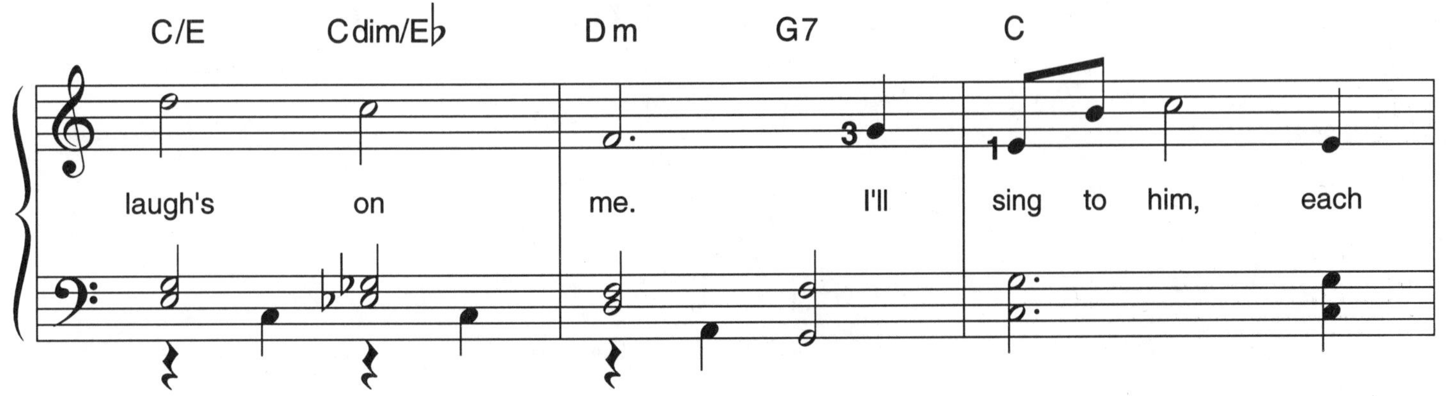
C/E Cdim/E♭ Dm G7 C
laugh's on me. I'll sing to him, each

G7 C C+ F Fdim
spring to him, and long for the day when I'll cling to him, be -

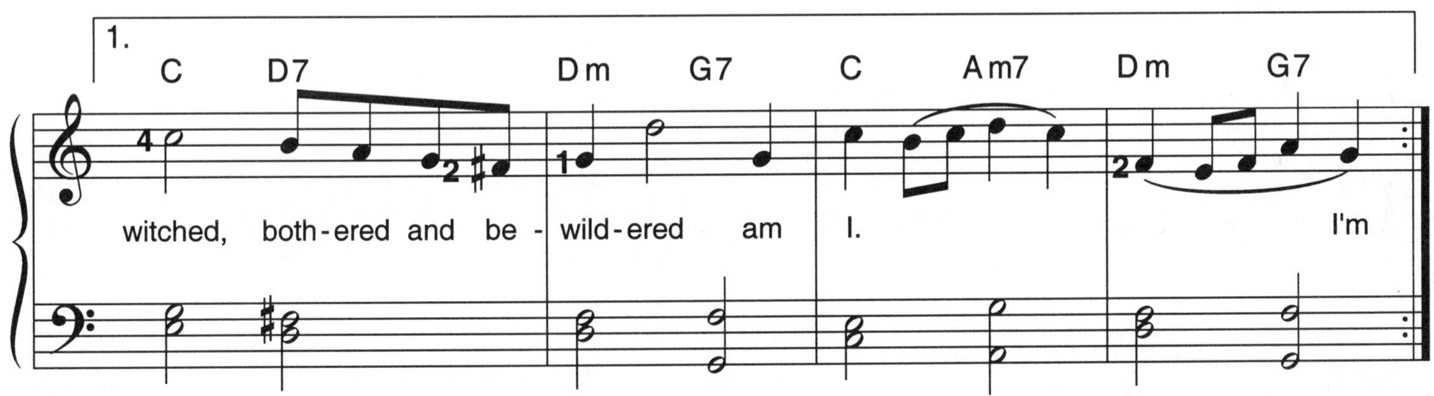
1.
C D7 Dm G7 C Am7 Dm G7
witched, both-ered and be - wild-ered am I. I'm

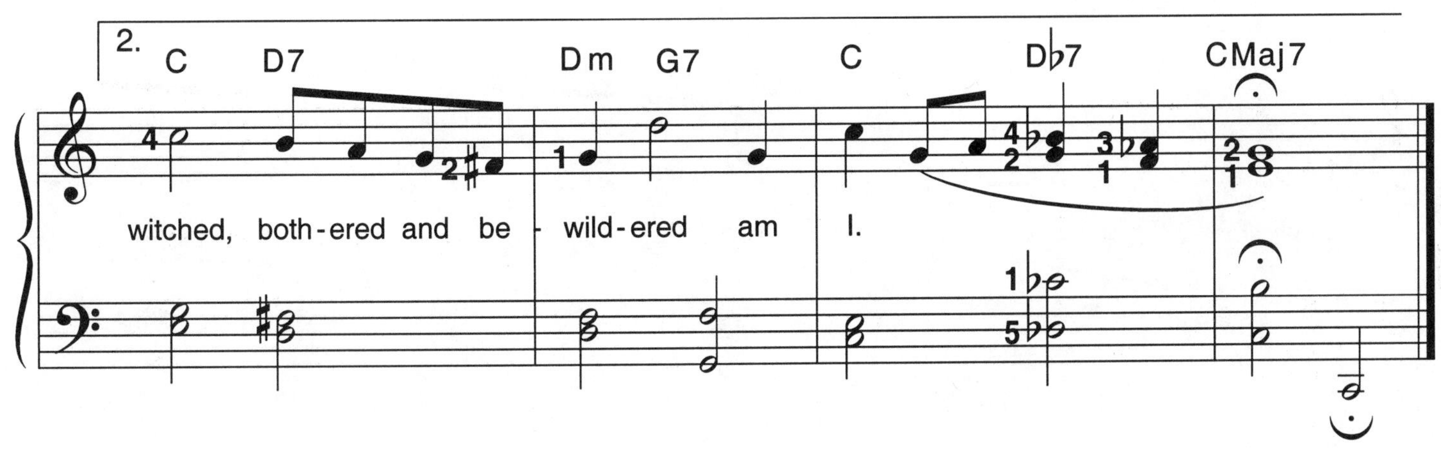
2.
C D7 Dm G7 C D♭7 CMaj7
witched, both-ered and be - wild-ered am I.

On A Clear Day (You Can See Forever)

John Cullum introduced this standard on Broadway when he sang it to Barbara Harris in *On a Clear Day You Can See Forever*. In the movie, Yves Montand sang it to Barbra Streisand.

Lyrics by ALAN JAY LERNER
Music by BURTON LANE
Arranged by Richard Bradley

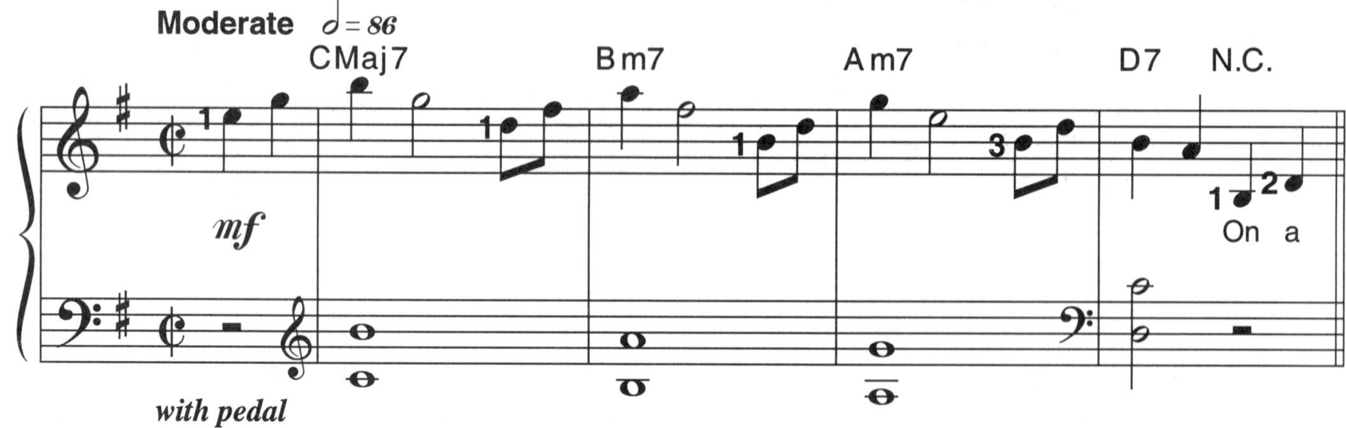

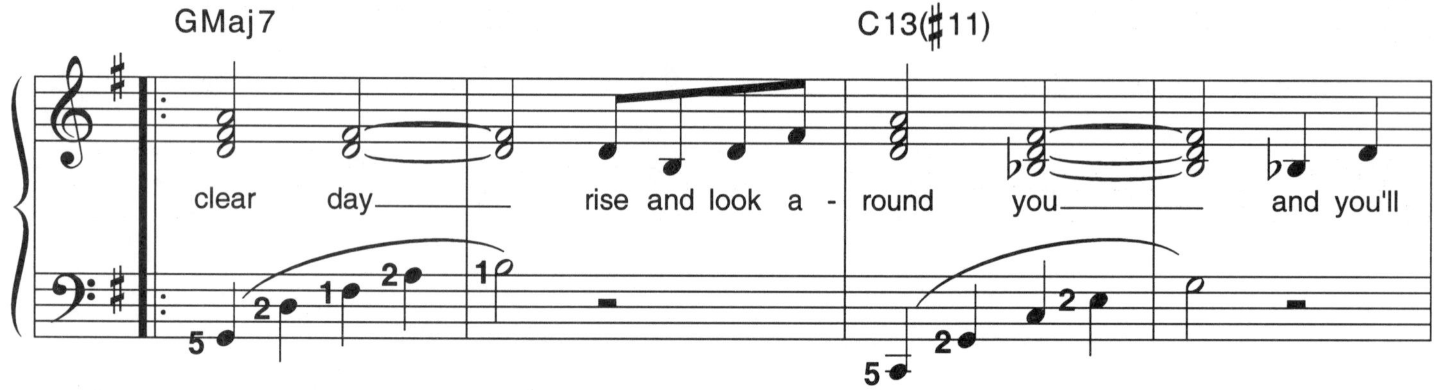

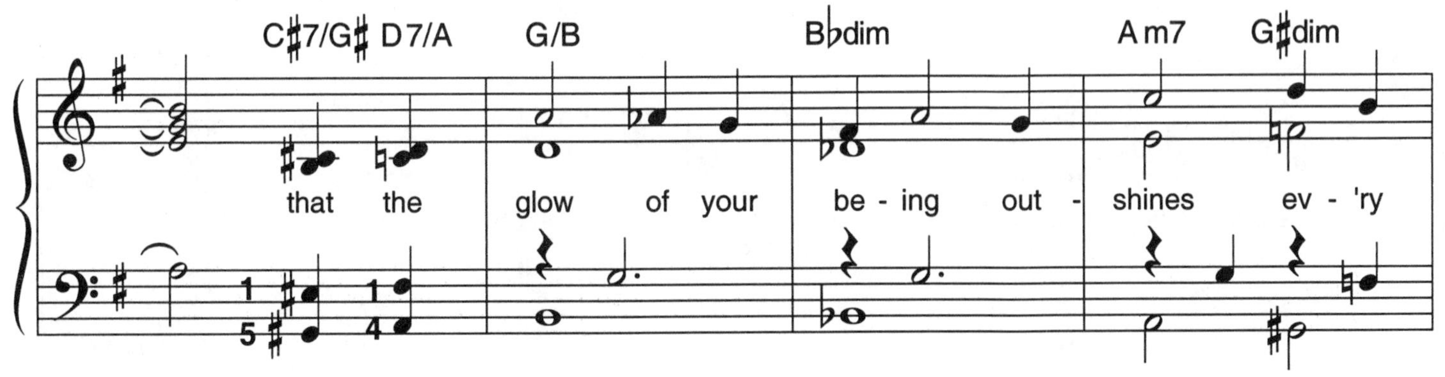
C♯7/G♯ D7/A
G/B
B♭dim
Am7
G♯dim
that the glow of your be - ing out - shines ev - 'ry

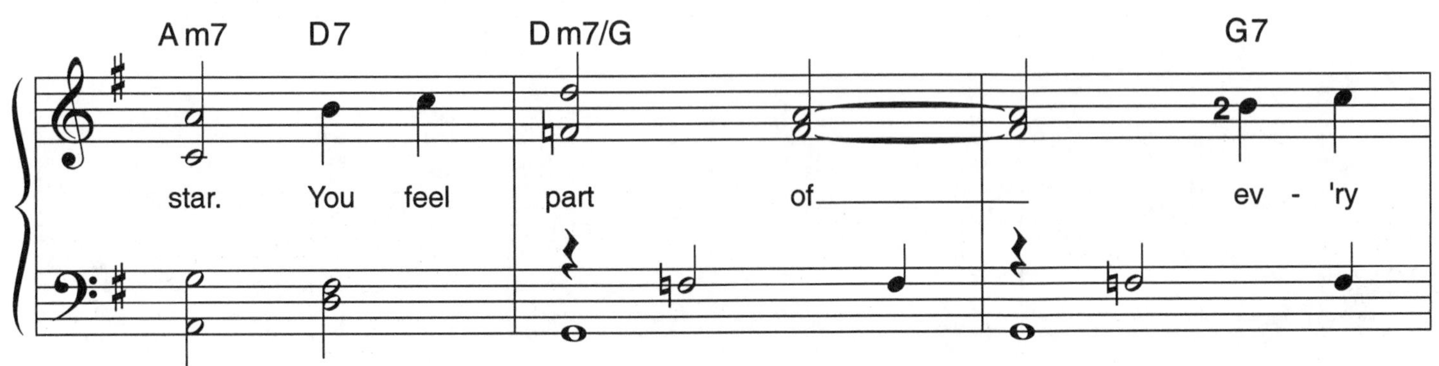
Am7
D7
Dm7/G
G7
star. You feel part of ev - 'ry

Dm7/G
G7
CMaj7
Bm7
mountain, sea and shore. You can hear, from far and

A7/C♯
D7
near, a world you've nev - er heard be - fore. And on a

Gdim GMaj7 G Bm7sus4 E9 Bm E9
clear day, on that clear day you can

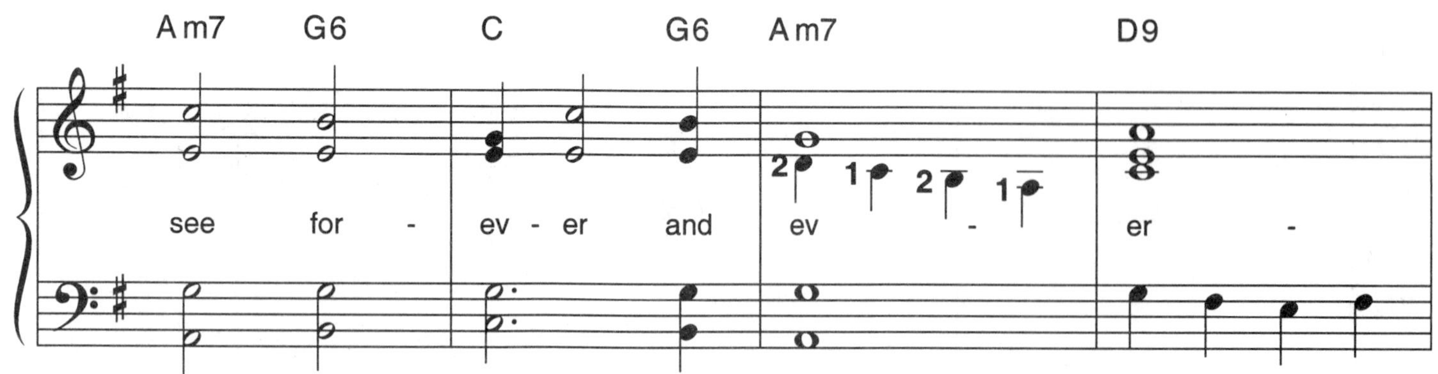
Am7 G6 C G6 Am7 D9
see for - ev - er and ev - er -

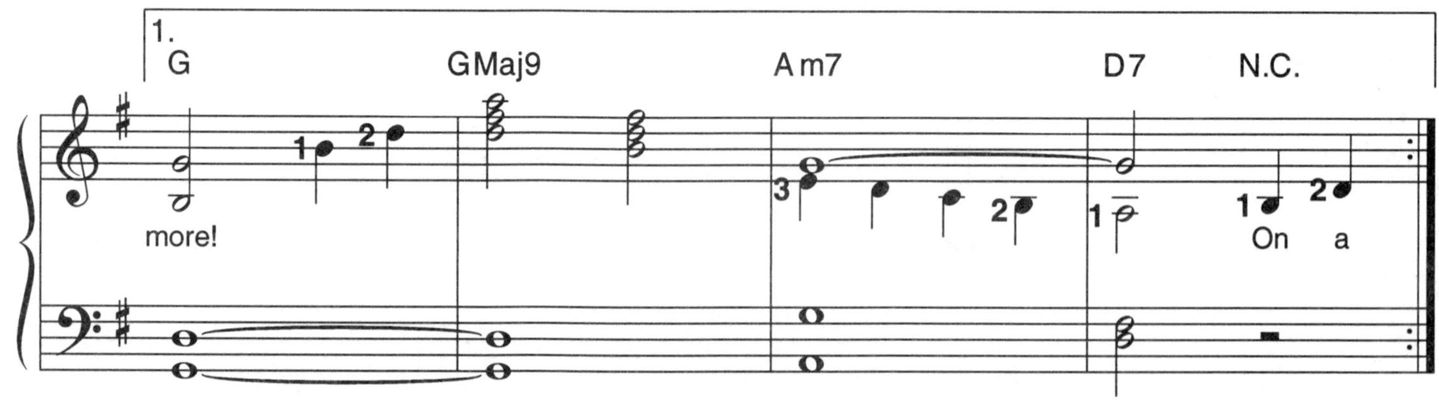
1.
G GMaj9 Am7 D7 N.C.
more! On a

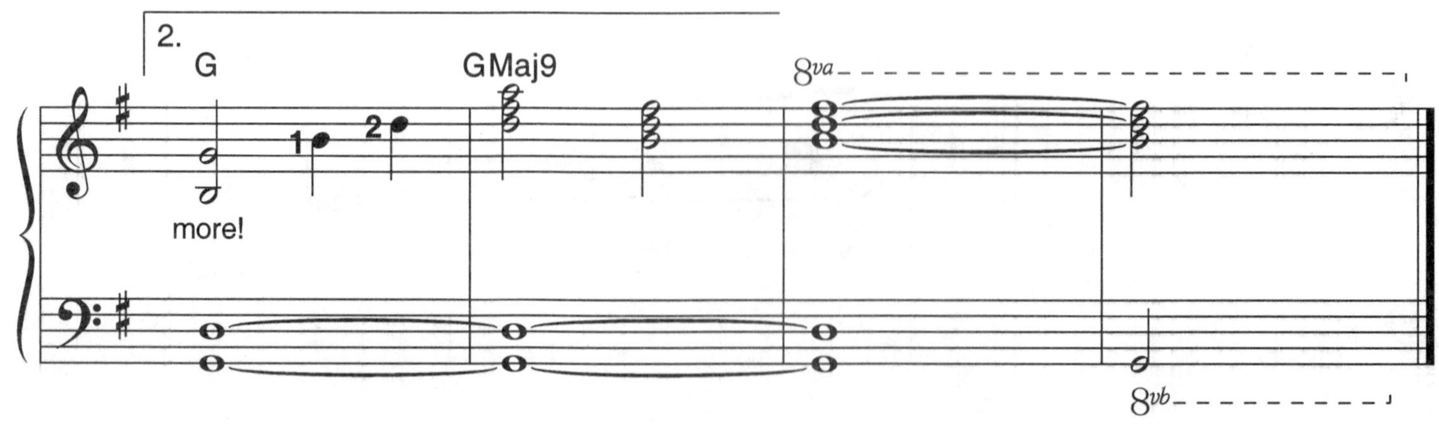
2.
G GMaj9
8va
more!
8vb

Singin' In The Rain

Although this standard is closely associated with Gene Kelly in the 1952 film *Singin' in the Rain*, it was originally introduced by Cliff Edwards (Ukulele Ike) in 1929 in the Oscar nominated movie *Hollywood Revue*.

Lyric by ARTHUR FREED
Music by NACIO HERB BROWN
Arranged by Richard Bradley

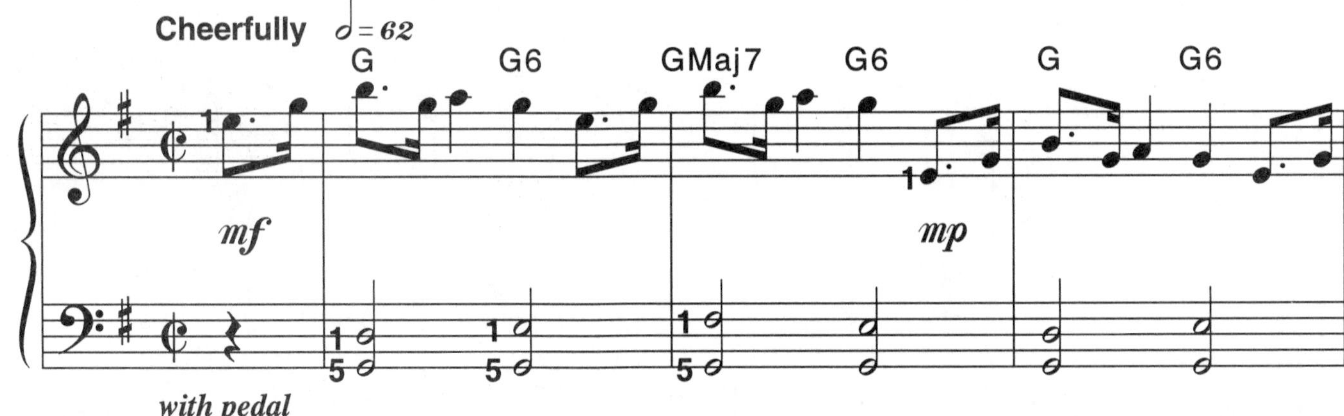

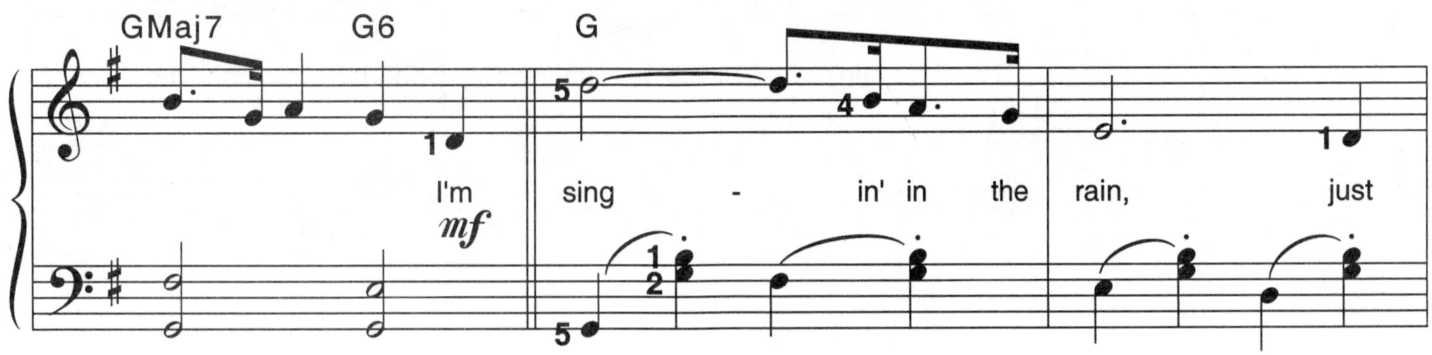

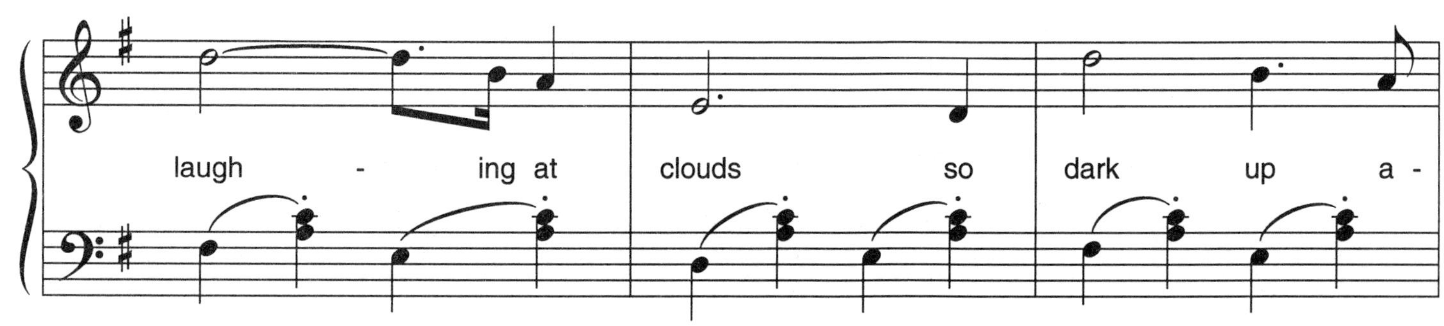
laugh - ing at
clouds so
dark up a -

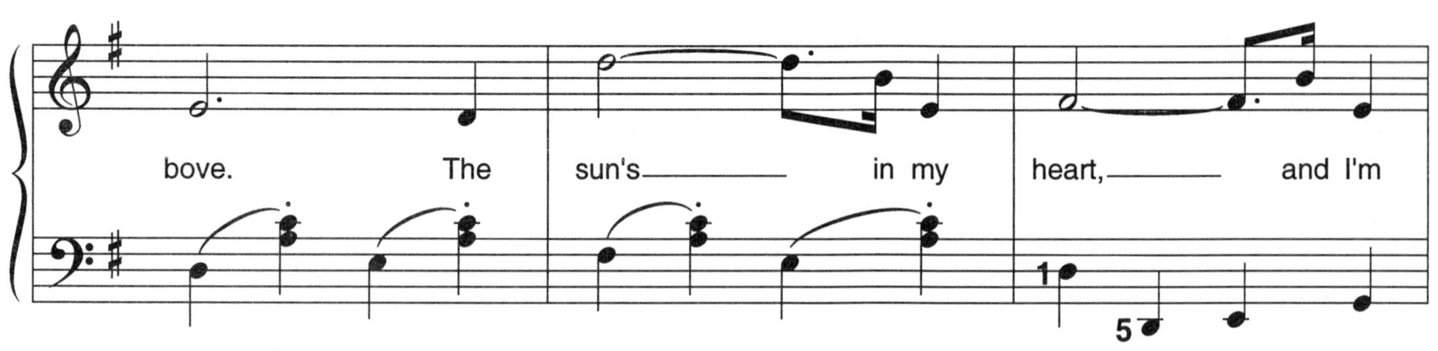
bove. The
sun's in my
heart, and I'm
1
5

G
read - y for
love. Let the
storm - y clouds
1
2

chase ev - 'ry
- one from the
place. Come

Fdim
D7
on with the
rain, I've a
smile on my
face. I'll
walk down the
lane with a
hap - py re -
frain, and
sing - in' just
sing - in' in the
rain.
G
G6
GMaj7
G6
G

Tomorrow

Tomorrow is the best remembered song from the Broadway musical *Annie*.

Lyrics by MARTIN CHARNIN
Music by CHARLES STROUSE
Arranged by Richard Bradley

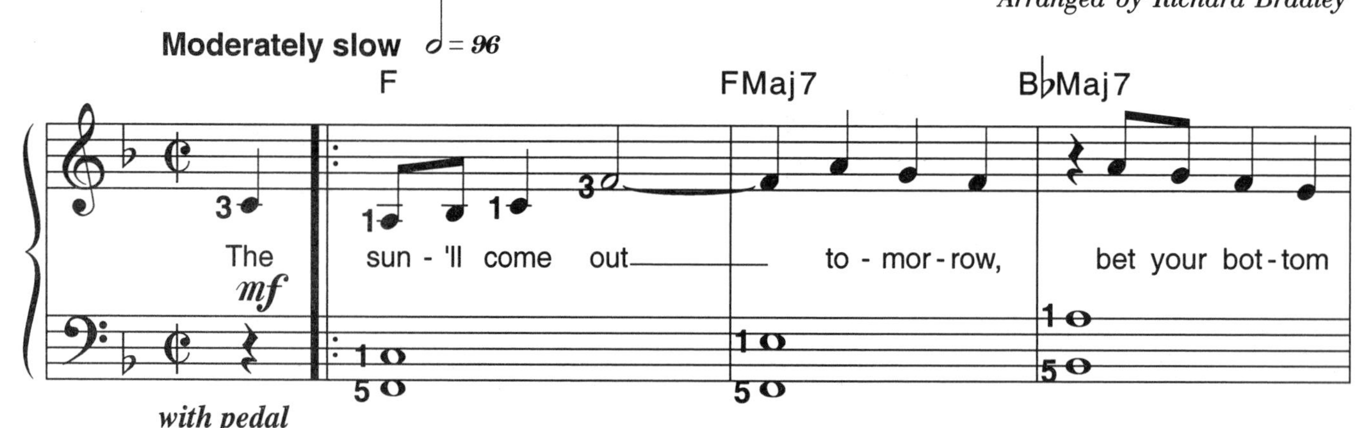

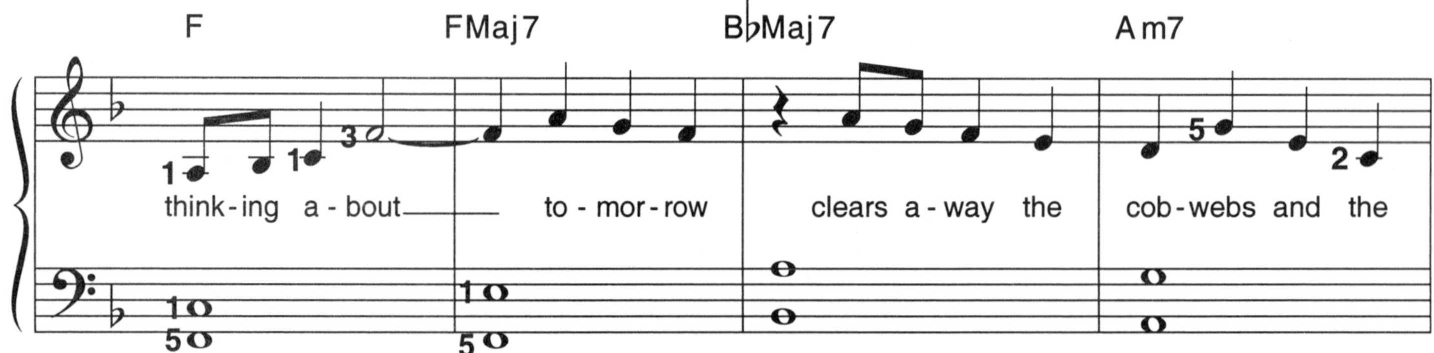

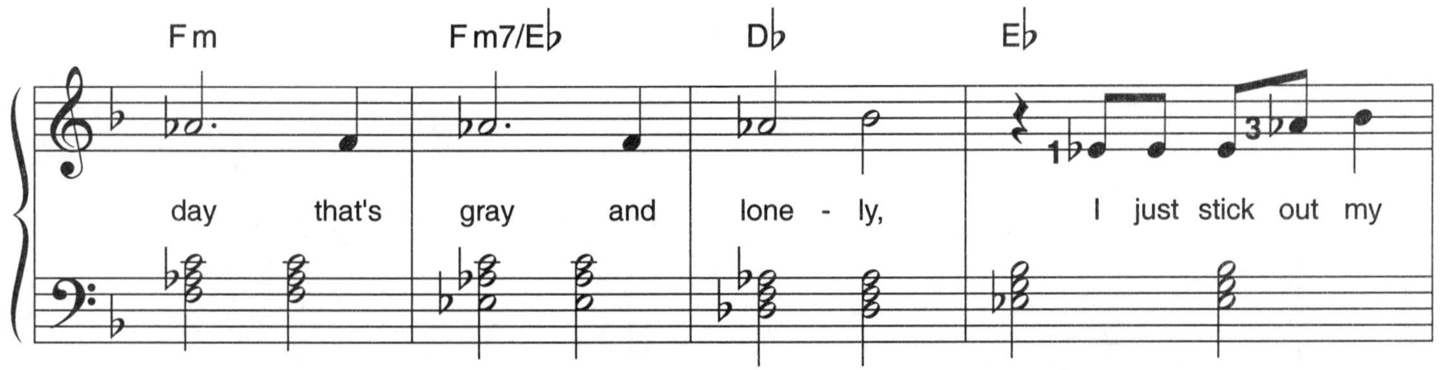
Fm
Fm7/E♭
D♭
E♭
day that's gray and lone - ly, I just stick out my

A♭
A♭Maj7/G
C7sus4
chin and grin and say:

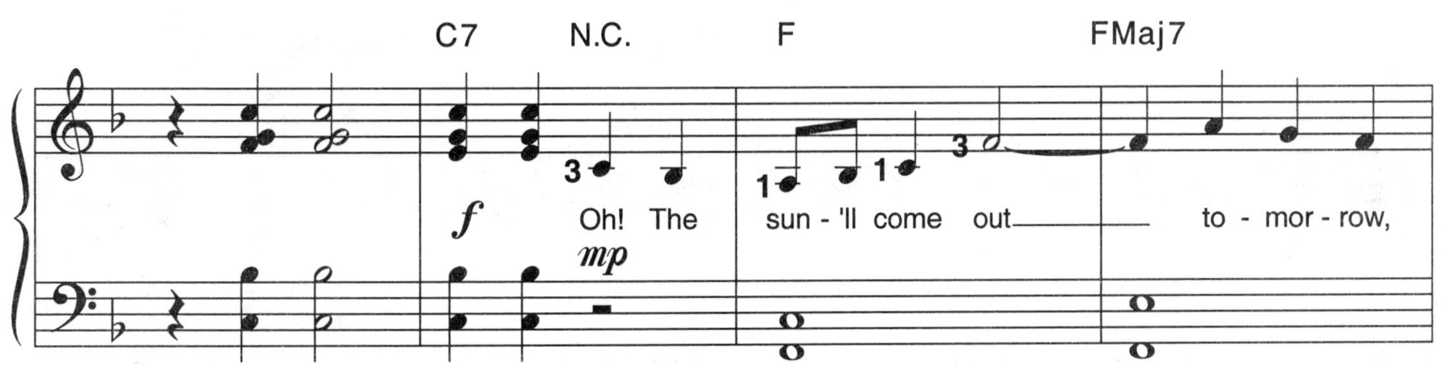
C7
N.C.
F
FMaj7
f
mp
Oh! The sun - 'll come out to - mor - row,

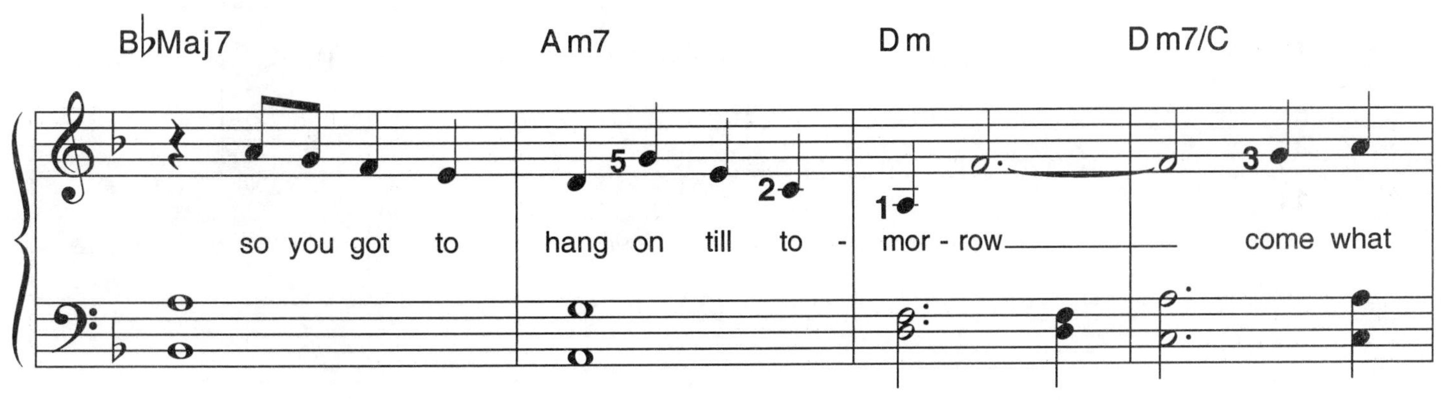
B♭Maj7
Am7
Dm
Dm7/C
so you got to hang on till to - mor - row come what

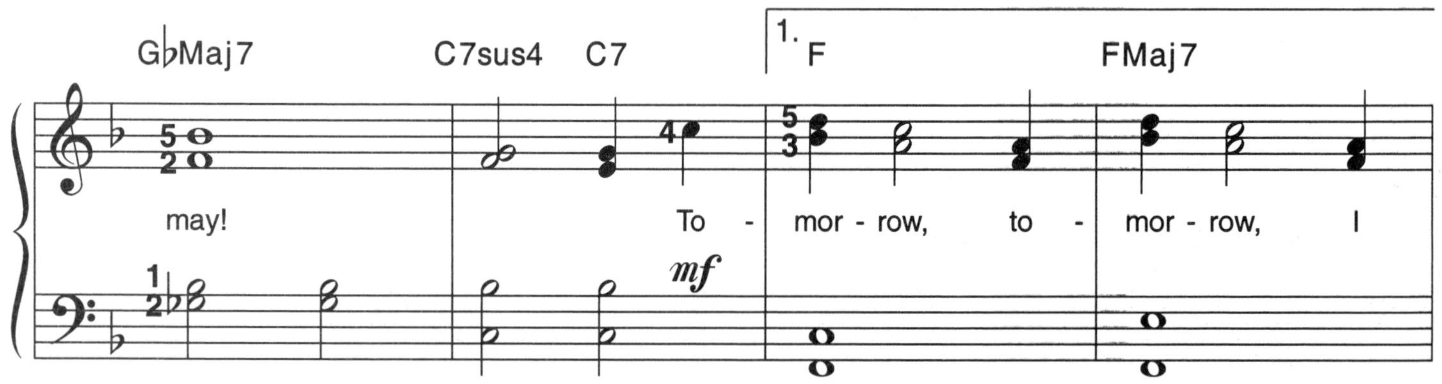
G♭Maj7
C7sus4
C7
1.
F
FMaj7
may!
To - mor - row, to - mor - row, I
mf

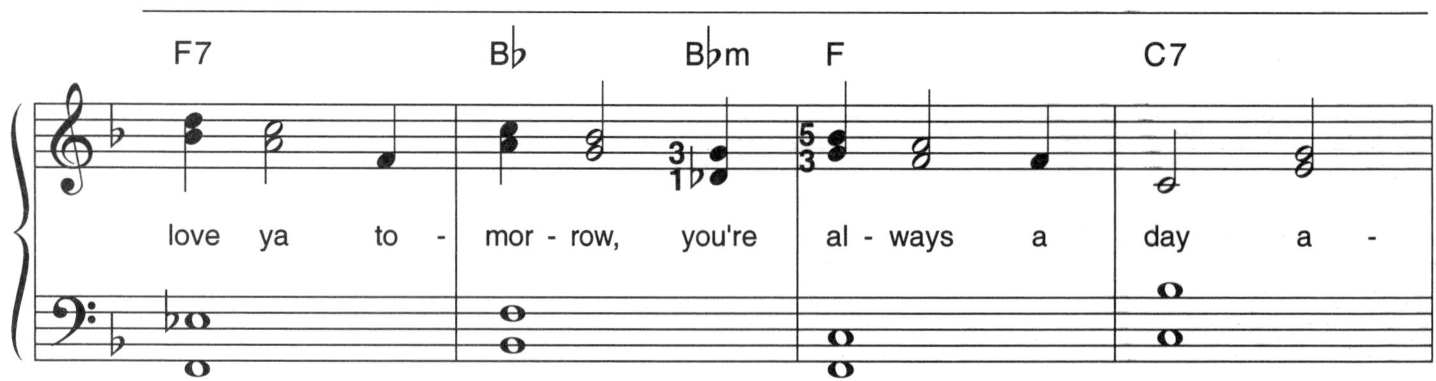
F7
B♭
B♭m
F
C7
love ya to - mor - row, you're al - ways a day a -

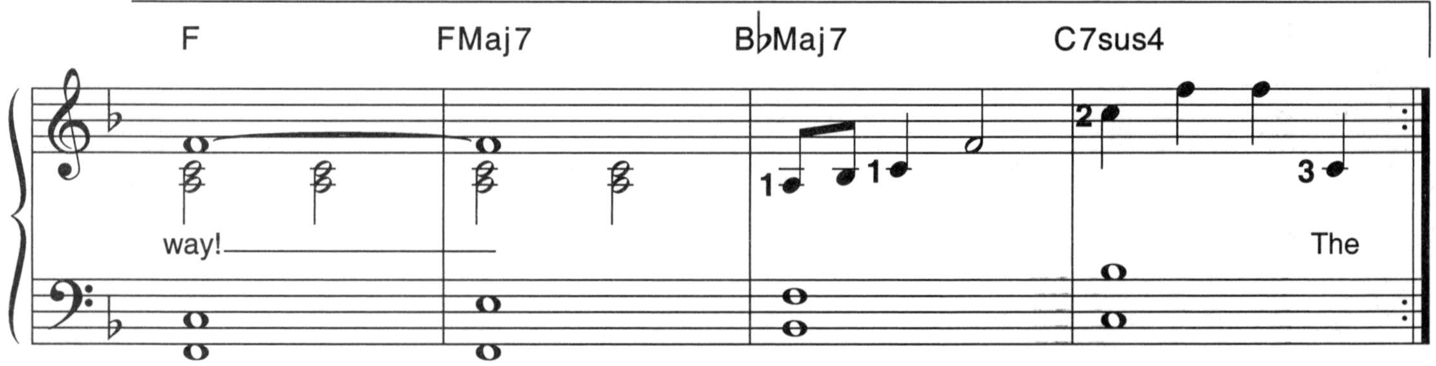
F
FMaj7
B♭Maj7
C7sus4
way!
The

2.
F
FMaj7
F7
B♭
B♭m
mor - row, to - mor - row, I love ya to - mor - row, you're

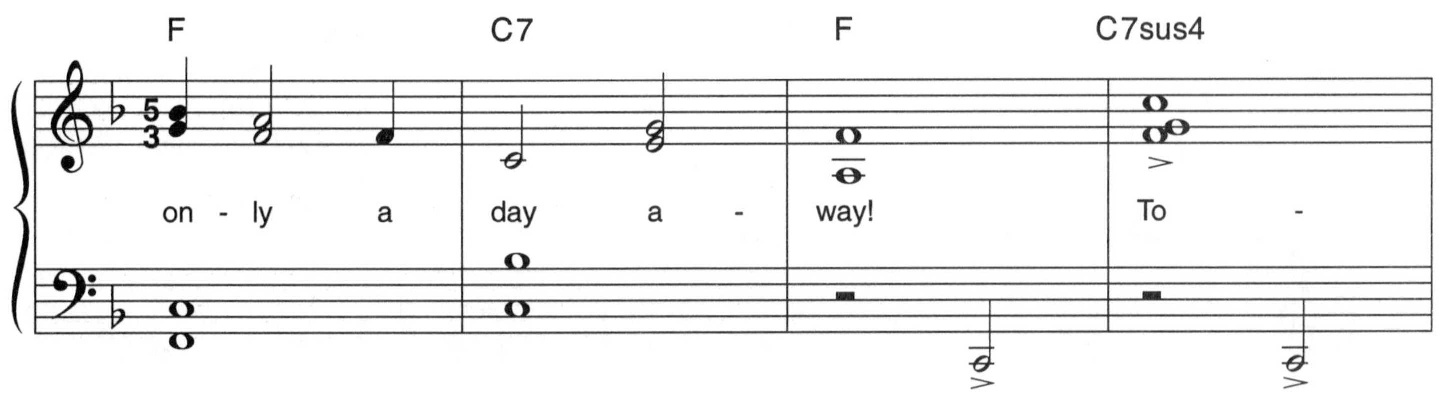
F
C7
F
C7sus4
on - ly a day a - way! To -

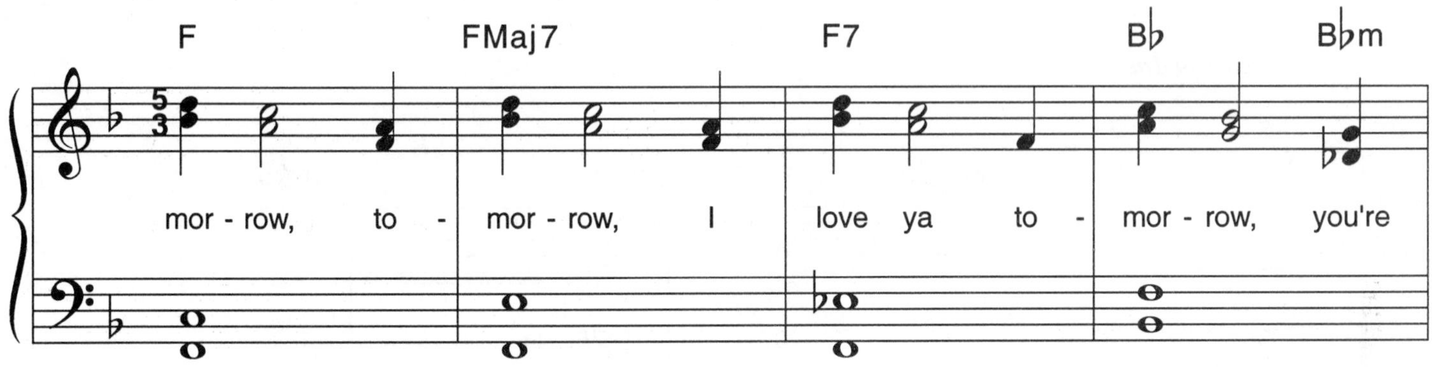
F
FMaj7
F7
B♭
B♭m
mor - row, to - mor - row, I love ya to - mor - row, you're

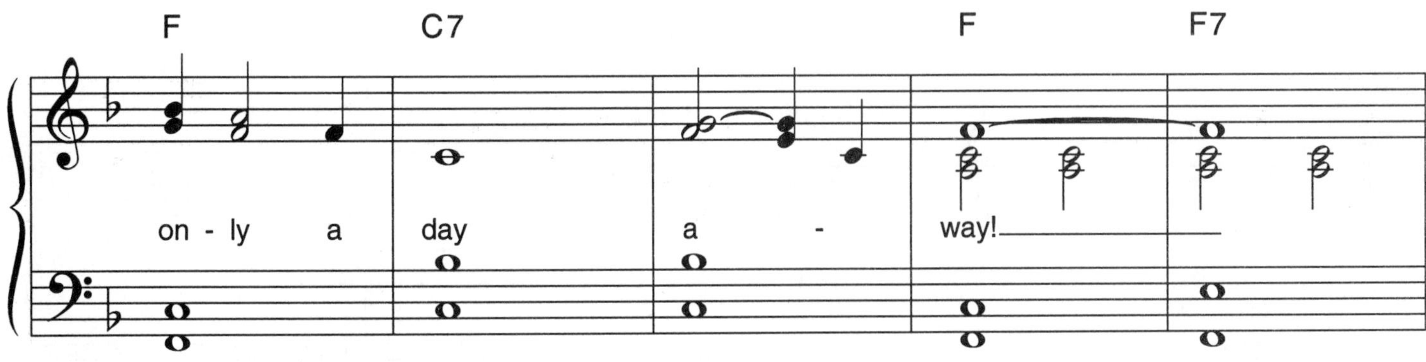
F
C7
F
F7
on - ly a day a - way!

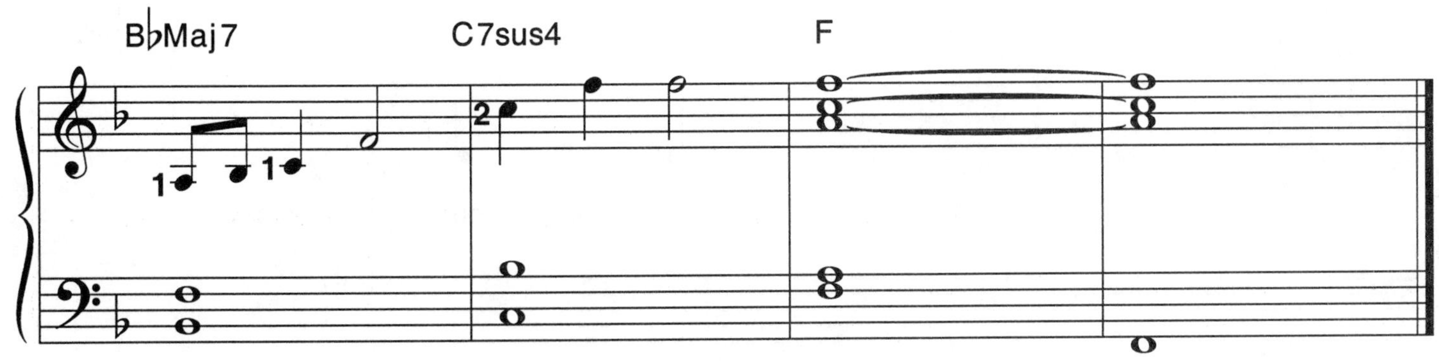
B♭Maj7
C7sus4
F

Charade

Andy Williams sang this Oscar nominated standard from the motion picture *Charade*.

Words by JOHNNY MERCER
Music by HENRY MANCINI
Arranged by Richard Bradley

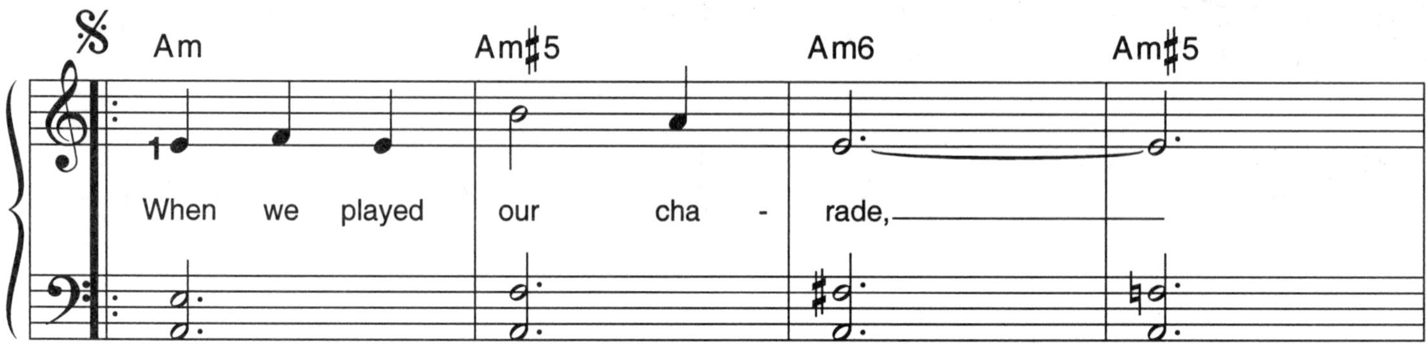

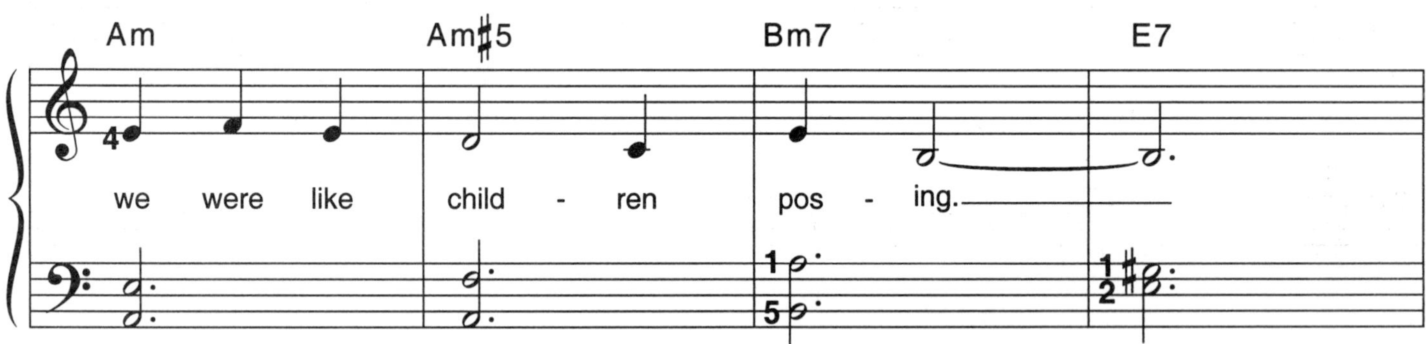

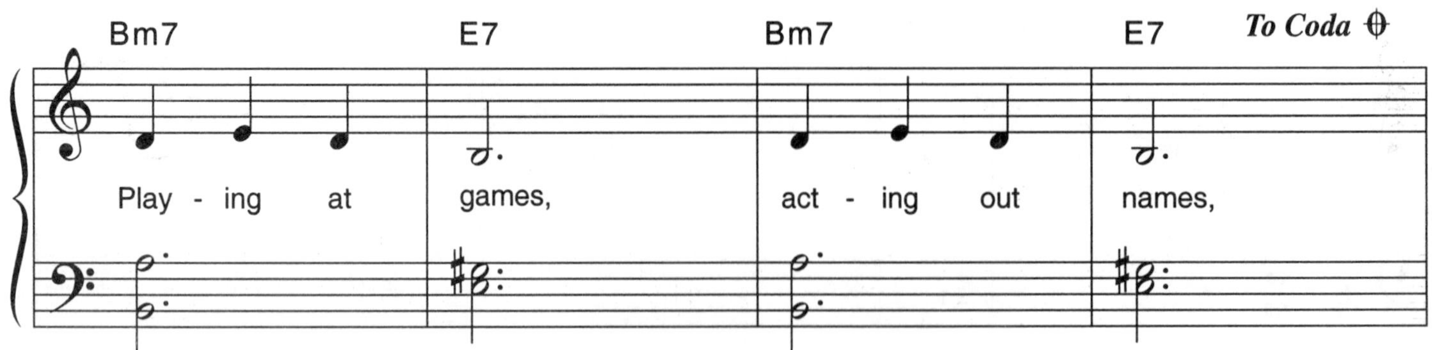

Bm7
E7
Am
Am♯5
4
2
guess - ing the parts we played.

1.
2.
Am6
Am♯5
Am♯5
Dm7
mf
2 1
1 2
Fate
1
5

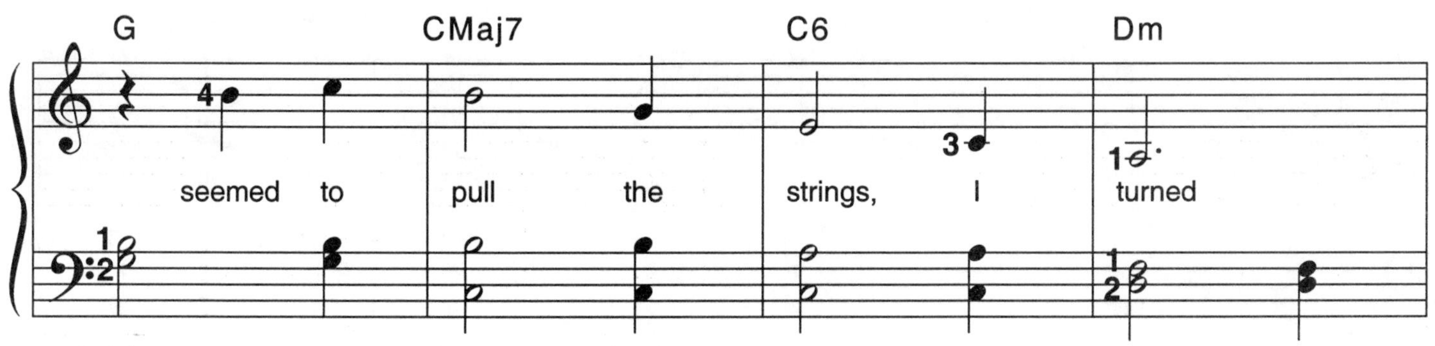
G
CMaj7
C6
Dm
4
3
1
seemed to pull the strings, I turned
1
2
1
2

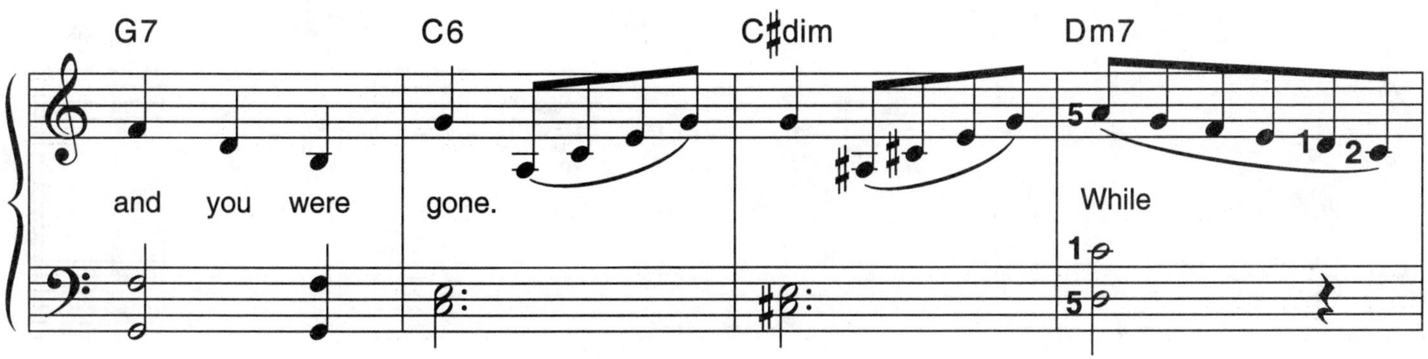
G7
C6
C♯dim
Dm7
5
1 2
and you were gone.
While
1
5

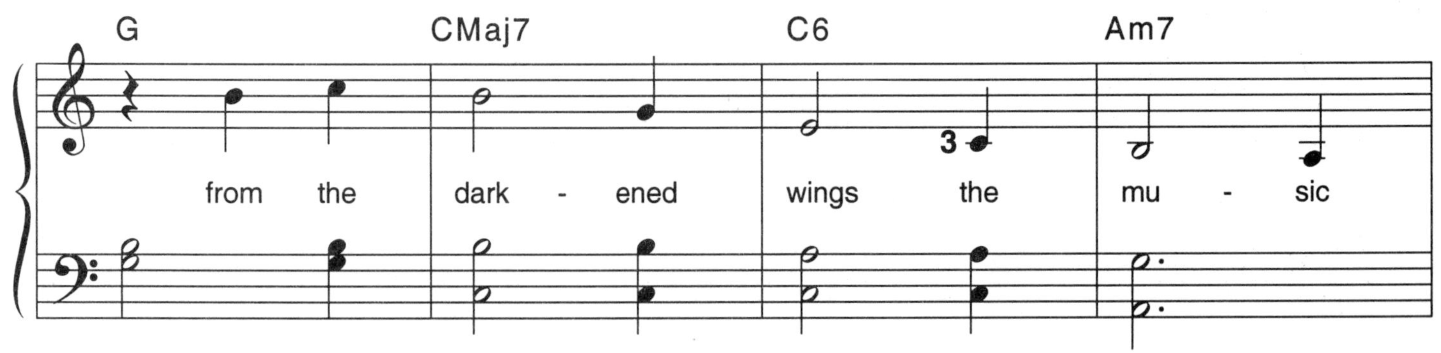
G
CMaj7
C6
Am7
3
from the dark - ened wings the mu - sic

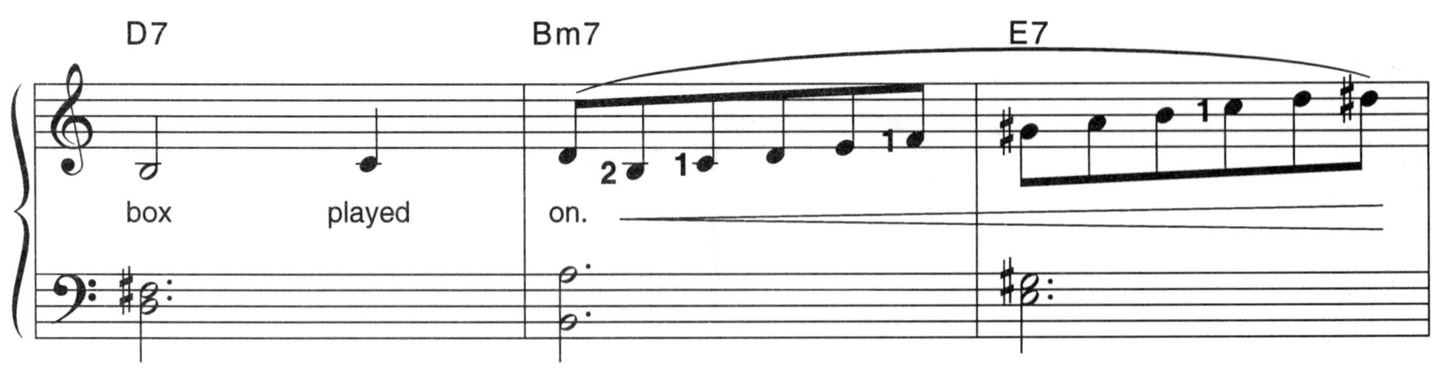
D7
Bm7
E7
2 1 1 1
box played on.

Am
Am♯5
Am6
Am♯5
4 5
f

D.S. 𝄋 al Coda 𝄌
Am
Am♯5
Am6
Am♯5
4
mp

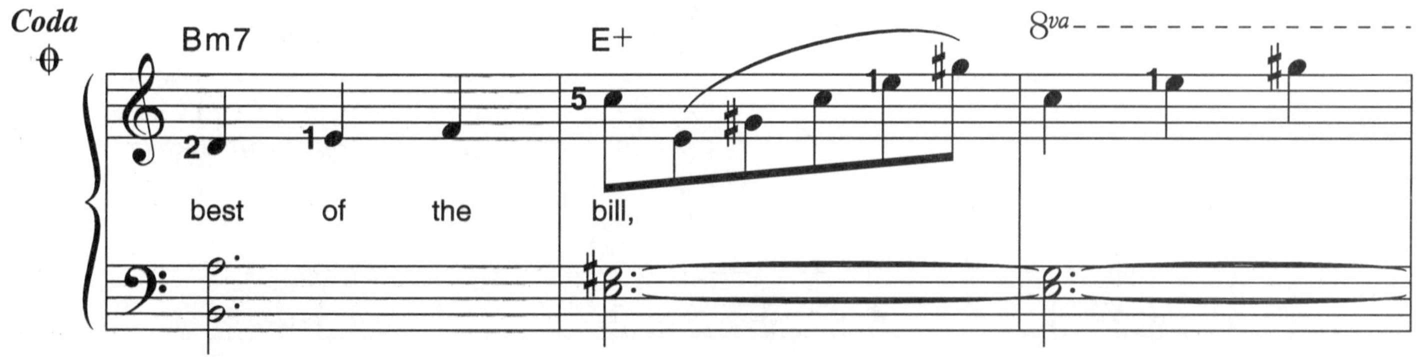

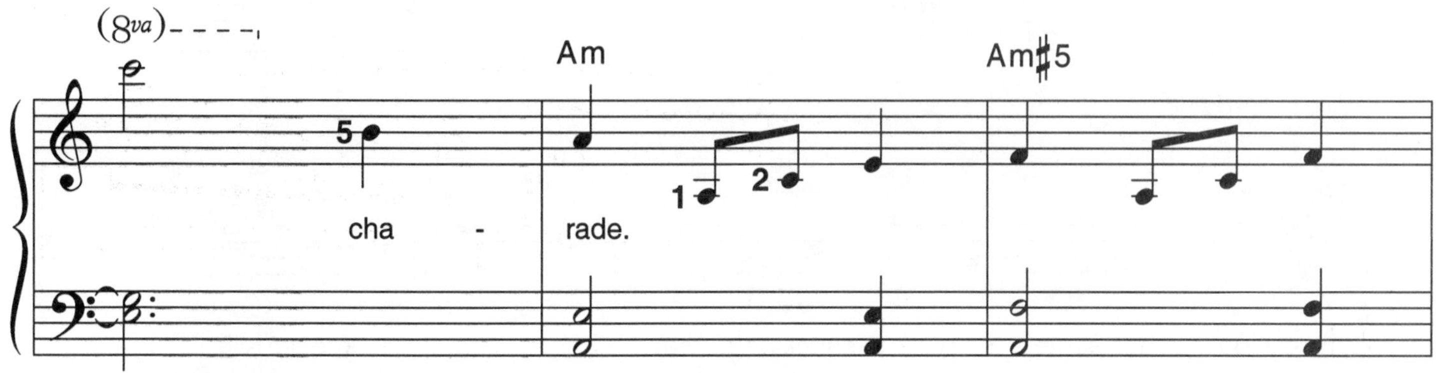

Verse 2:
Oh, what a hit we made.
We came on next to closing.
Best on the bill, lovers until
Love left the masquerade.

Verse 3:
Sad little serenade,
Song of my heart's composing.
I hear it still, I always will,
Best of the bill,
Charade.

Anything Goes

Ethel Merman introduced this standard in the Broadway musical *Anything Goes*.

Words and Music by
COLE PORTER
Arranged by Richard Bradley

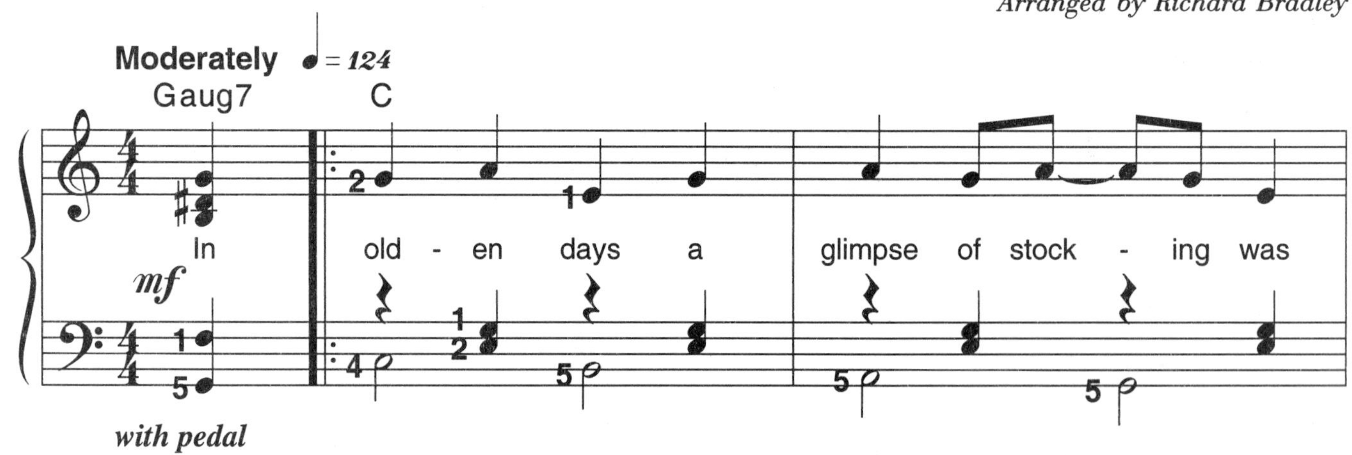

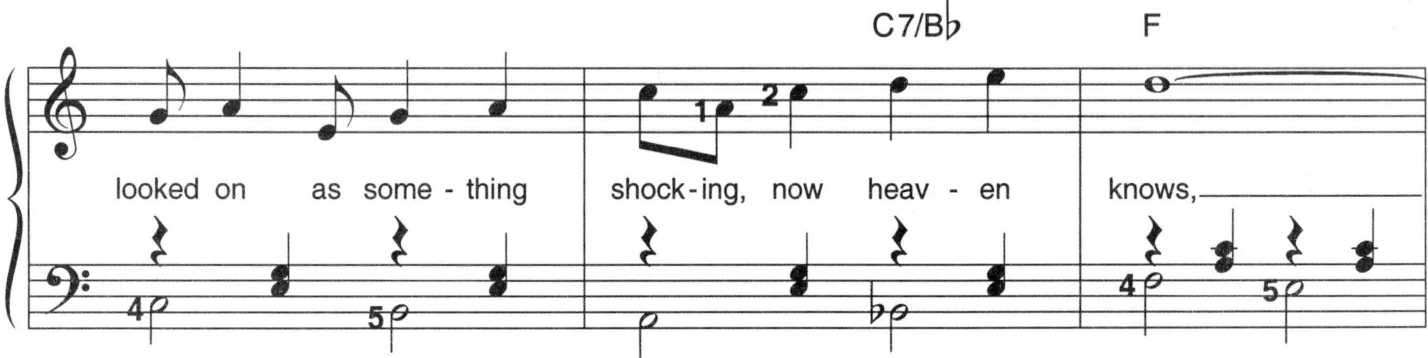

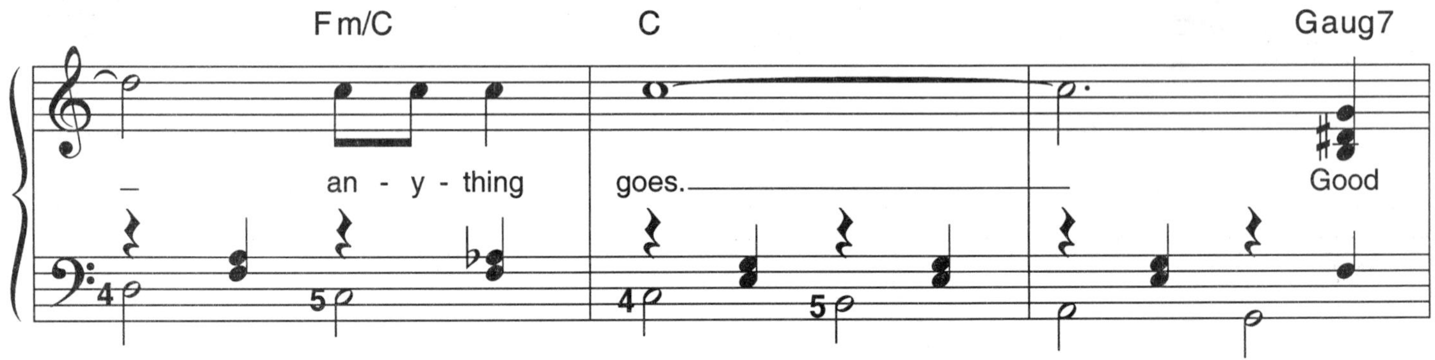

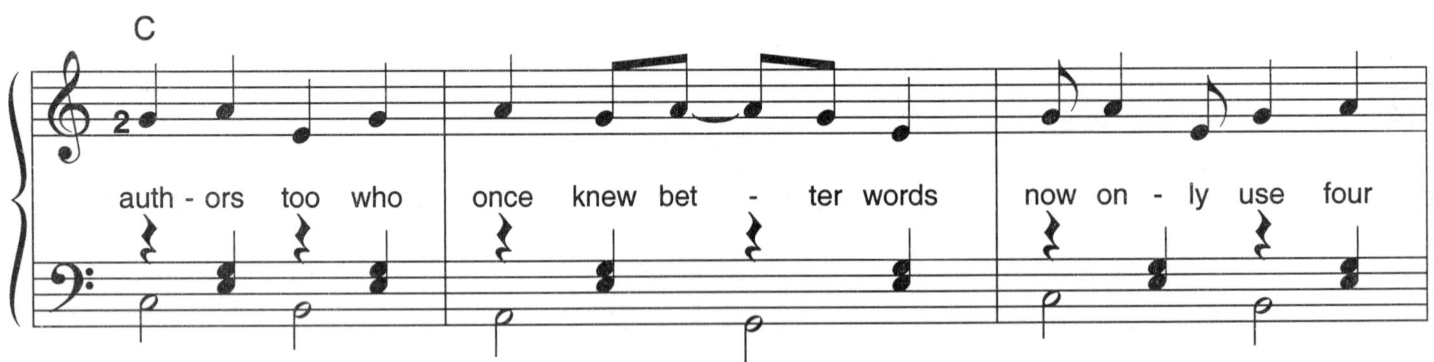

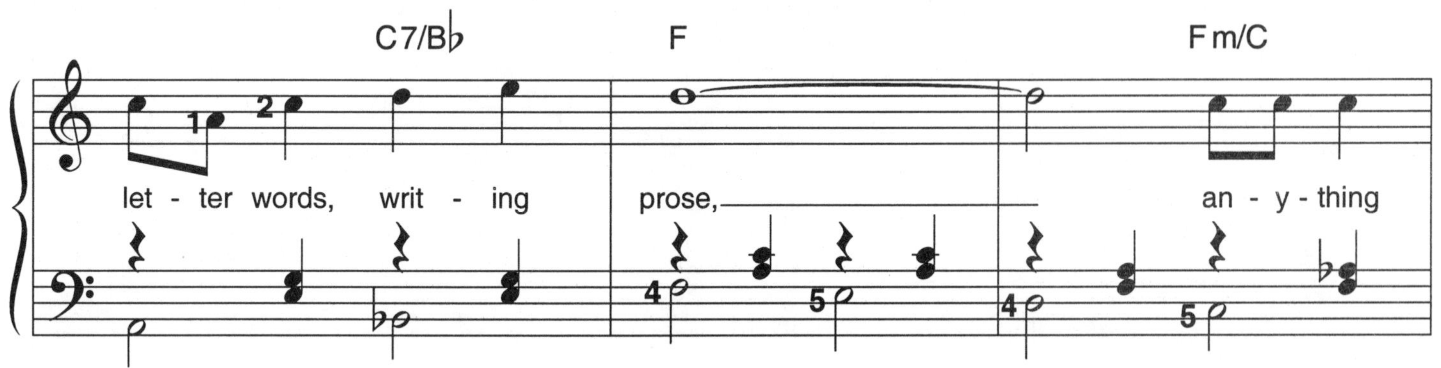
C7/B♭
F
Fm/C
let - ter words, writ - ing prose, an - y - thing

C
B7
E
goes. The world has gone mad to - day and good's

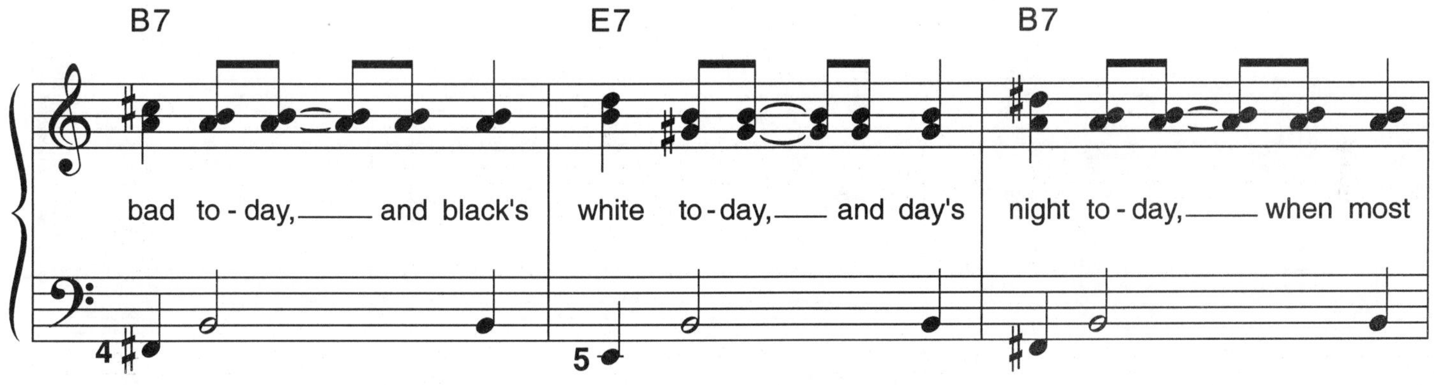
B7
E7
B7
bad to - day, and black's white to - day, and day's night to - day, when most

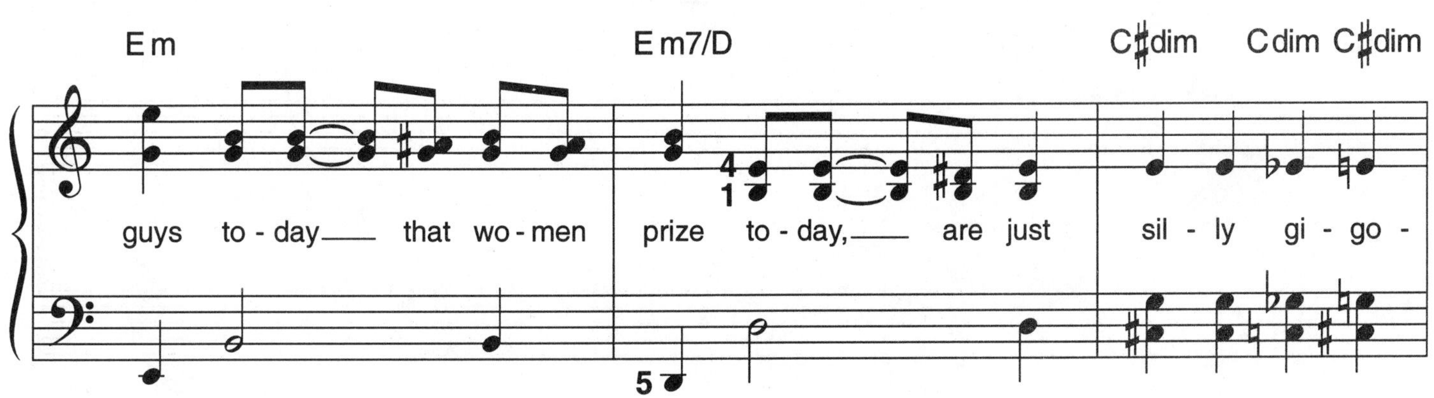
Em
Em7/D
C♯dim
Cdim
C♯dim
guys to - day that wo - men prize to - day, are just sil - ly gi - go -

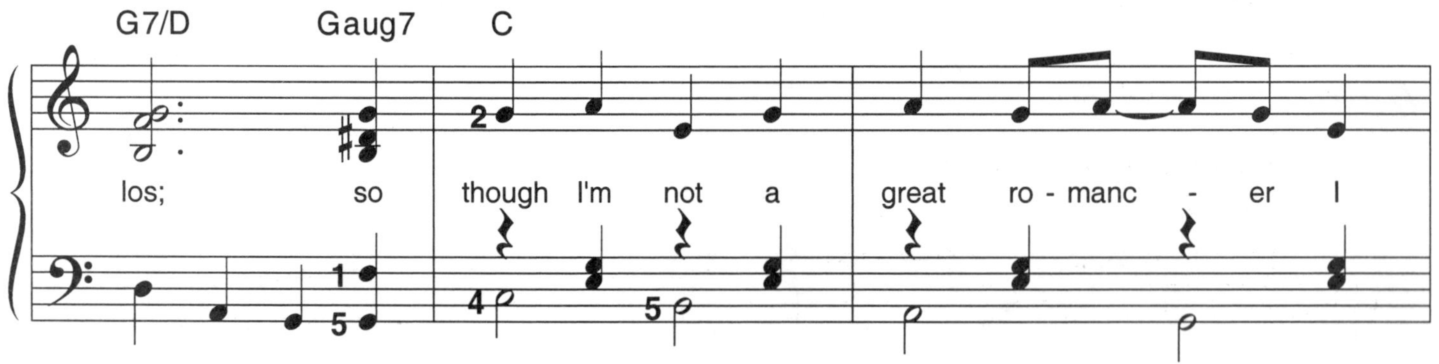
G7/D
Gaug7
C
los; so though I'm not a great ro - manc - er I

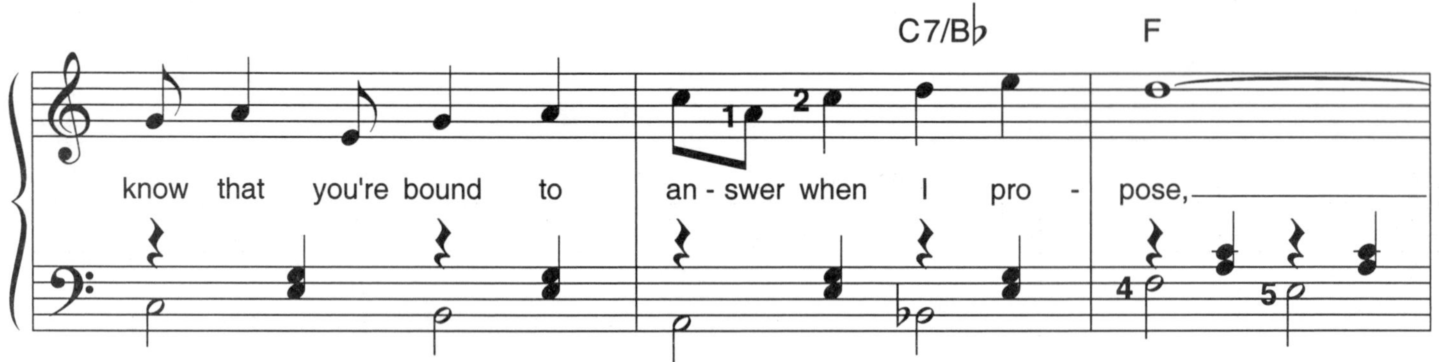
C7/B♭
F
know that you're bound to an - swer when I pro - pose,

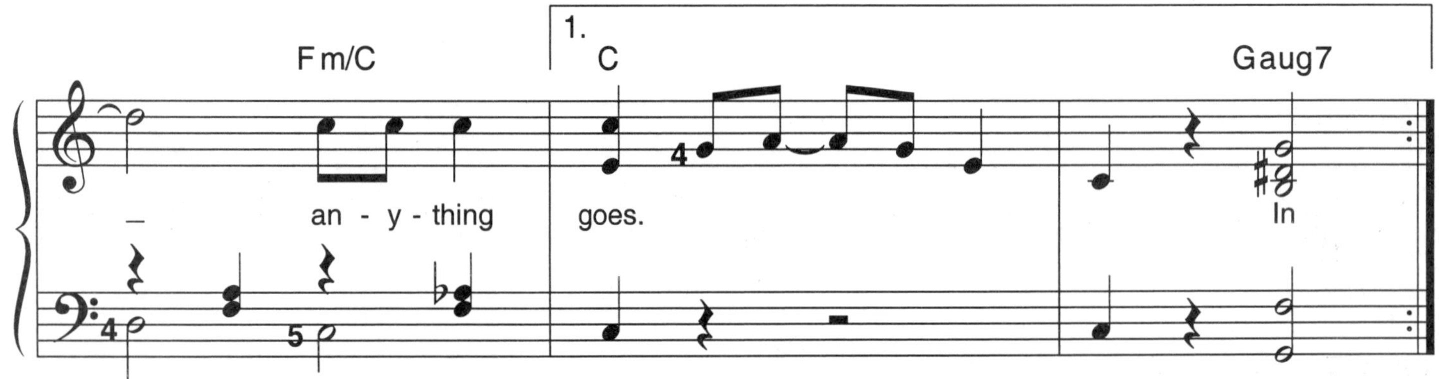
Fm/C
1.
C
Gaug7
— an - y - thing goes. In

2.
C
goes.

How Do You Keep The Music Playing?

This beautiful standard from the motion picture *Best Friends* was nominated for the best song Oscar in 1982.

Words by ALAN and MARILYN BERGMAN
Music by MICHEL LEGRAND
Arranged by Richard Bradley

Moderately slow ♩ = 106

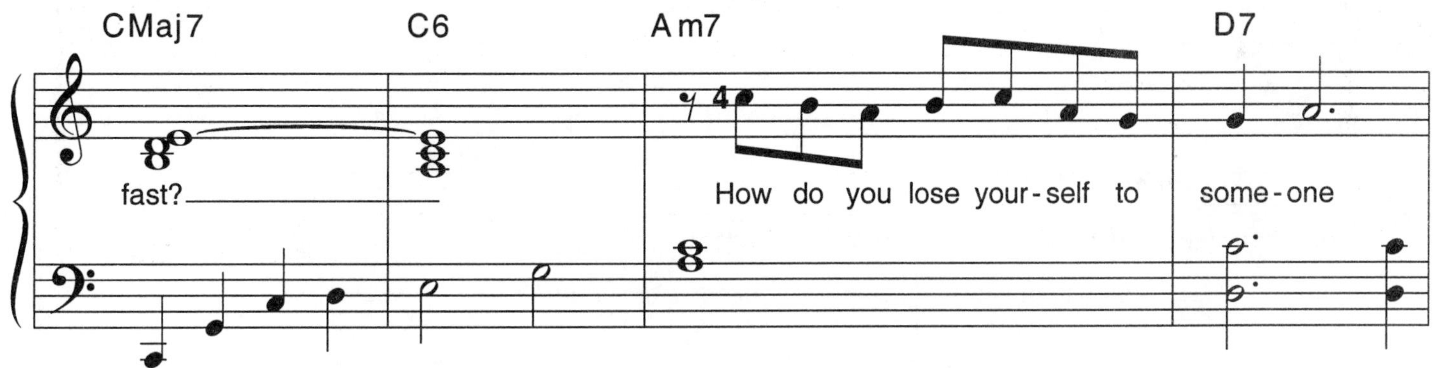

B7
Em
A7
Dm7
new things to say?
And since we know we're al-ways
mp
G7
C
chang - ing,
how can it be the
same?
F
Em
Dm
mf And tell me how, year af - ter
year, you're sure your heart will fall a -
Dm7
G7
C
part each time you
hear her
name?
I
mp
f
Am7
D7
GMaj7
G6
know the
way I feel for you, it's now or
nev - er. The

C
F♯m7(♭5)
B7
more I love, the more that I'm a - fraid that in your eyes I may not see for -
Em7
Em7(♭5)
A7
Dm7
ev - er for - ev - er.
If we can be the best of
mf
G7
C
lov - ers,
yet be the best of
friends,
F
Em
Em7
A7
Dm7
if we can try with ev - 'ry day to make it bet - ter as it grows,
G7(♭9)
Dm7
G7
C
with an - y luck, then I sup - pose the mu - sic nev - er ends.
mp
p

Theme From Ice Castles
(Through The Eyes Of Love)

Melissa Manchester sang this Oscar nominated song in the film *Ice Castles*.

Lyrics by CAROL BAYER SAGER
Music by MARVIN HAMLISCH
Arranged by Richard Bradley

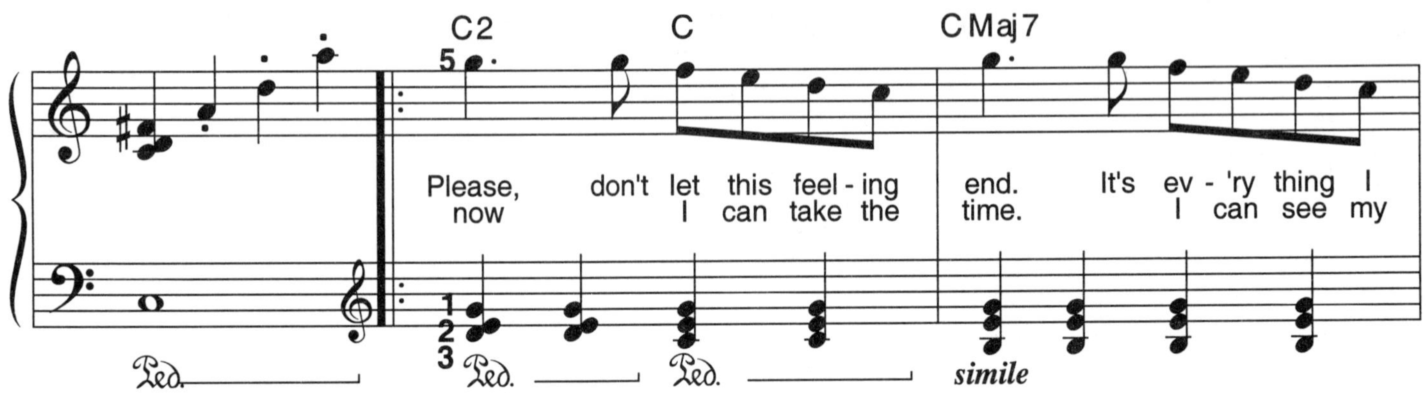

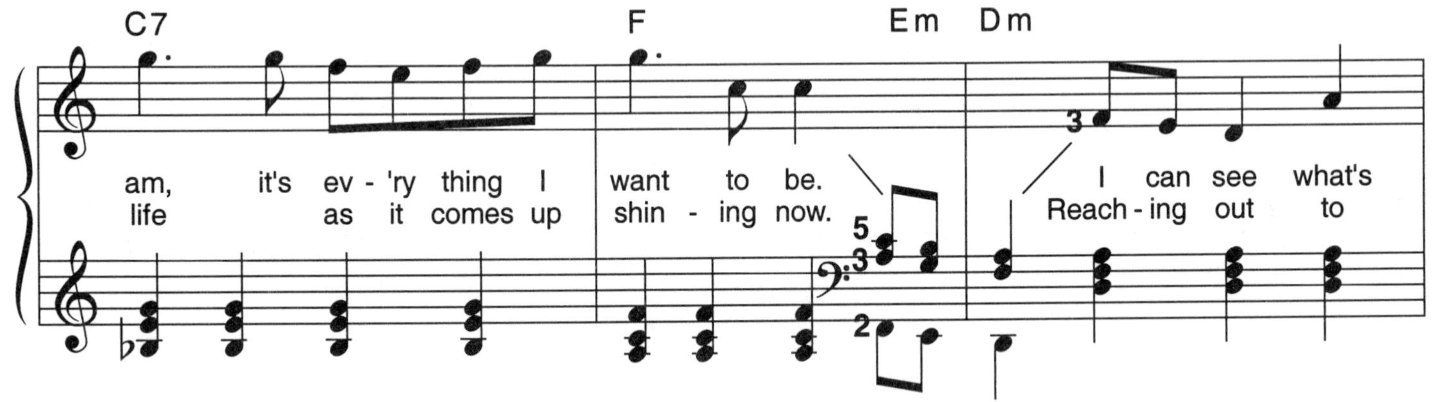

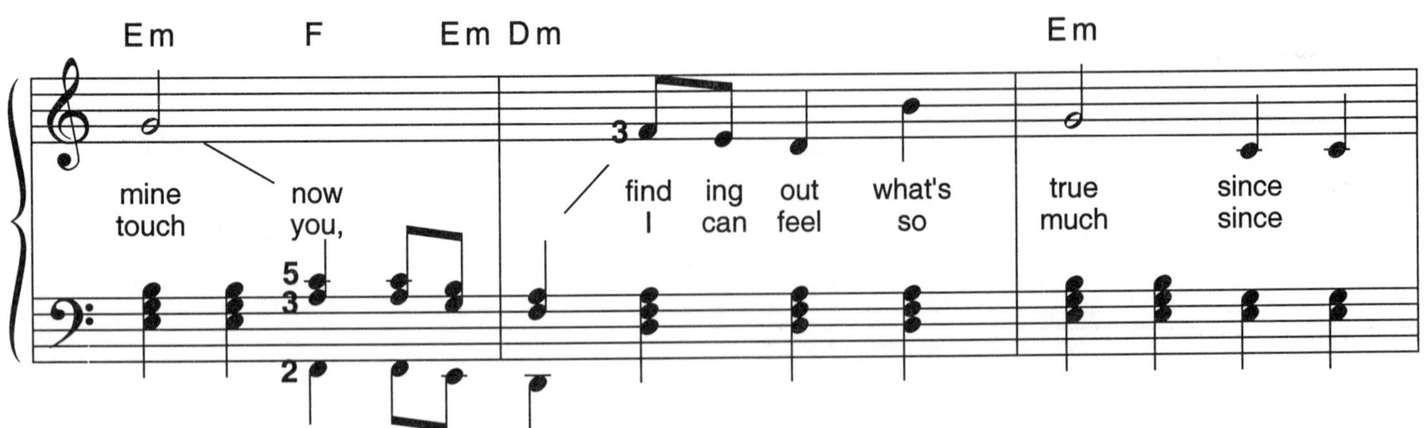

F
E
Am
D7
I
I
found
found
you
you
look - ing
look - ing

Dm
1.
G7
through the eyes of
through the eyes of
love.
And
cresc.

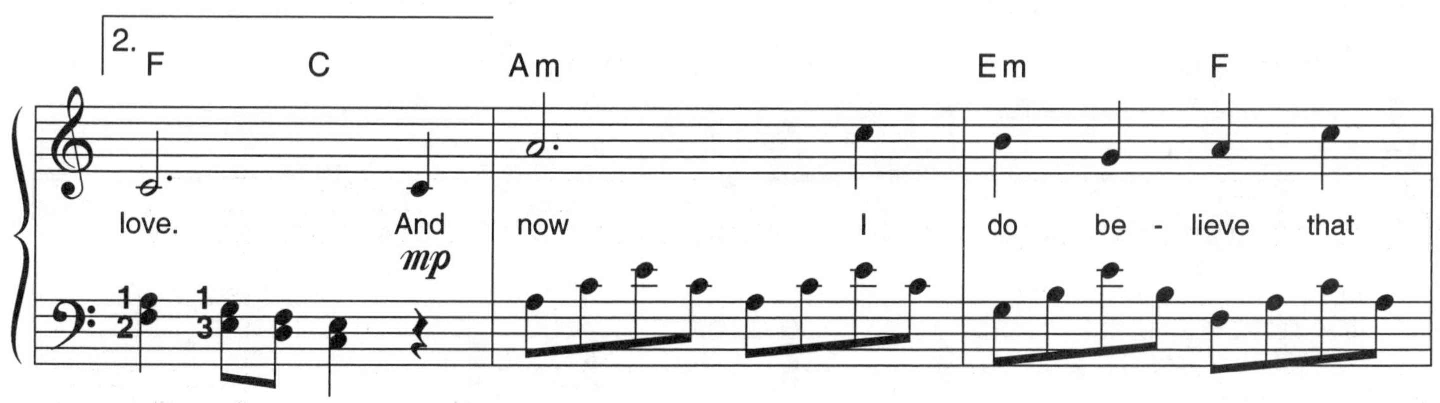
2.
F
C
Am
Em
F
love.
And
mp
now
I
do be - lieve that

Em
Dm
C
ev - en in the storm we'll find some
light.

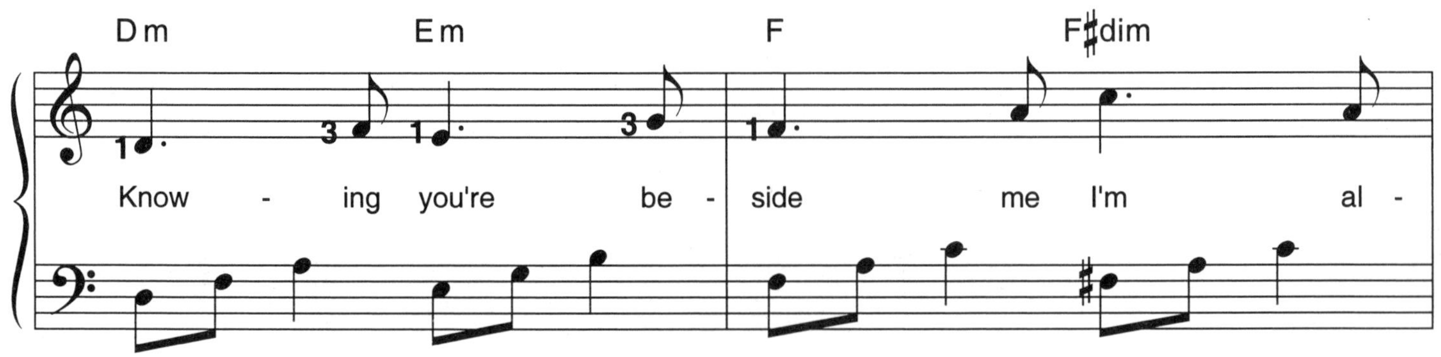
Dm
Em
F
F♯dim
Know - ing you're be - side me I'm al -

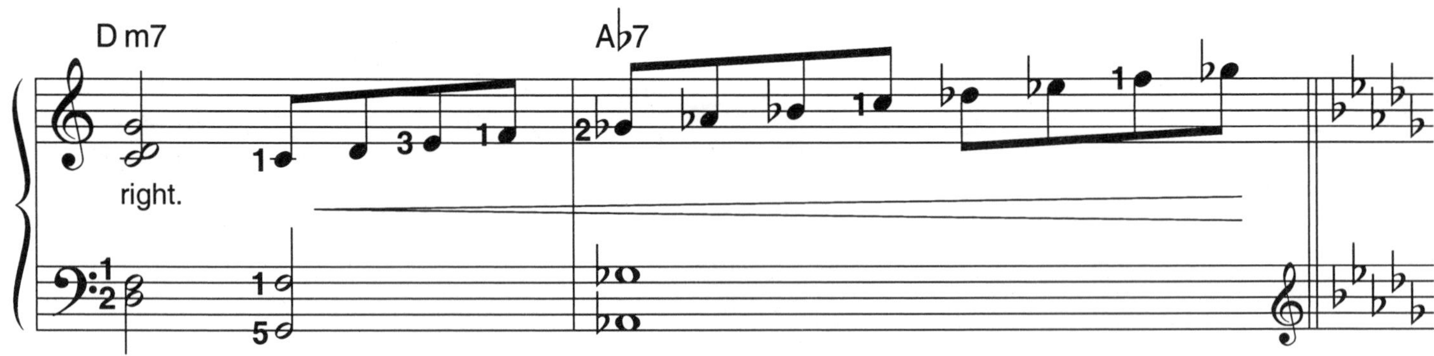
Dm7
A♭7
right.

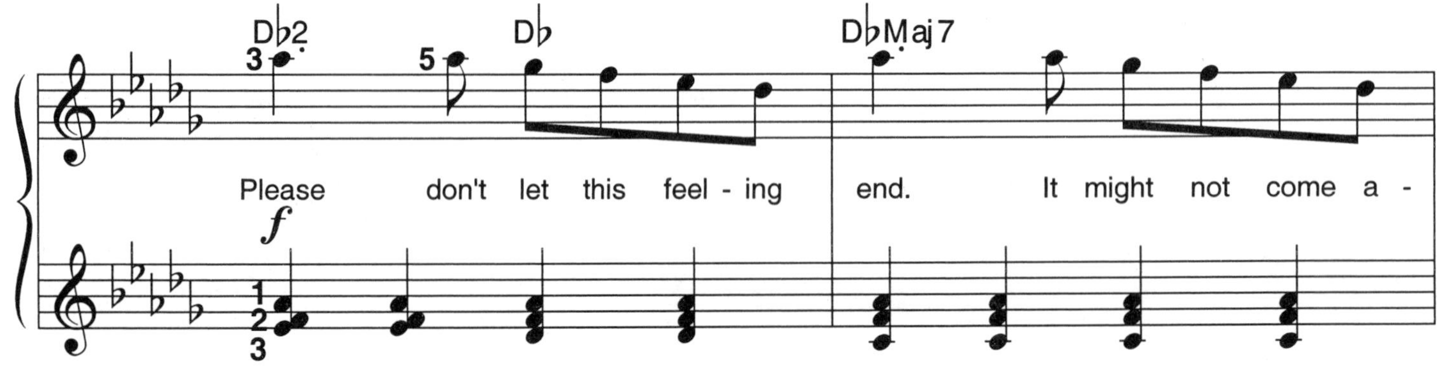
D♭2
D♭
D♭Maj7
Please don't let this feel - ing end. It might not come a -

D♭7
G♭
Fm
gain, and I want to re - mem - ber

E♭m
Fm
G♭
Fm
E♭m
how it feels to touch you,
how I feel so
Fm
G♭
F
much since I found
B♭m
E♭7
E♭m
D♭
you look-ing through the eyes of love.

The Girl From Ipanema

(Garôta De Ipanema)

Recorded by Astrud Gilberto, Peggy Lee, The Morgan-James Duo and many others.

Original Words by VINICIUS DE MORAES
English Words by NORMAN GIMBEL
Music by ANTONIO CARLOS JOBIM
Arranged by Richard Bradley

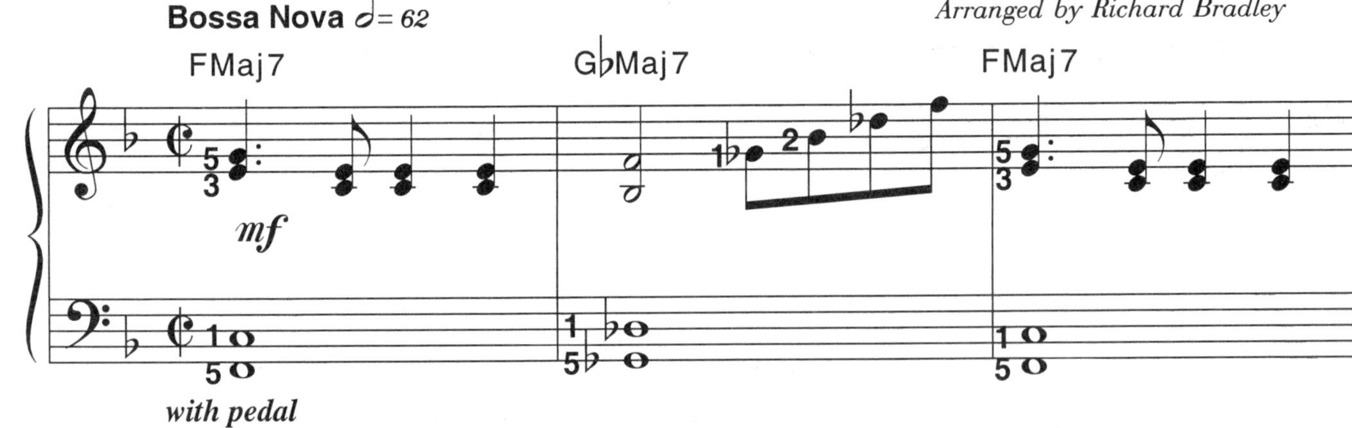

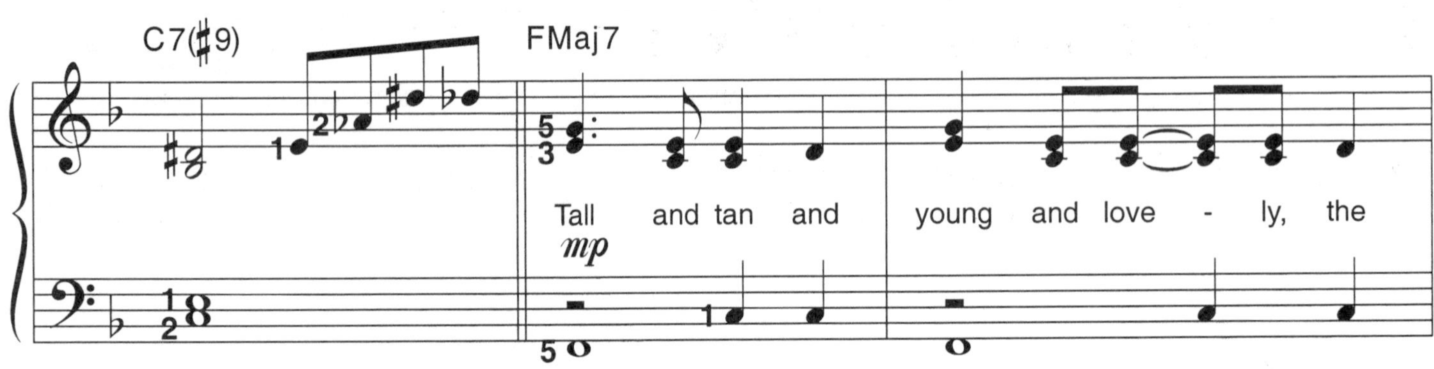

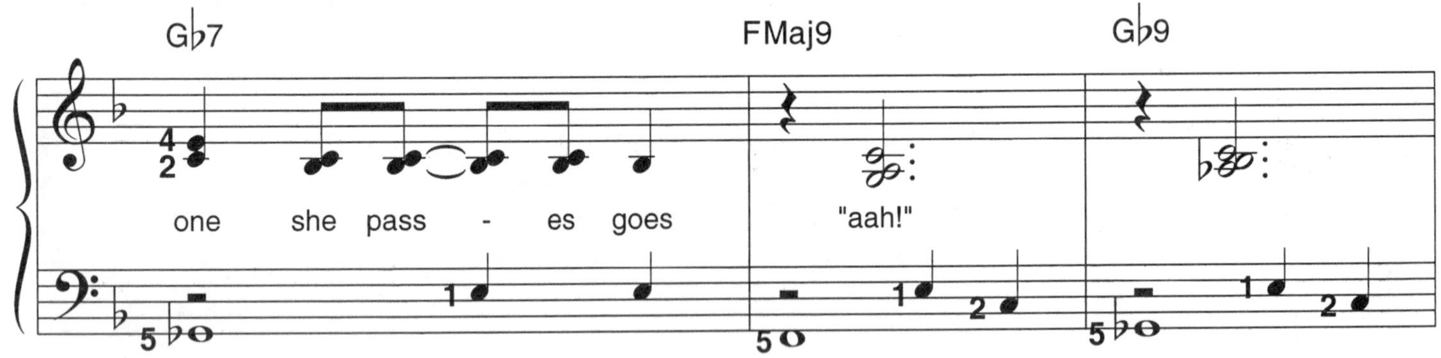

FMaj7
G7
When she walks she's like a sam-ba that swings so cool and

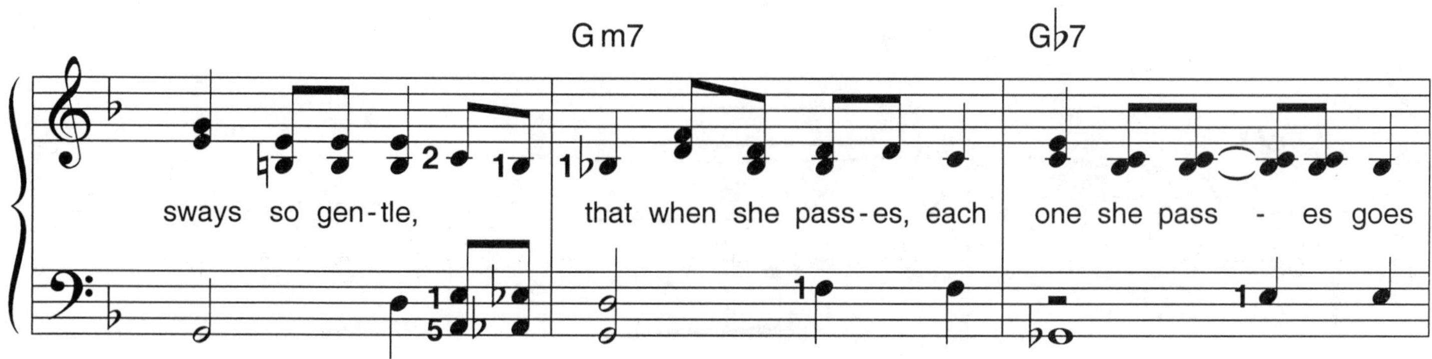
Gm7
G♭7
sways so gen-tle, that when she pass-es, each one she pass - es goes

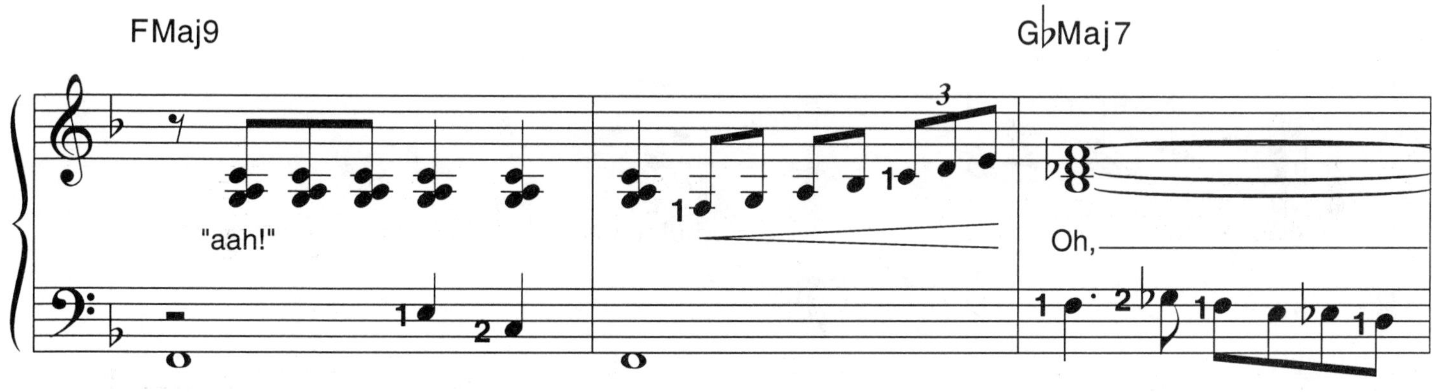
FMaj9
G♭Maj7
"aah!"
Oh,

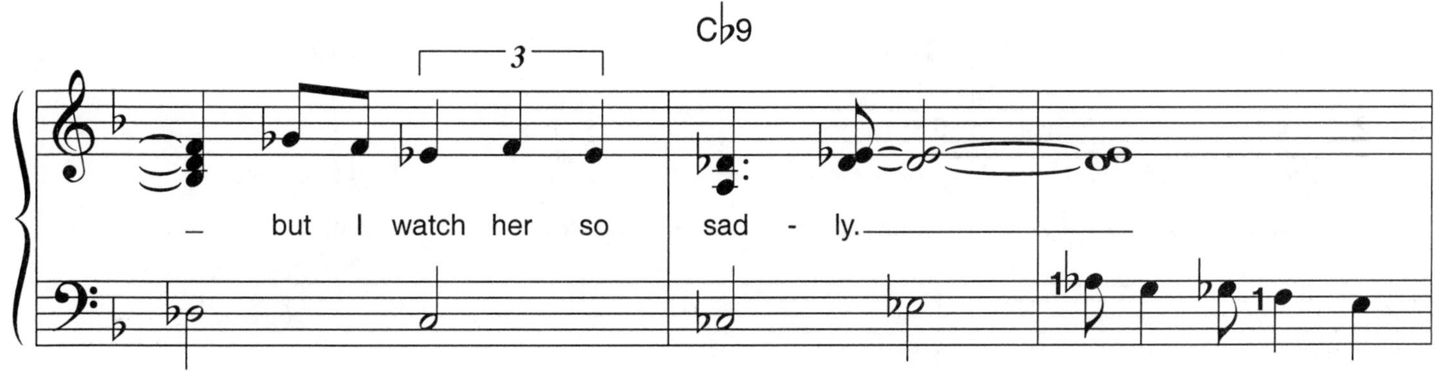
C♭9
but I watch her so sad - ly.

F♯m9
D9
How
can I tell her I
love her?

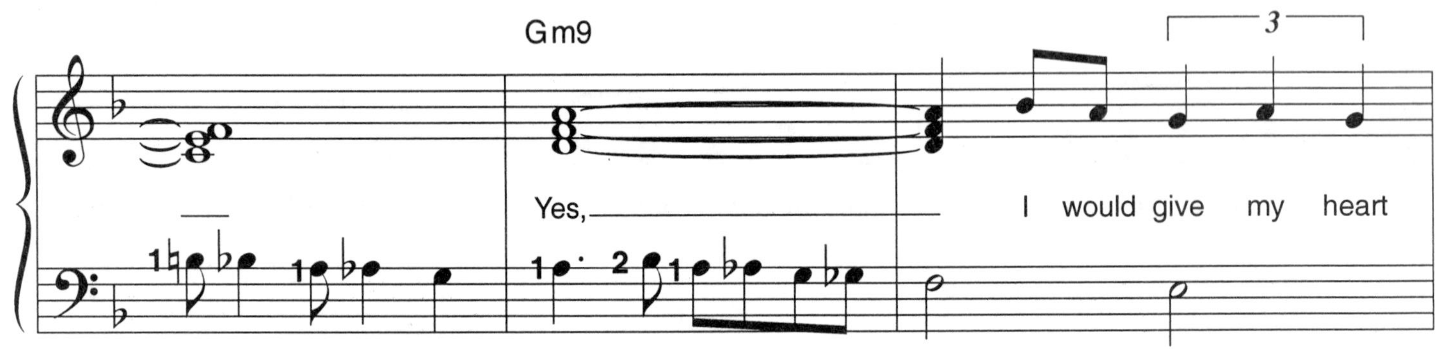
Gm9
Yes,
I would give my heart

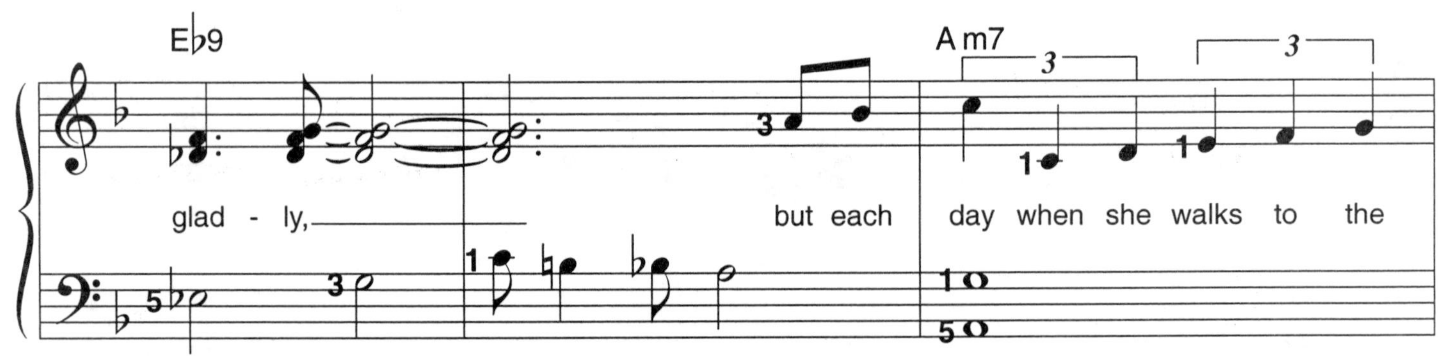
E♭9
Am7
glad - ly,
but each
day when she walks to the

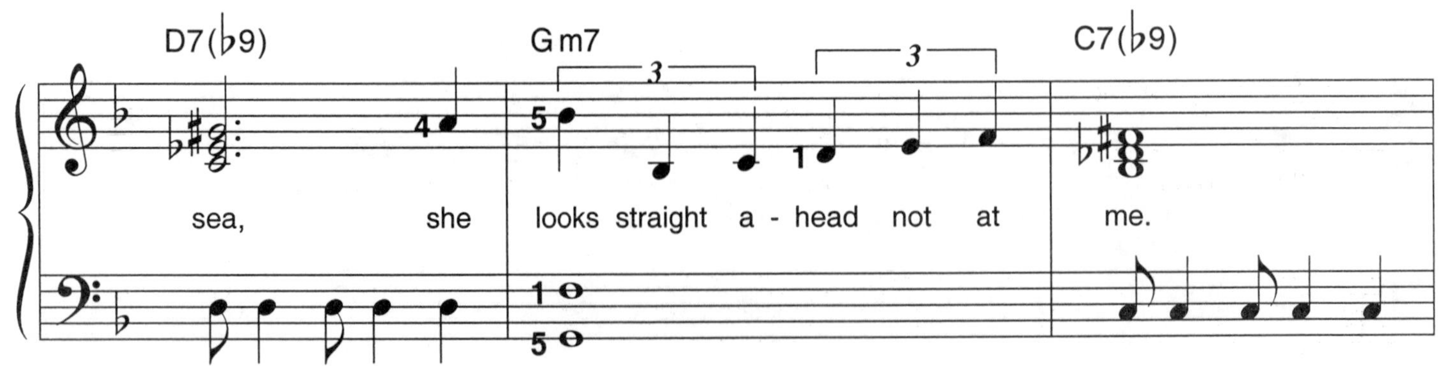
D7(♭9)
Gm7
C7(♭9)
sea, she
looks straight a - head not at
me.

FMaj7
G7
Tall and tan and young and love - ly, the girl from I - pa -
mp

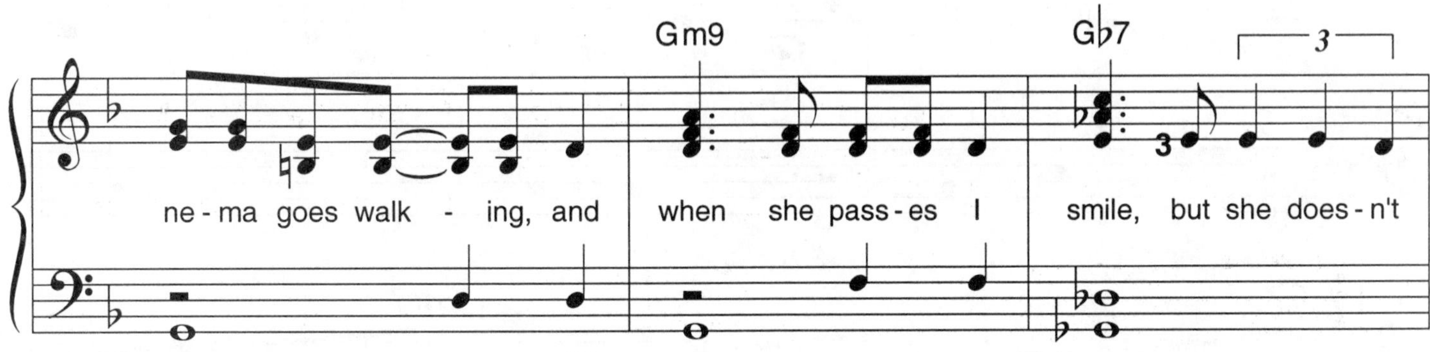
Gm9
G♭7
ne - ma goes walk - ing, and when she pass - es I smile, but she does - n't

FMaj7
G♭7
FMaj7
see.

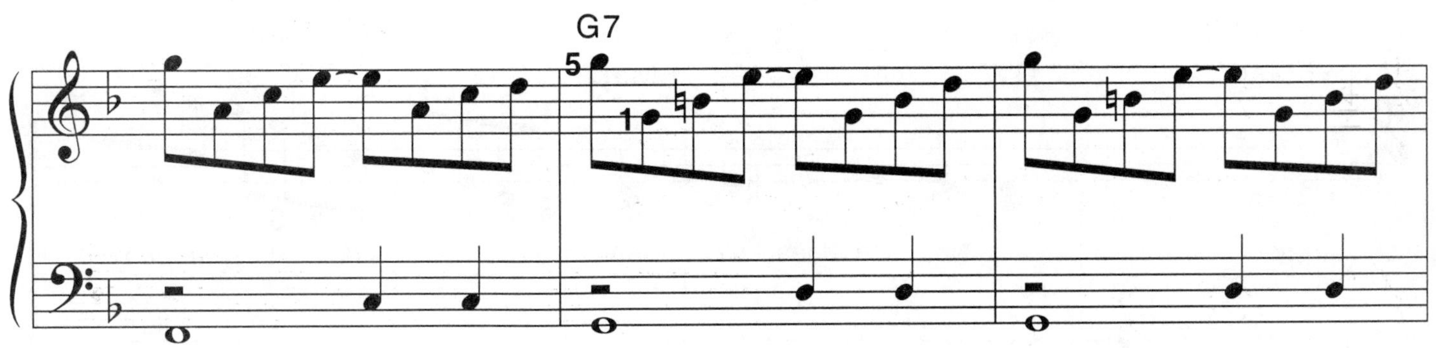
G7

Gm7
G♭7
FMaj7
G♭7
FMaj7
G7
Gm7
G♭7
FMaj7
G♭7
She just does - n't
FMaj7
see.
G♭7
No, she does - n't
FMaj7
see.
rit.
molto rit

On Green Dolphin Street

(Instrumental version)

George Shearing is among the many jazz artists who have recorded this standard from the film *Green Dolphin Street*.

Lyrics by NED WASHINGTON
Music by BRONISLAU KAPER
Arranged by Richard Bradley

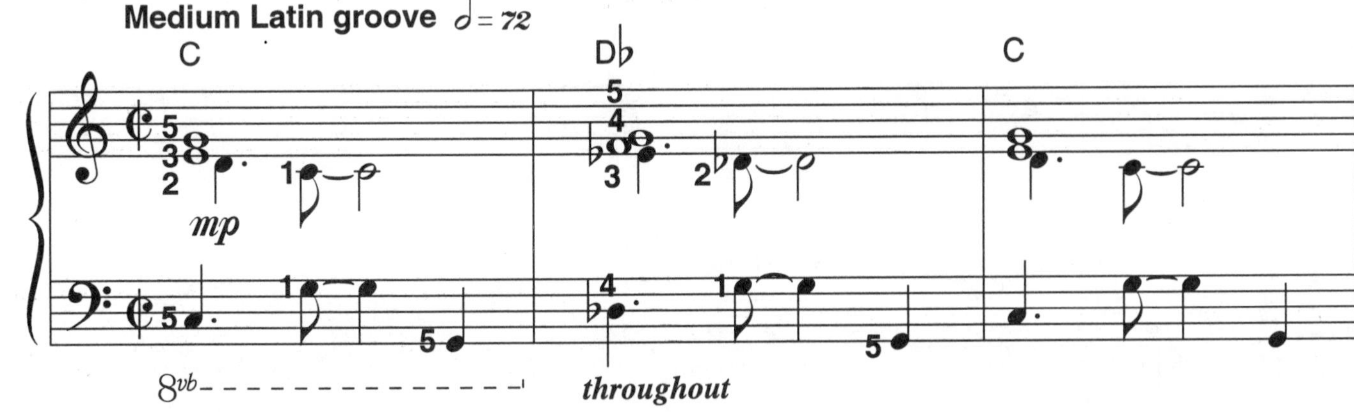

Swing
Dm7
G7
Latin
C
CMaj9 C6
f
Swing
Fm7
B♭7
Latin
E♭
Dm7
G7
C6
mf
Cm7
C13♯11
D♭
C
C
Em7
E♭m7

LYRICS
Lover, one lovely day.
Love came, planning to stay.
Green Dolphin Street supplied the setting
The setting for nights beyond forgetting.
And through these moments apart
Mem'ries live in my heart.
When I recall the love I found on,
I could kiss the ground
On Green Dolphin Street.

Ain't Misbehavin'

Louis Armstrong and "Fats" Waller are among those who have recorded this familiar tune.

Words by ANDY RAZAF
Music by THOMAS "FATS" WALLER
and HARRY BROOKS
Arranged by Richard Bradley

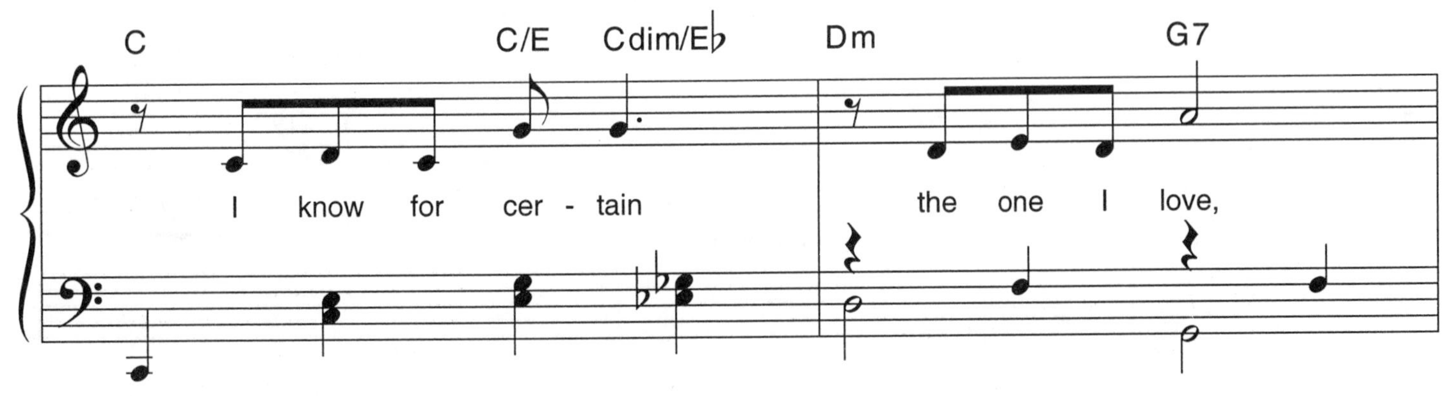
C C/E Cdim/E♭ Dm G7
I know for cer - tain the one I love,

C C7/E F Fm
I'm thru with flirt - in', it's just you I'm think - ing of,

C Am7 Dm G7
ain't mis - be - hav - in', I'm sav - in' my love for

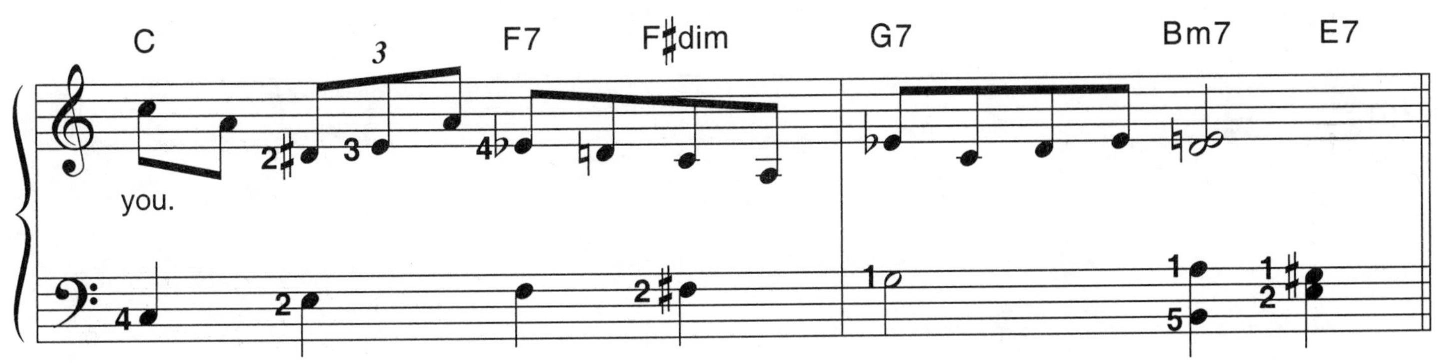
C F7 F♯dim G7 Bm7 E7
you.

Am
Am(♯5)
Like Jack Hor - ner
in the cor - ner,
3
3

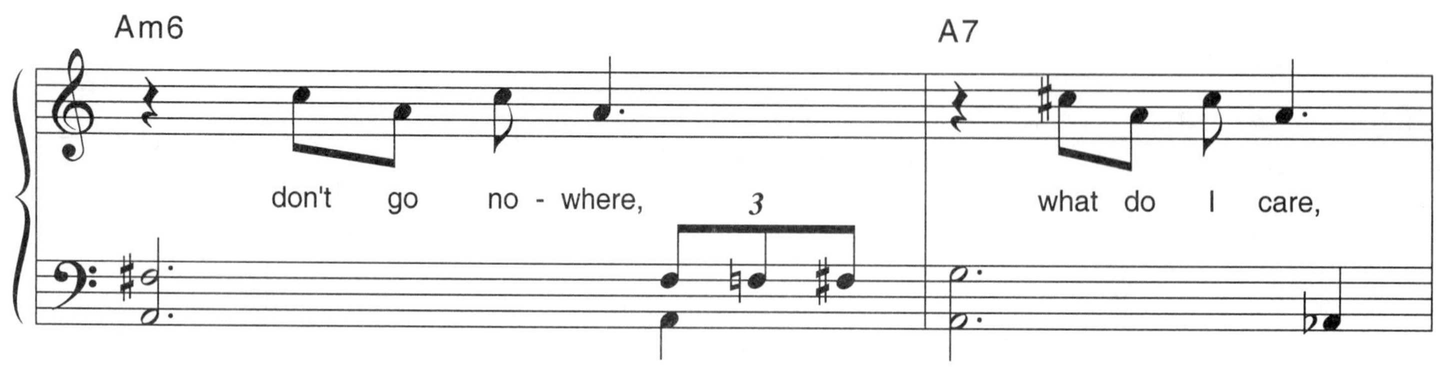
Am6
A7
don't go no - where,
what do I care,
3

G
Em
Am7
D7
your kiss - es
are worth wait - ing
3
3
3

G7
A7
D9
G9
for, be - lieve me.

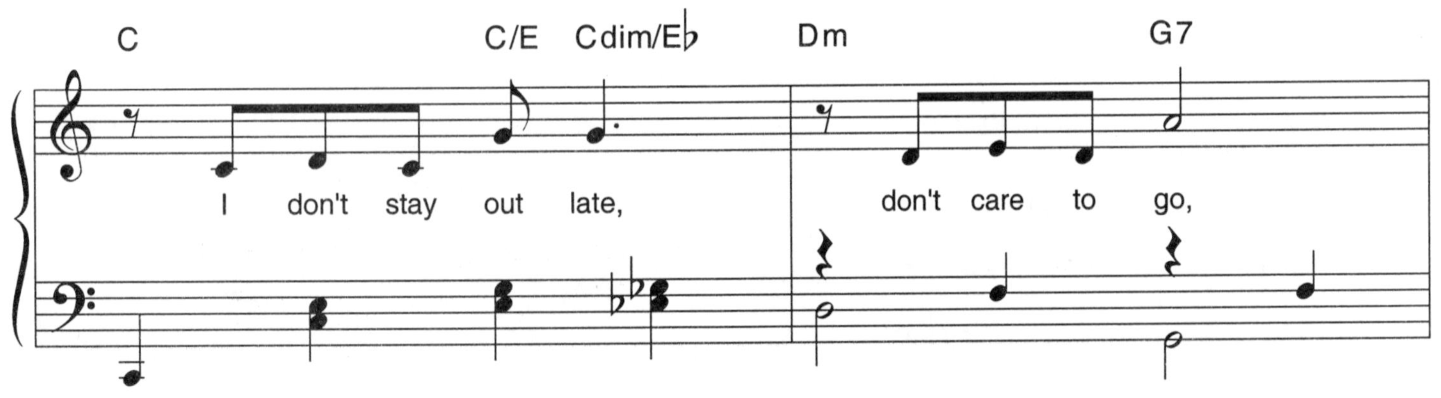
C
C/E
Cdim/E♭
Dm
G7
I don't stay out late,
don't care to go,

C
C7/E
F
Fm
3
I'm home a - bout eight, just
me and my ra - di - o,

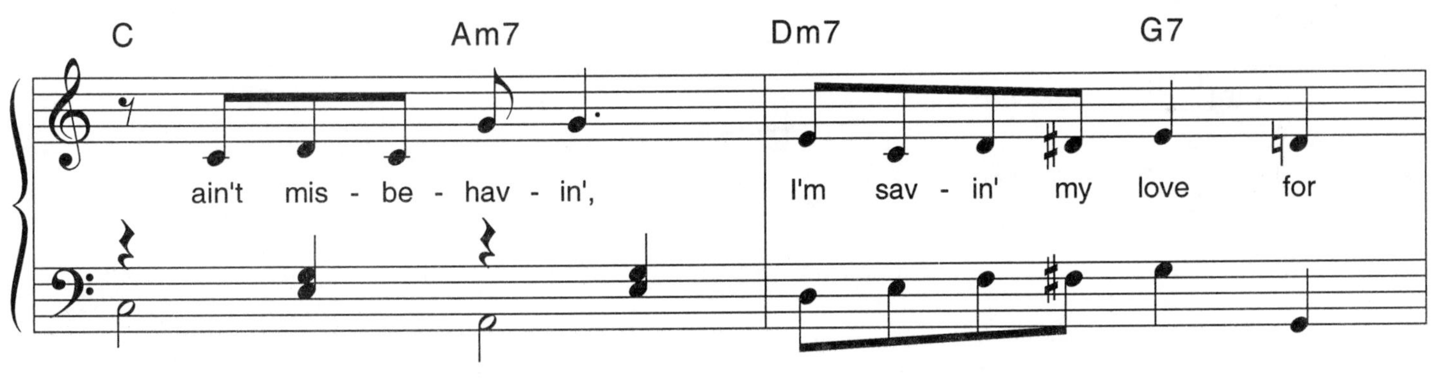
C
Am7
Dm7
G7
ain't mis - be - hav - in',
I'm sav - in' my love for

C
F7
F♯dim
C
D♭9
C13
3
2
3
4
you.

The Shadow Of Your Smile

(Love Theme from "The Sandpiper")

Frequently recorded in a jazz style, this standard won the Best Song Oscar for 1965.

Lyrics by PAUL FRANCIS WEBSTER
Music by JOHNNY MANDEL
Arranged by Richard Bradley

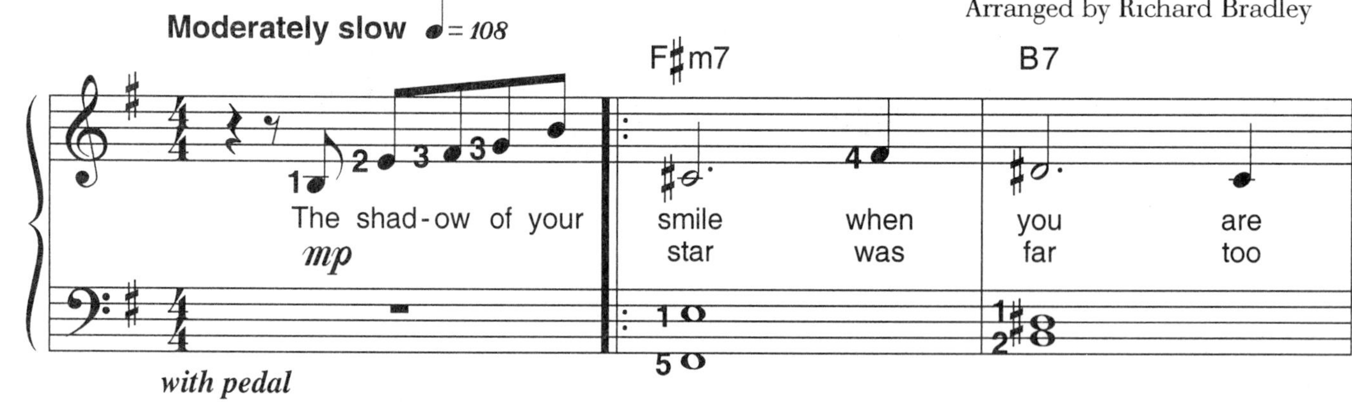

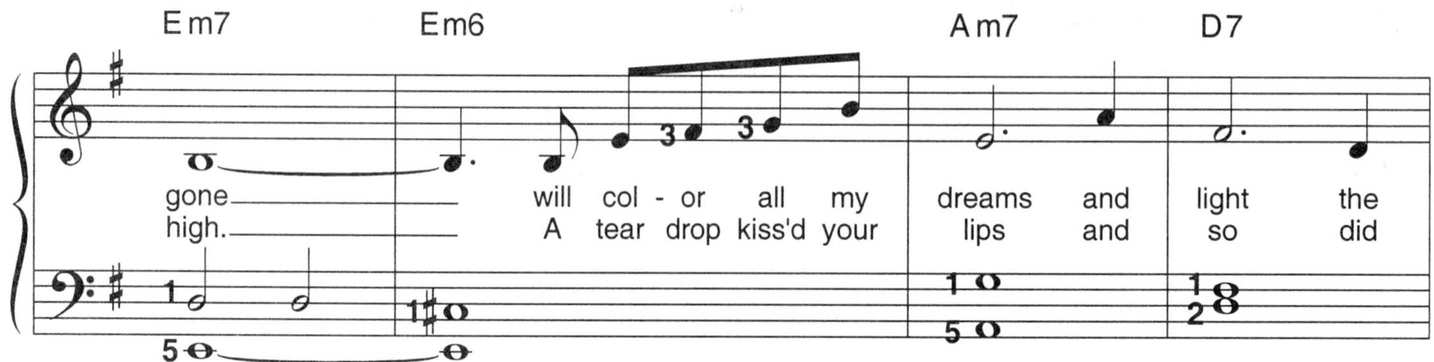

2.
F♯m7
B7
N.C.
B m7(♭5)
me
Our wist - ful lit - tle
I.

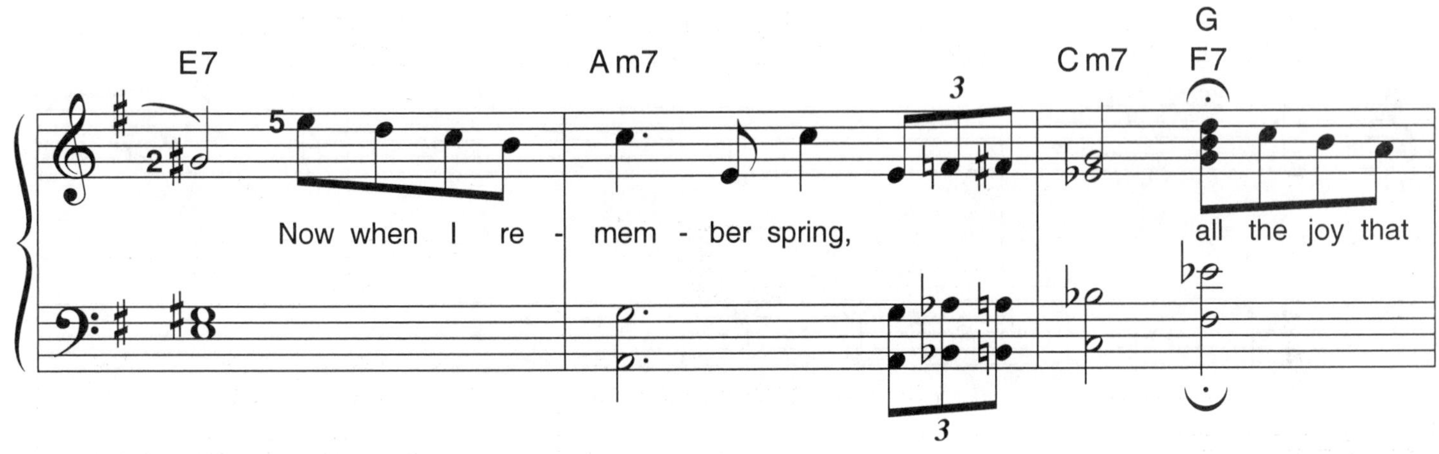
E7
Am7
Cm7
G
F7
Now when I re - mem - ber spring,
all the joy that

Bm7
E7
A7
love can bring,
I will be re - mem - ber - ing

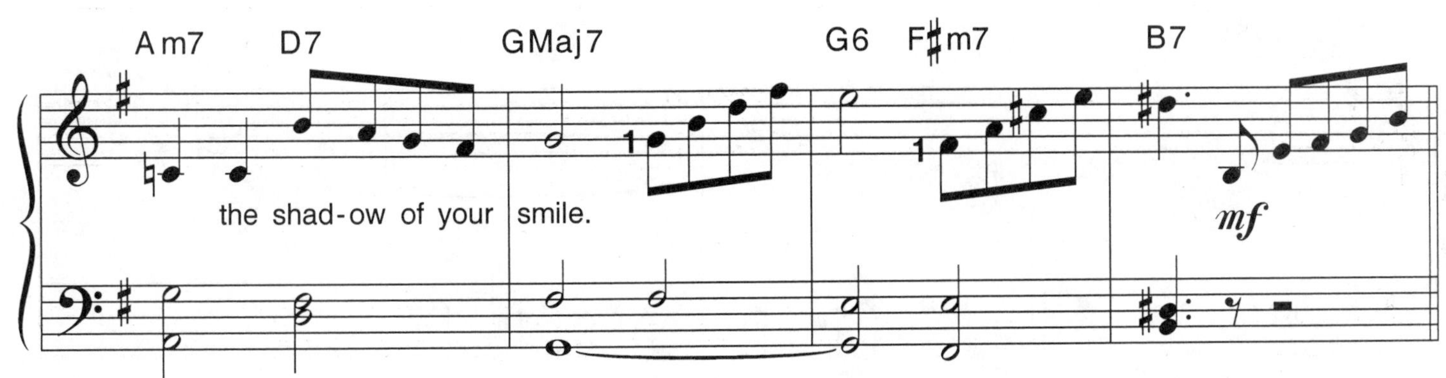
Am7
D7
GMaj7
G6
F♯m7
B7
the shad-ow of your smile.
mf

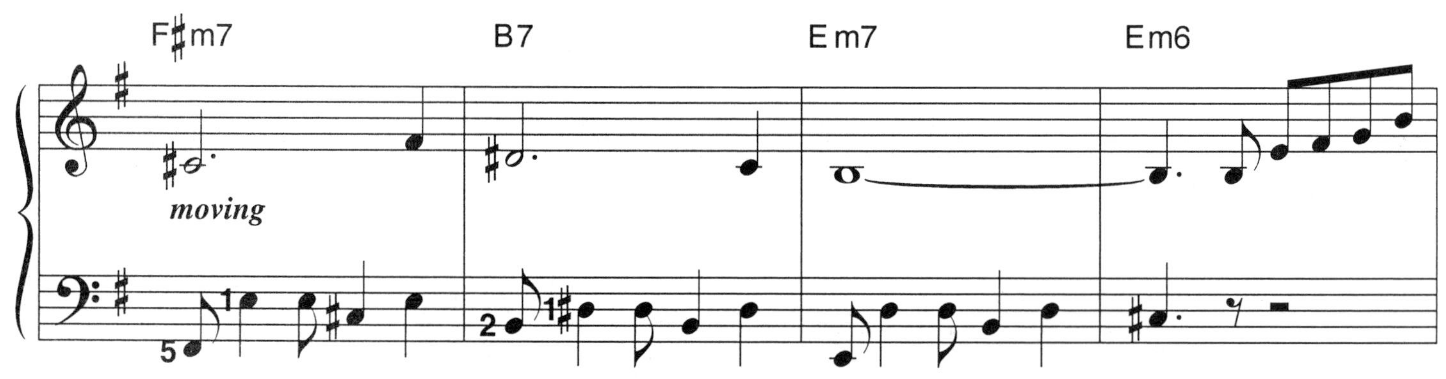
F♯m7
B7
Em7
Em6
moving
1
5
2
1

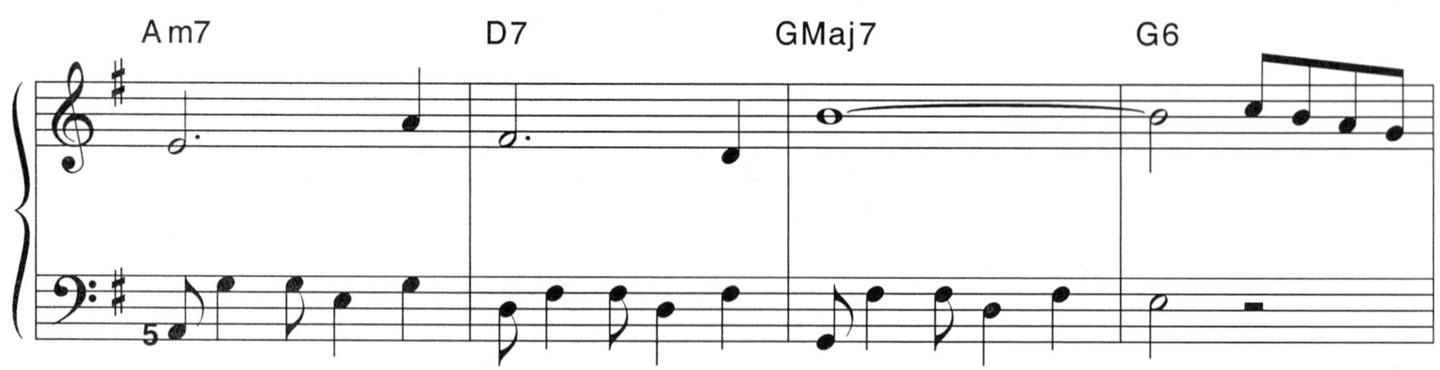
Am7
D7
GMaj7
G6
5

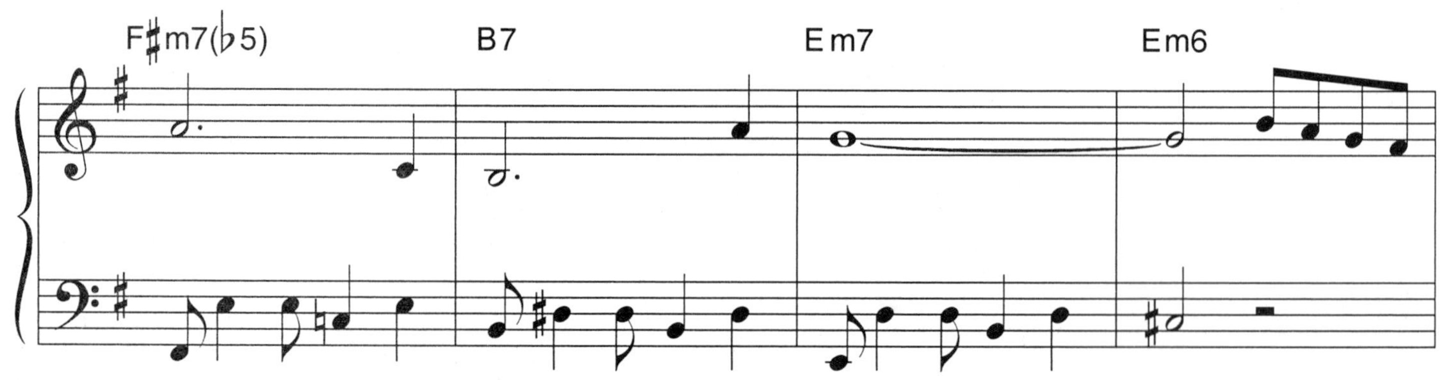
F♯m7(♭5)
B7
Em7
Em6

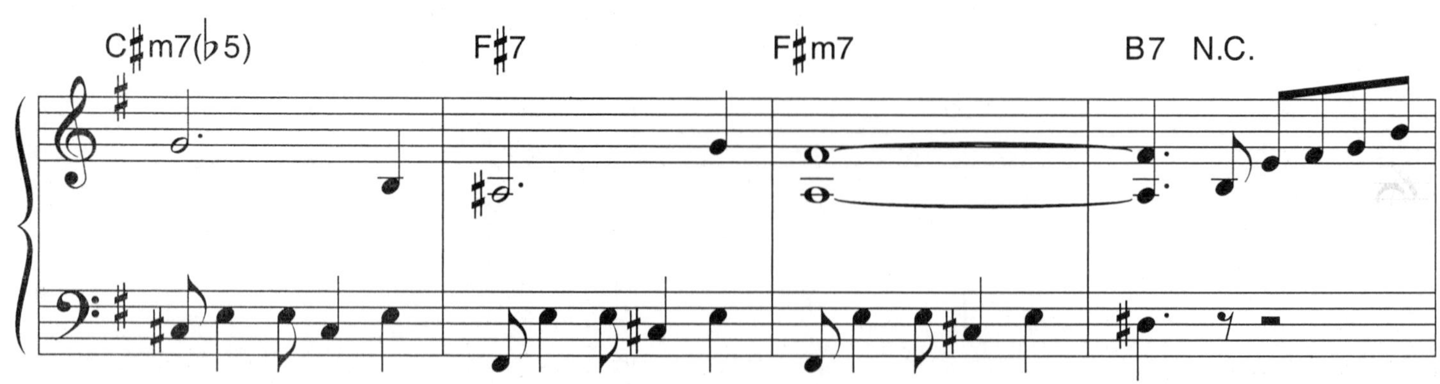
C♯m7(♭5)
F♯7
F♯m7
B7 N.C.

F♯m7
B7
Em7
Em6
Am7
D7
Bm7(♭5)
E7
f
Am7
3
broadly
3
Cm7
G
F7
Bm7
E7
mf
A7
Am7
D7
mp
GMaj7
GMaj9
1
1
Ped.

Maple Leaf Rag

Early recordings include composer Scott Joplin, The New Orleans Rhythm Kings and Red Nichol's Famous Pennies.

By SCOTT JOPLIN
Arranged by Richard Bradley

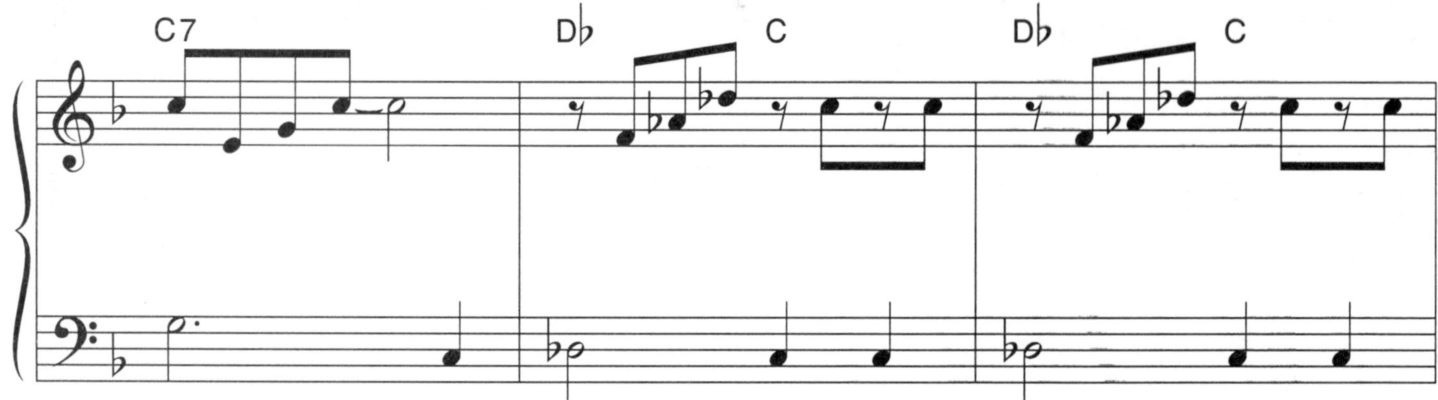

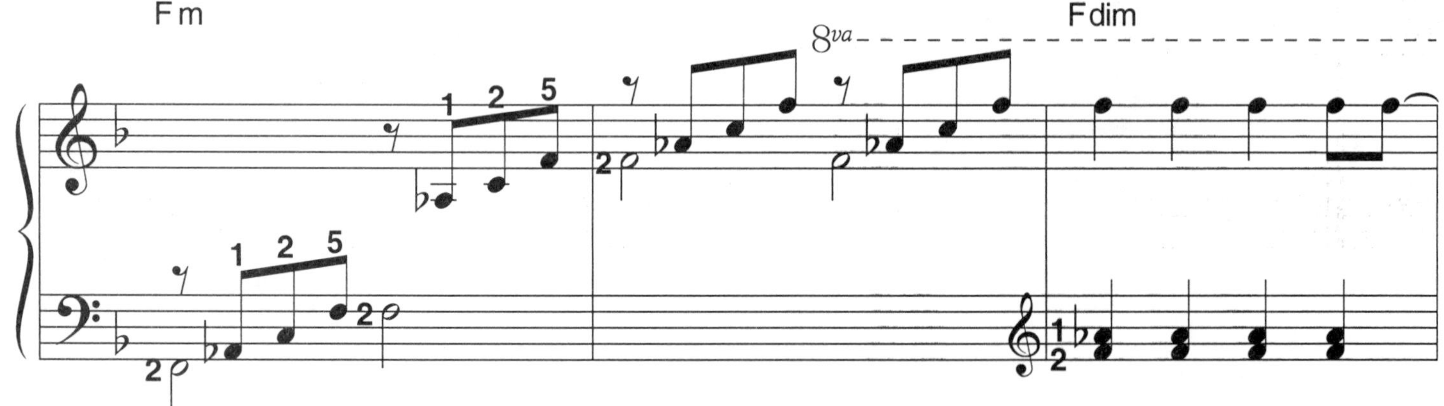

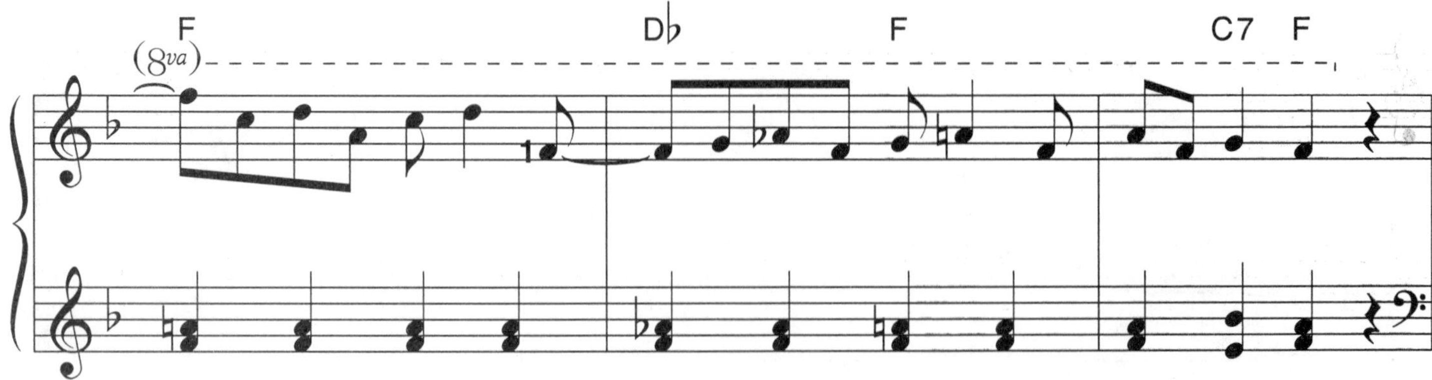

Fdim
F
D♭
F

1.
C7
F
2.
To next strain
C7
F
3.
Fine
C7
F

C7
F

C7

F
C7

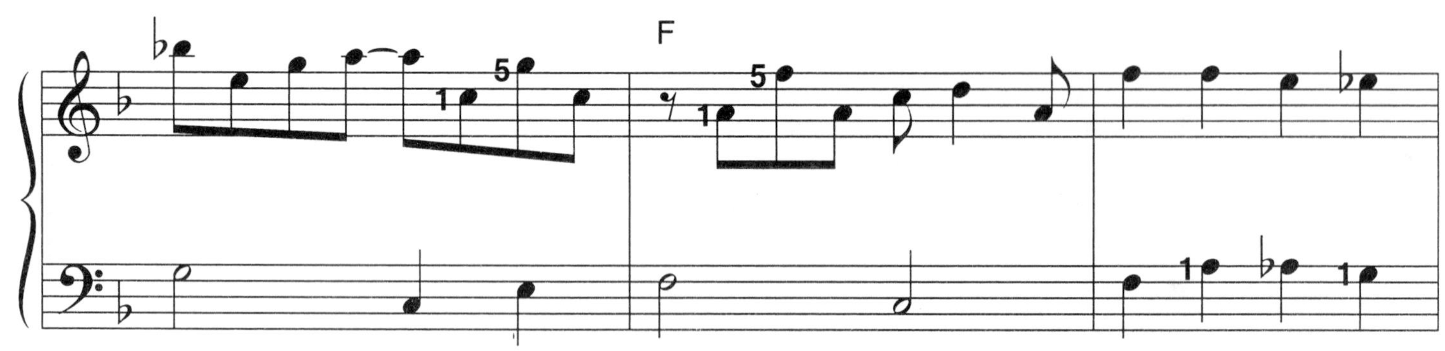
F

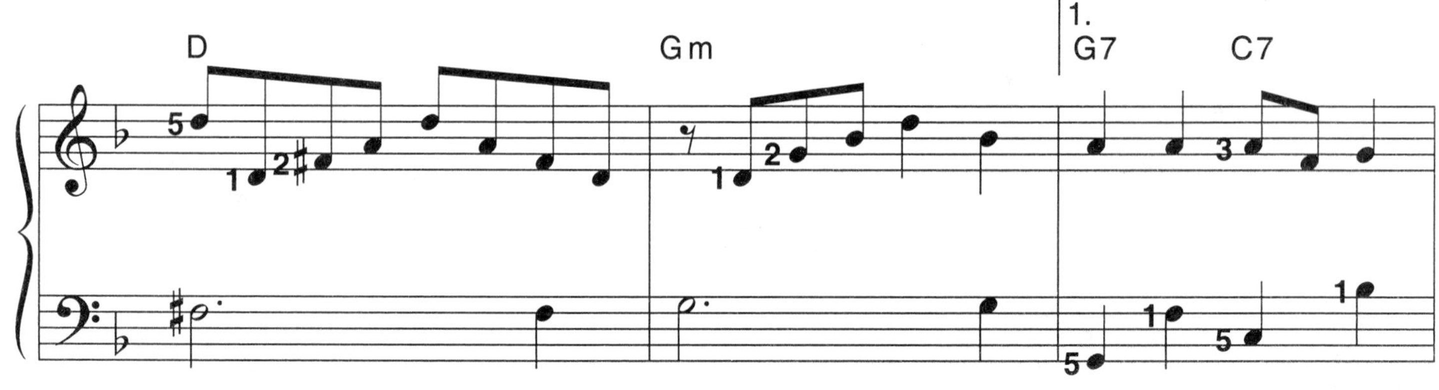
D
Gm
1.
G7
C7

F
2.
G7
C7
F
D.S. 𝄋 al Fine

I Got It Bad
(And That Ain't Good)

Ivie Anderson provided the vocal on the original recording by Duke Ellington & his Orchestra.

By DUKE ELLINGTON
and PAUL FRANCIS WEBSTER
Arranged by Richard Bradley

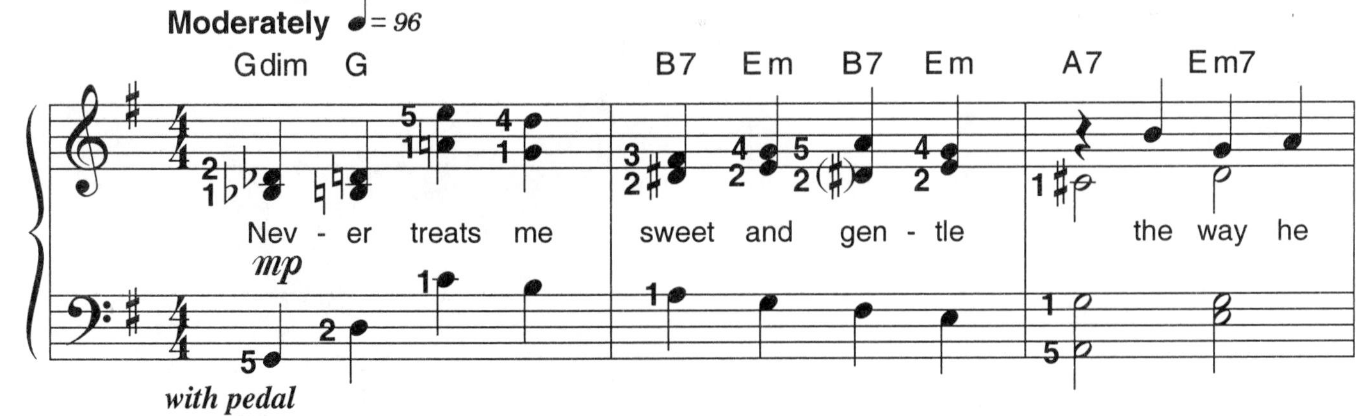

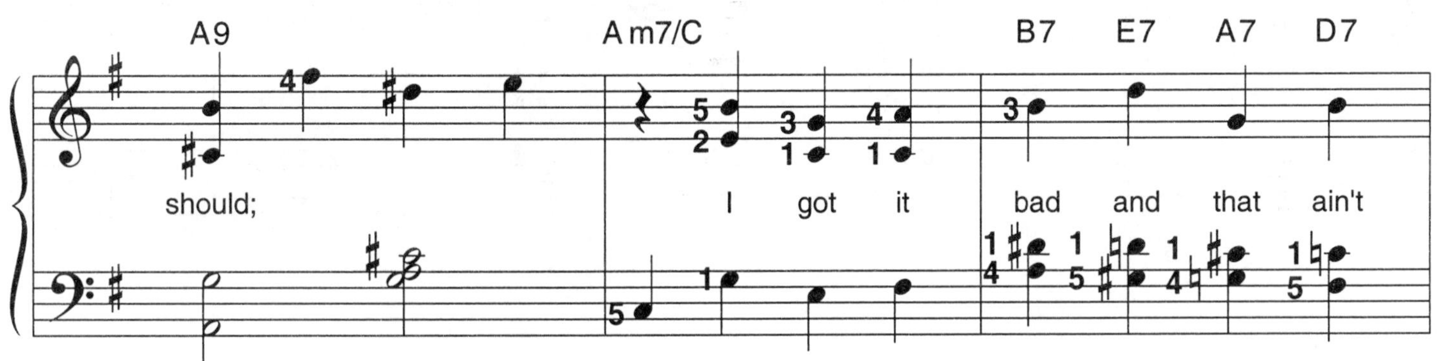

Am7/C
B7
B♭7
A7
A♭7
G
Am7
I got it bad and that ain't good!

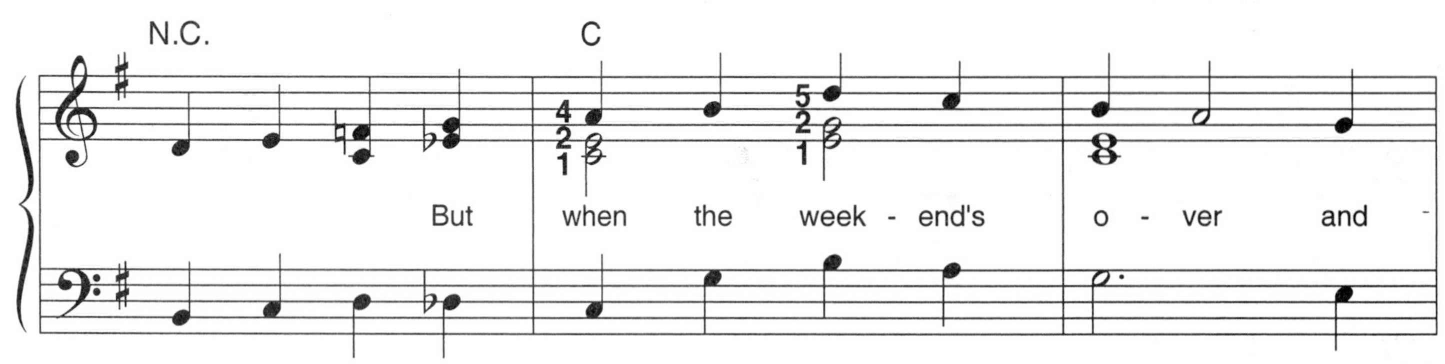
N.C.
C
But when the week - end's o - ver and

F7
B7
Em
Em7
Mon - day rolls a - round I end up like I

A9
F13(♯11)
E♭7(♯5)
D7
start out, just cry - in' my heart out.

Verse 2:
Like a lonely weeping willow lost in the wood,
I got it bad and that ain't good!
And the things I tell my pillow, no woman should.
I got it bad and that ani't good!
Though folks with good intensions tell me to save my tears,
I'm glad I'm mad about him, I can't live without him.
Lord above me, make him love me the way he should;
I got it bad and that ain't good!

Satin Doll

Originally recorded by
Duke Ellington & his Orchestra.
Words and Music by
BILLY STRAYHORN, DUKE ELLINGTON
and JOHNNY MERCER
Arranged by Richard Bradley
Moderate swing ♩= 116
CMaj7 Dm7 Em7 A7(♭9) Dm7
mf
Cig - a - rette hold - er
G7 Em7 A7
which wigs me o - ver her should - er, she digs me
Am7 D7 A♭m7 D♭7 CMaj7 Dm7 D♯m7
out cat - tin' that sat - in doll.
Em7 A7(♭9) Dm7 G7
Ba - by shall we go out skip - pin'

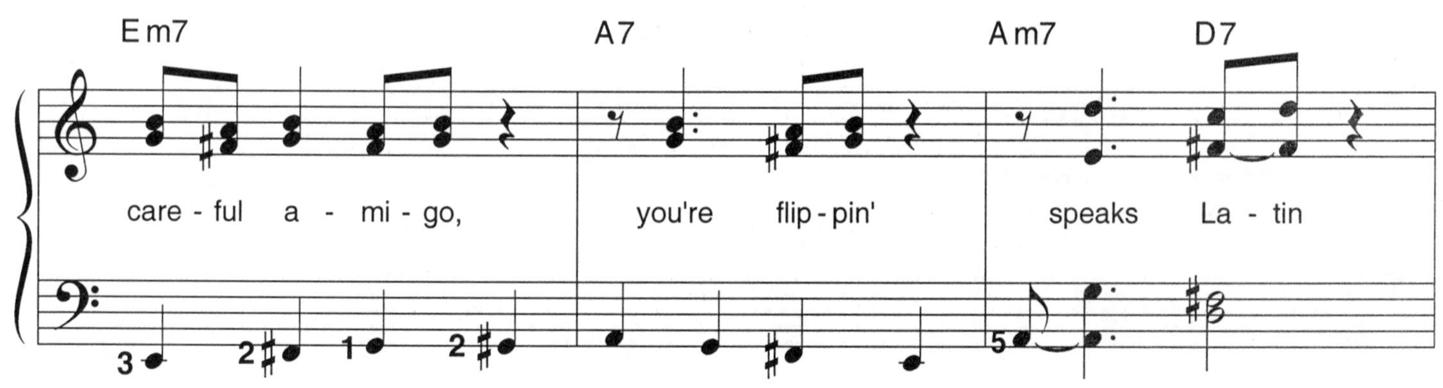
Em7
A7
Am7
D7
care - ful a - mi - go, you're flip - pin' speaks La - tin

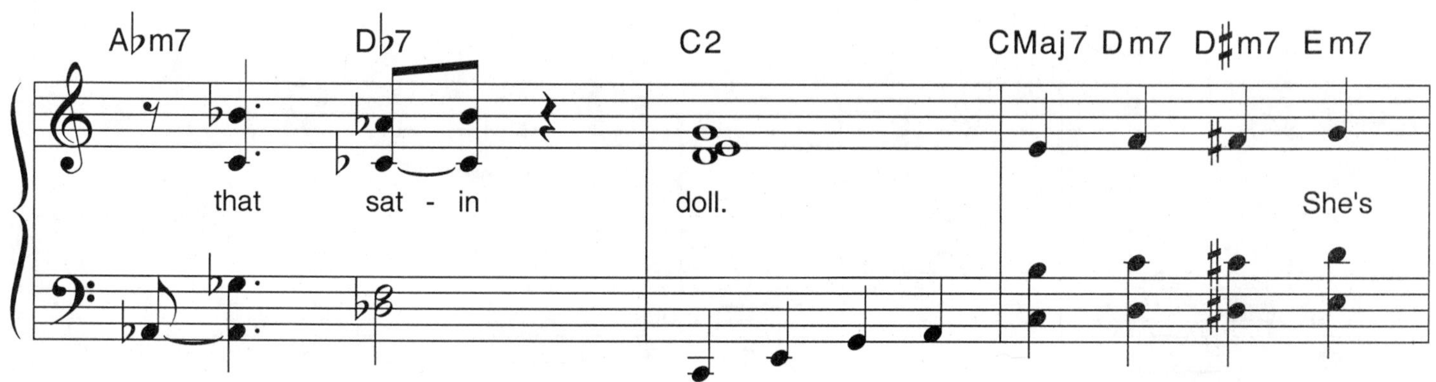
A♭m7
D♭7
C2
CMaj7 Dm7 D♯m7 Em7
that sat - in doll. She's

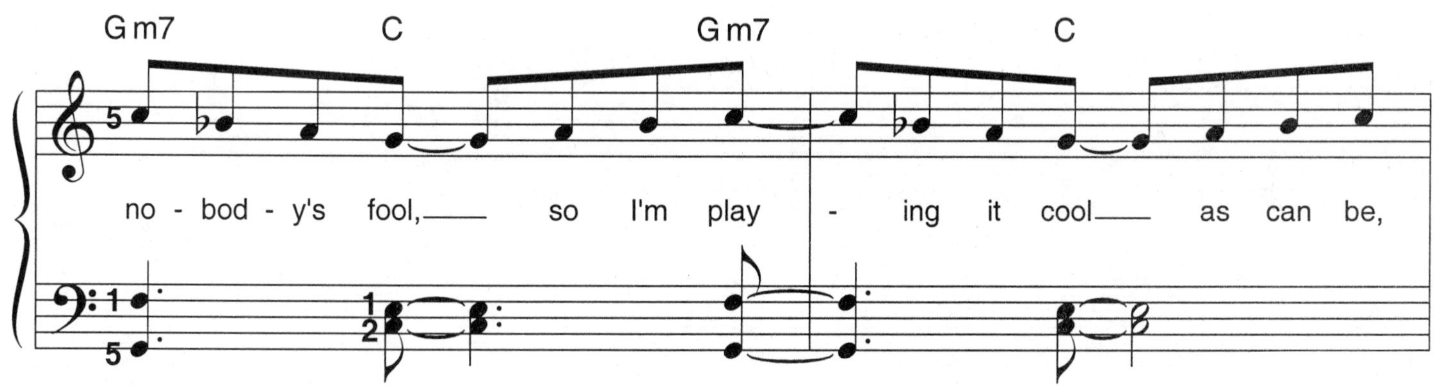
Gm7
C
Gm7
C
no - bod - y's fool, so I'm play - ing it cool as can be,

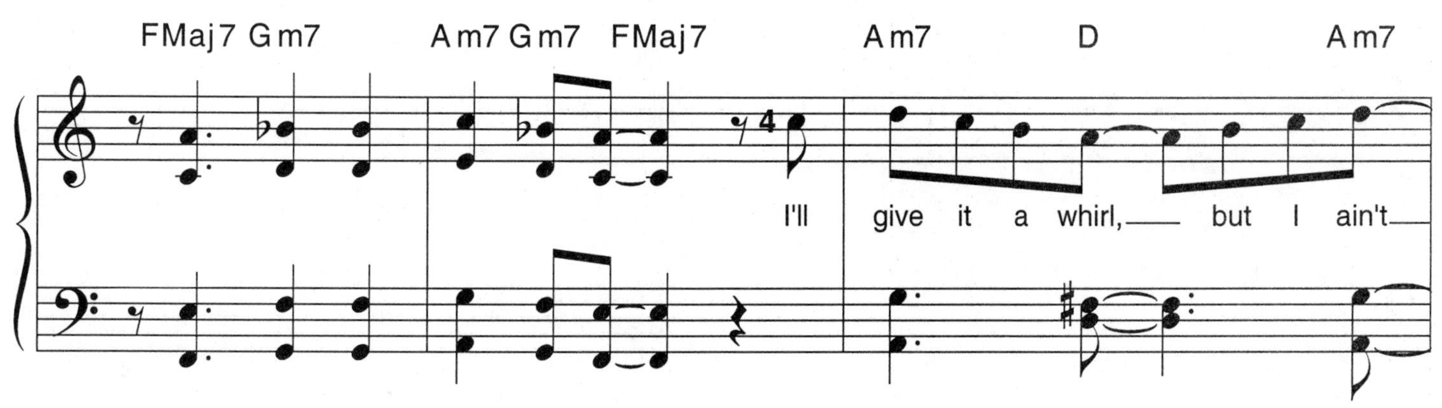
FMaj7 Gm7
Am7 Gm7 FMaj7
Am7
D
Am7
I'll give it a whirl, but I ain't

D
Dm7
G7 N.C.
– for no girl — catch-ing me. —
Switch-E-Roo-ney!

Dm9
Em9
f

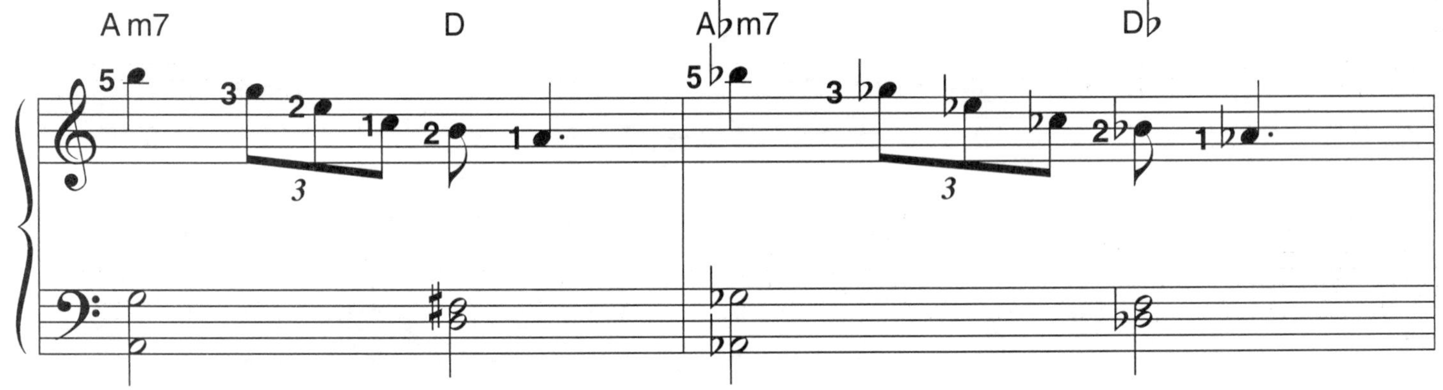
Am7
D
A♭m7
D♭

C7
B7
B♭7
A7

Dm7
G7
Em7
Tel - e - phone num - bers
well you know
do - ing my rhum - bas
mf
A7
Am7
D7
A♭m7
D♭7
with u - no,
and that 'n'
my sat - in
CMaj7
Dm7
D♯m7
Em7
A7(♭9)
Dm7
doll.
G7
Em7
A7
Am7
D7
A♭m7
D♭7
C6/9

Caravan

Original recording by
Duke Ellington & his Orchestra.

By
DUKE ELLINGTON,
JUAN TIZOL and IRVING MILLS
Arranged by Richard Bradley

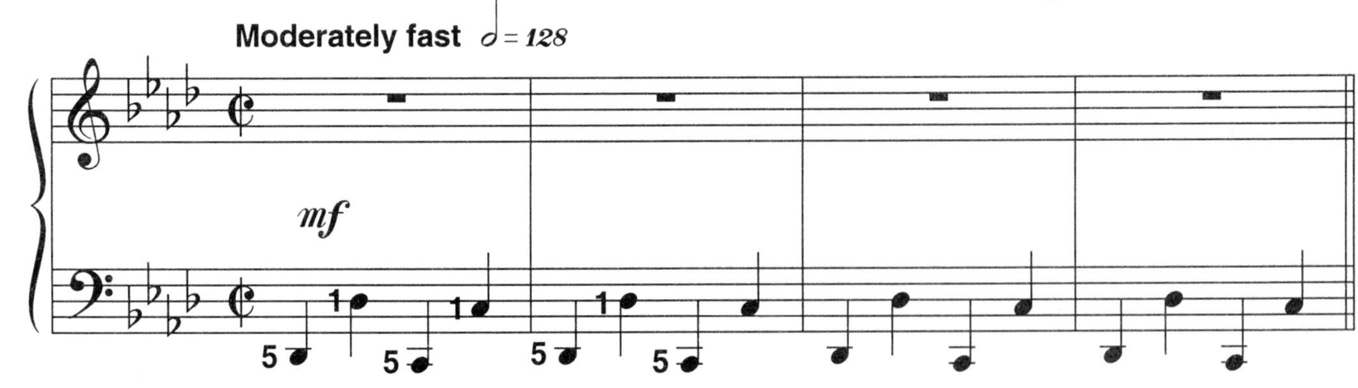

Fm
Fm♯5
Fm6
Fm♯5
Fm
Fm♯5
Fm6
Fm♯5

To Coda

Fm
Fm♯5
Fm6
Fm♯5
Fm
Fm♯5
Fm6
Fm♯5

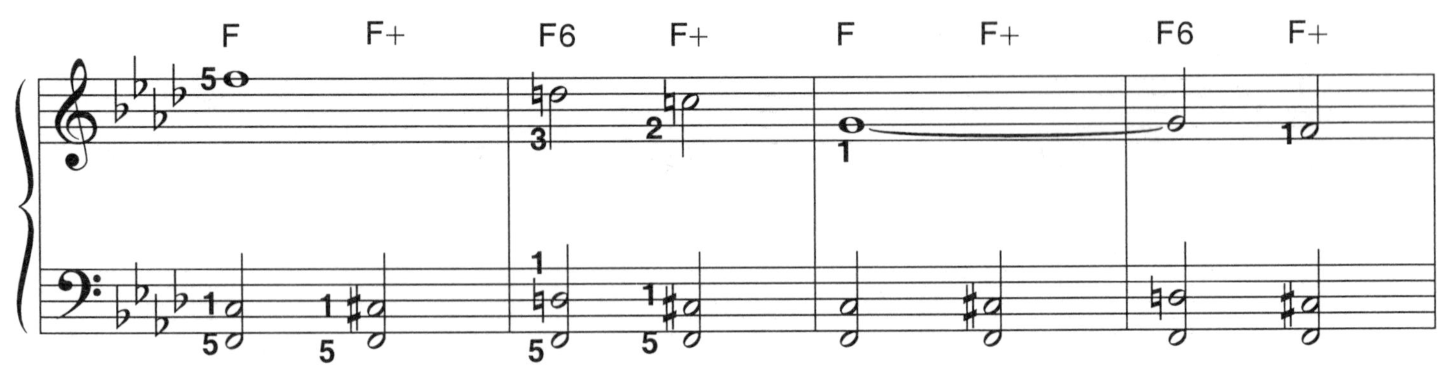
F
F+
F6
F+
F
F+
F6
F+

B♭
B♭+
B♭6
B♭+
B♭
B♭+
B♭6
B♭+

E♭
E♭+
E♭6
E♭+
E♭
E♭+
E♭6
E♭+

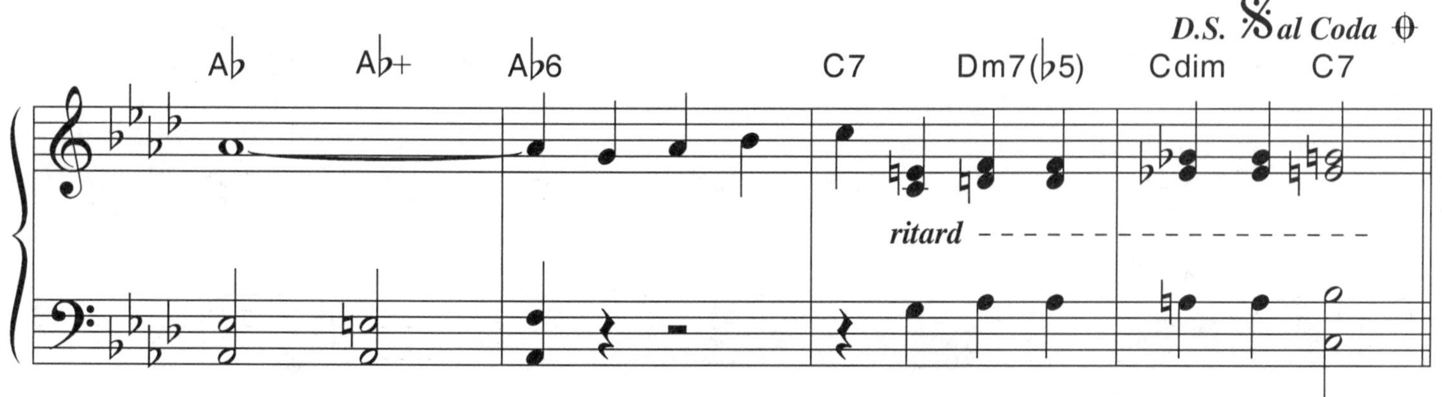
D.S. 𝄋 al Coda 𝄌
A♭
A♭+
A♭6
C7
Dm7(♭5)
Cdim
C7
ritard

Fm
Fm♯5
Fm6
Fm♯5
Fm
Fm♯5
5

Fm6
Fm♯5
Fm
Fm♯5
Fm6
Fm♯5

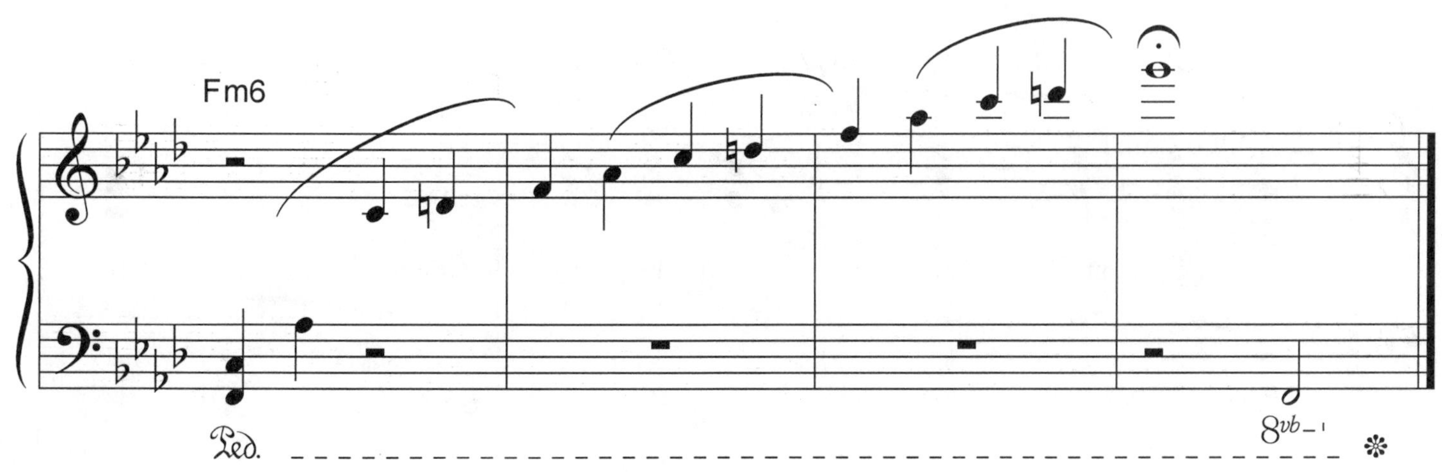
Fm6
Ped.
8vb

Mood Indigo

Originally recorded by Duke Ellington & his Orchestra in the thirties, it was re-recorded by them decades later with a vocal by Rosemary Clooney.

Words and Music by
DUKE ELLINGTON, IRVING MILLS
and ALBANY BIGARD
Arranged by Richard Bradley

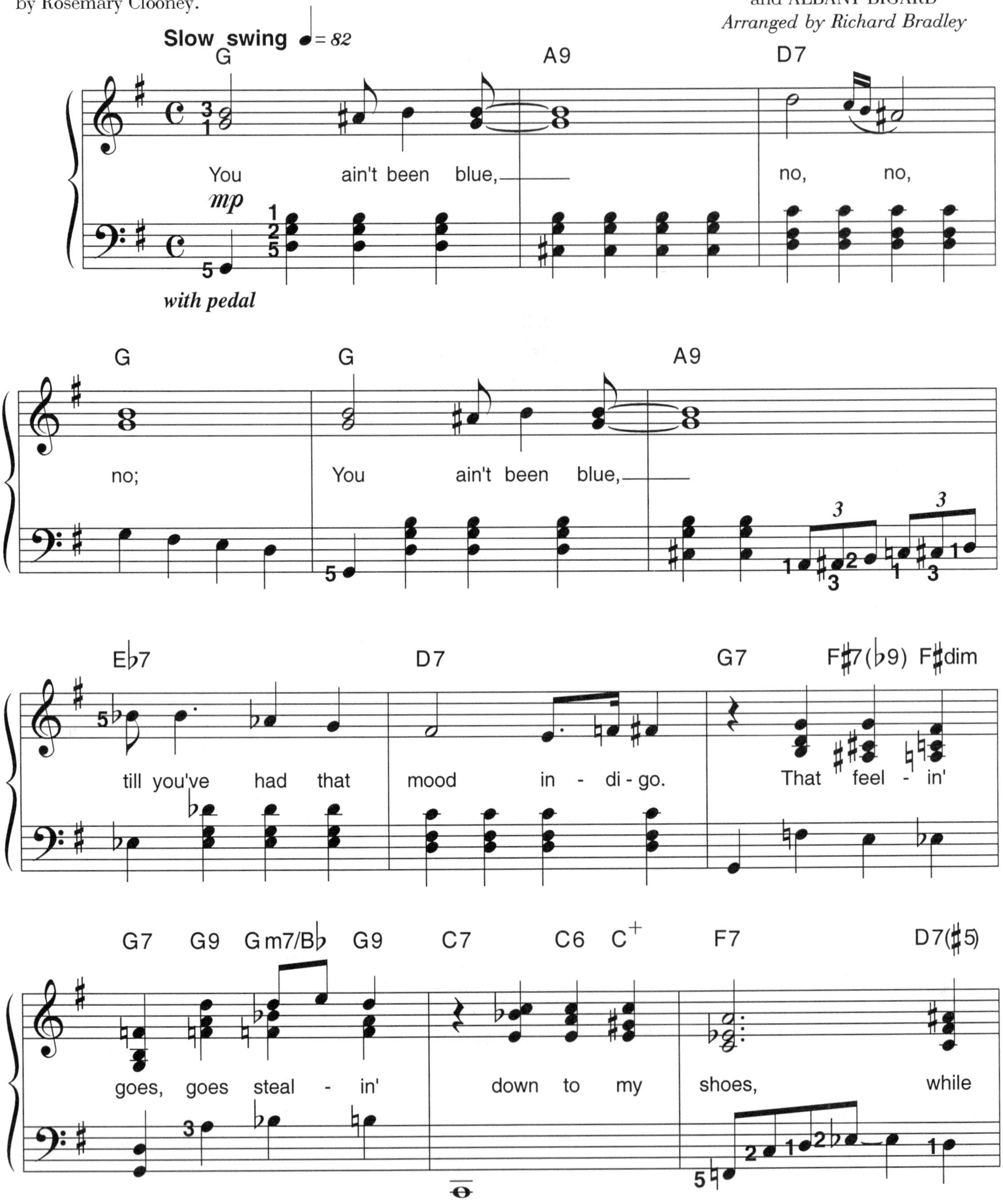
Slow swing ♩= 82
G A9 D7
You ain't been blue, no, no,
mp
with pedal
G G A9
no; You ain't been blue,
E♭7 D7 G7 F♯7(♭9) F♯dim
till you've had that mood in - di - go. That feel - in'
G7 G9 Gm7/B♭ G9 C7 C6 C+ F7 D7(♯5)
goes, goes steal - in' down to my shoes, while

Mood Indigo - 3 - 1

G
A9
D7
To Coda
I sit and sigh,
"Go 'long,
G
G
A9
A7(♭9) A7
blues."
Al - ways get that
mood in - di - go
D7
G
D7
G
since my ba - by said good - bye.
In the eve - nin'
A9
A7(♭9) A7
E9
E♭9
D9
when lights are low,
I'm so lone - ly I could cry;

G9
4
'Cause there's no - bod - y who cares a - bout me,

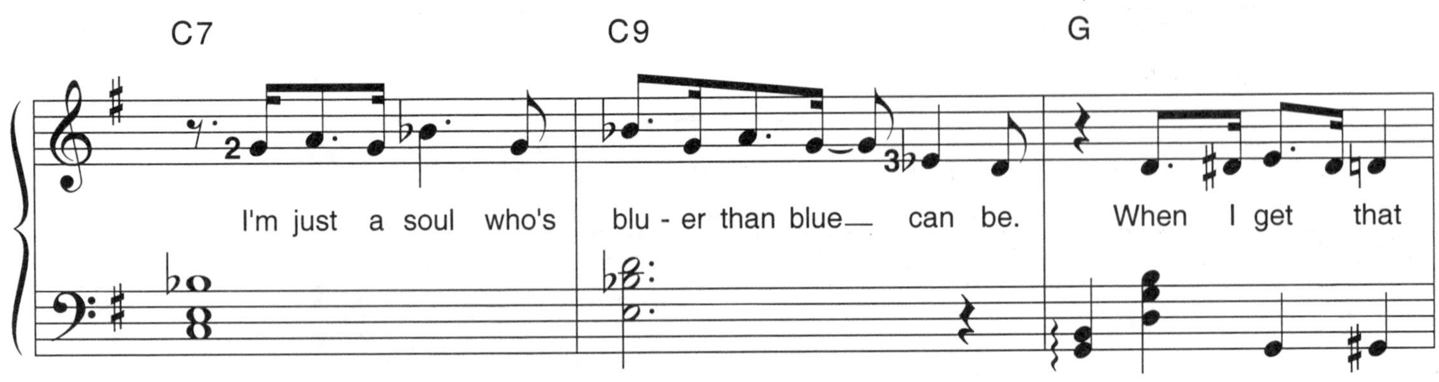
C7
C9
G
2
3
I'm just a soul who's blu - er than blue can be. When I get that

D.C. al Coda
A9
A7(♭9) A7
D7
G
D7
mood in - di - go, I could lay me down and die.

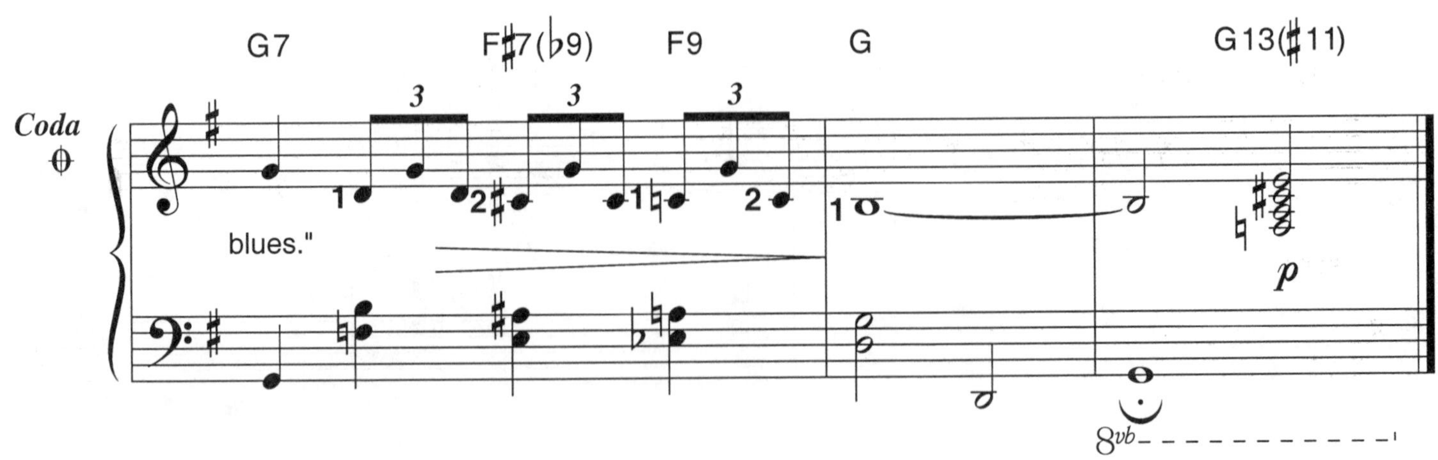
Coda
G7
F♯7(♭9)
F9
G
G13(♯11)
3
3
3
1
2
1
2
1
blues."
p
8vb

At Last

Originally recorded by Glenn Miller & his Orchestra, *At Last* is sung by Etta James on the soundtrack of *Living Out Loud.*

Lyric by MACK GORDON
Music by HARRY WARREN
Arranged by Richard Bradley

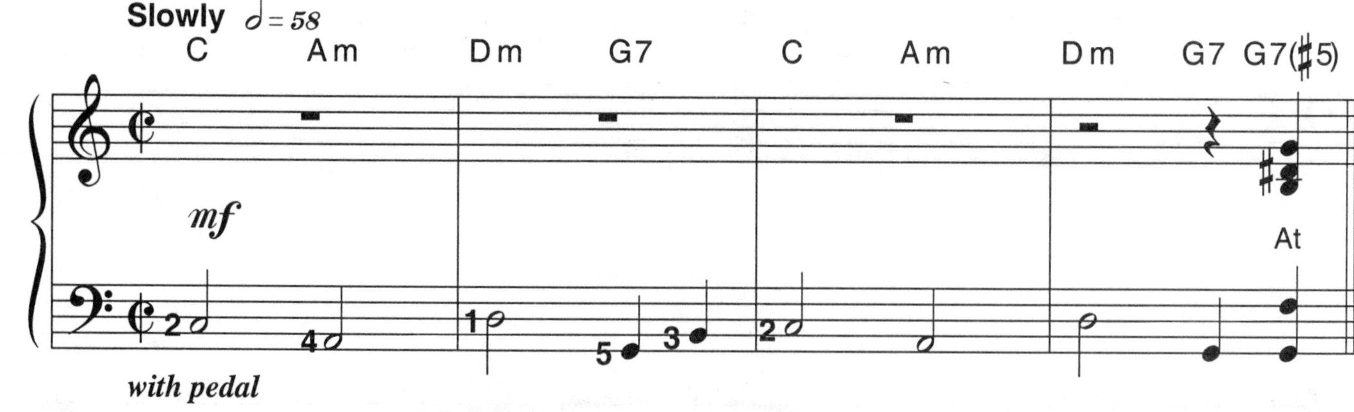

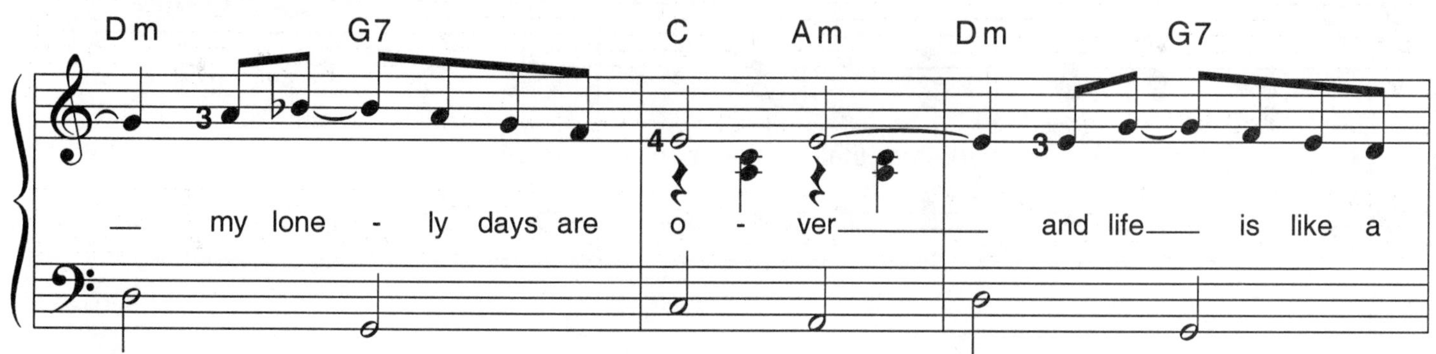

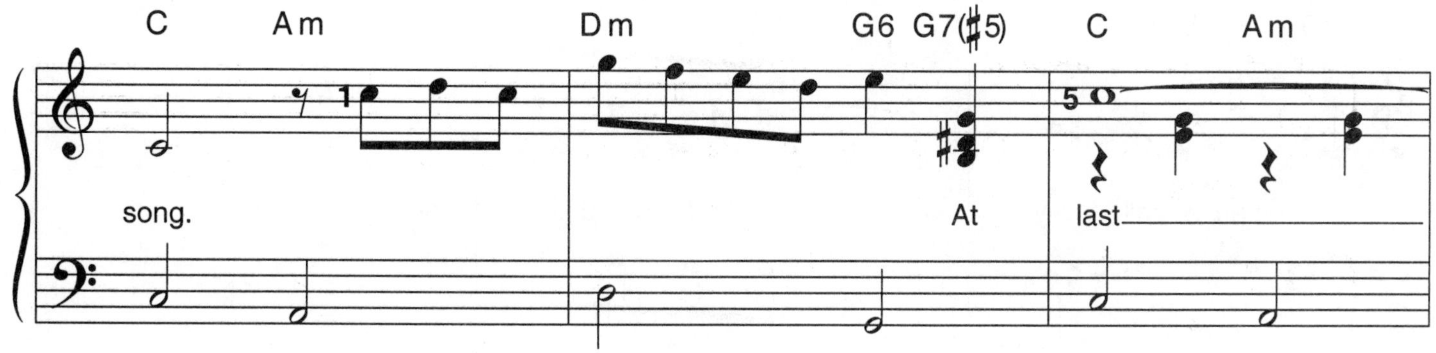

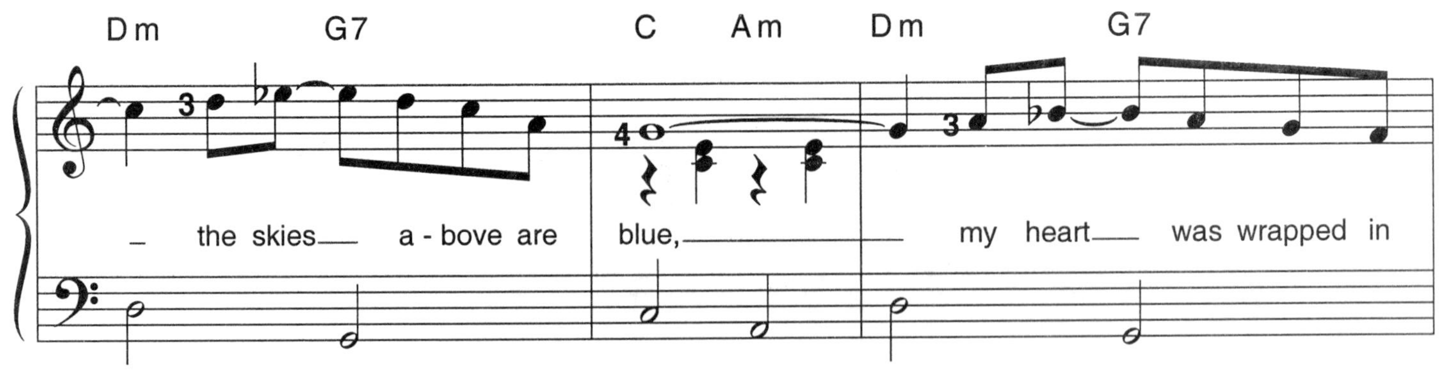
Dm G7 C Am Dm G7
3 4 3
– the skies a - bove are blue, my heart was wrapped in

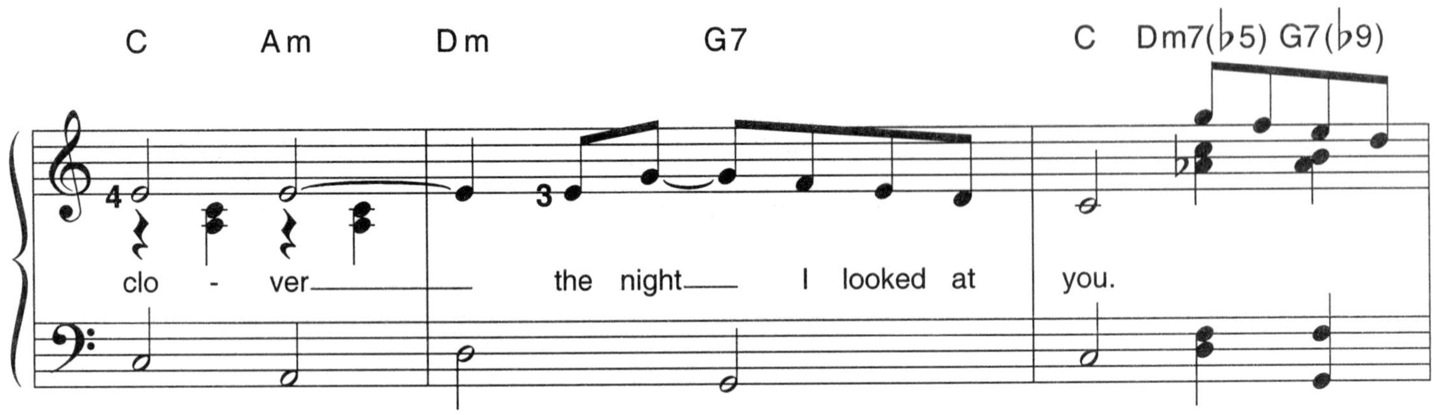
C Am Dm G7 C Dm7(♭5) G7(♭9)
4 3
clo - ver the night I looked at you.

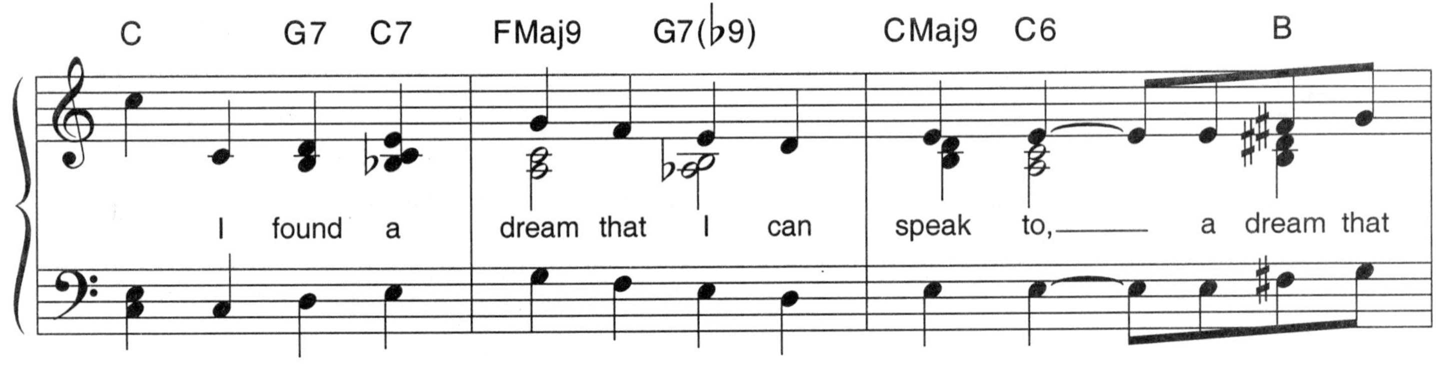
C G7 C7 FMaj9 G7(♭9) CMaj9 C6 B
I found a dream that I can speak to, a dream that

Am9 B7(♭9) Em N.C. Am7(♭5) D7
1
I can call my own, I found a thrill to press my

GMaj7
C
Am7
D7(♭9)
G6
G7(♯5)
cheek to, a thrill I've nev - er known. You

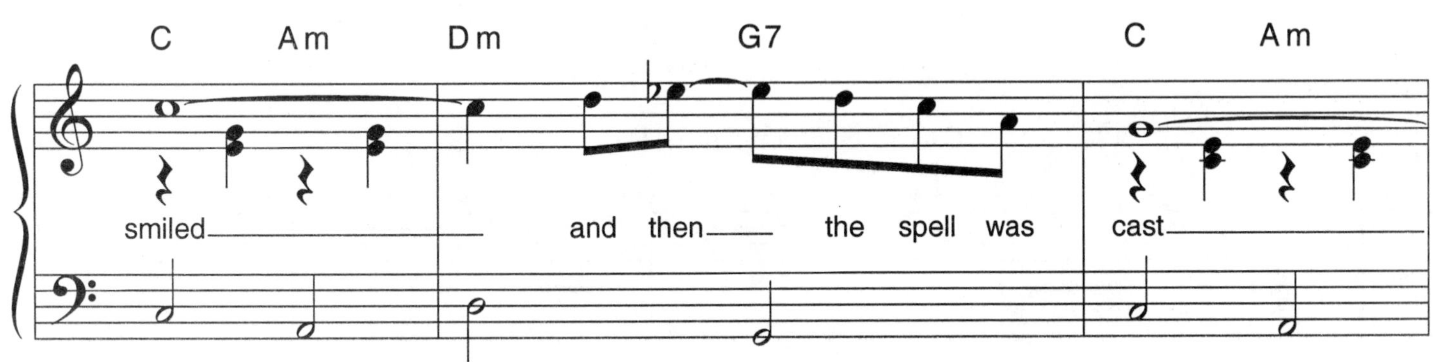
C
Am
Dm
G7
C
Am
smiled and then the spell was cast

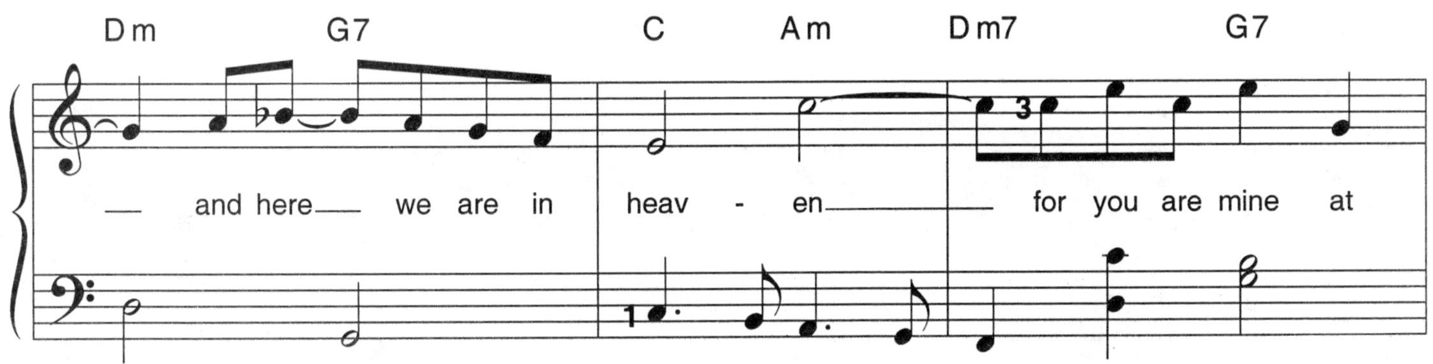
Dm
G7
C
Am
Dm7
G7
and here we are in heav - en for you are mine at

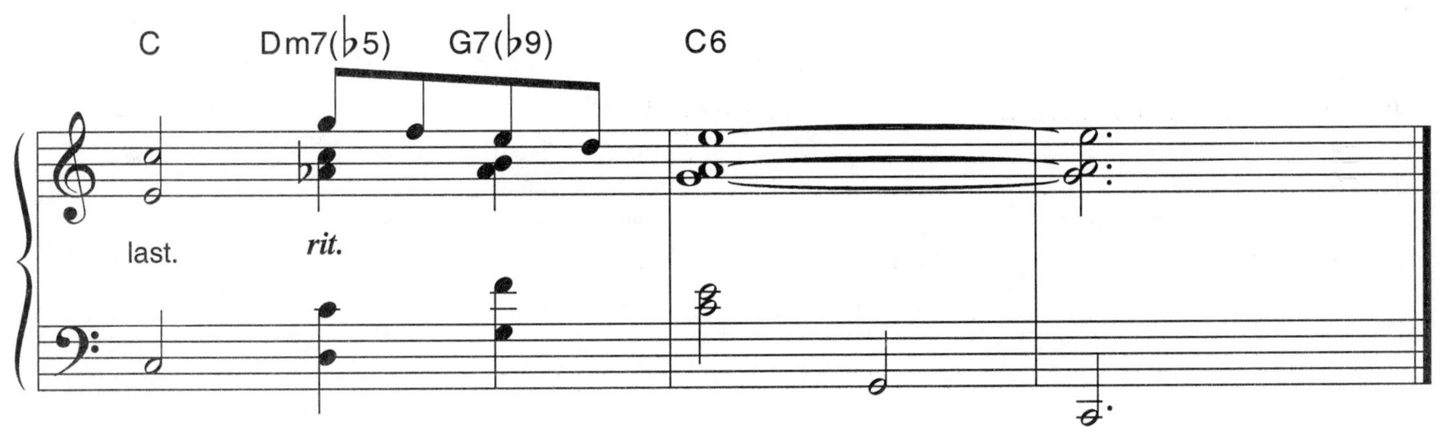
C
Dm7(♭5)
G7(♭9)
C6
last.
rit.

Twelfth Street Rag

Early recordings include Abe Lyman's Sharps & Flats, "Fats" Waller & his Rhythm and Pee Wee Hunt & his Orchestra.

By EUDAY L. BOWMAN
Arranged by Richard Bradley

D9
D7
D9
G

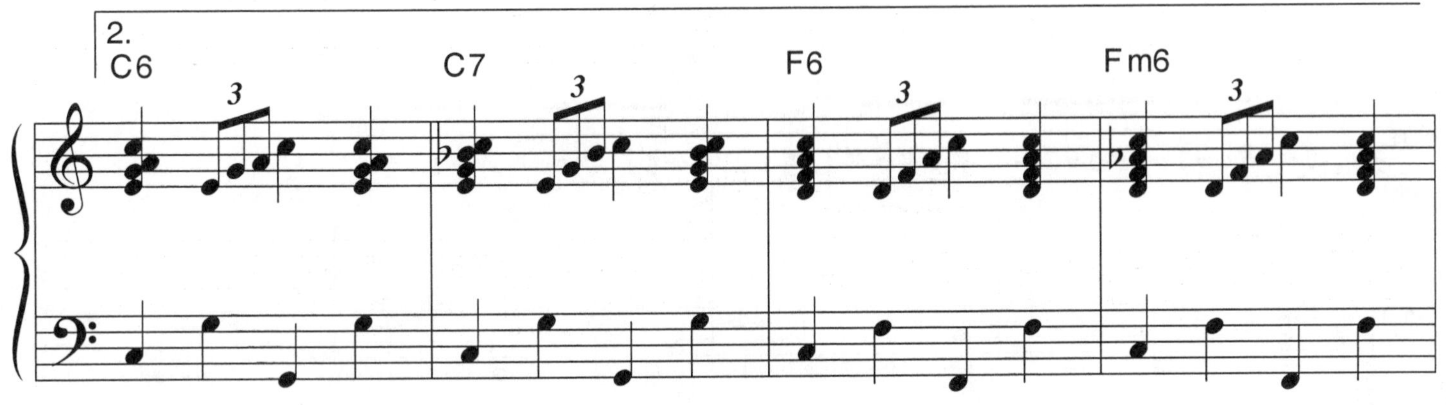
2.
C6
C7
F6
Fm6

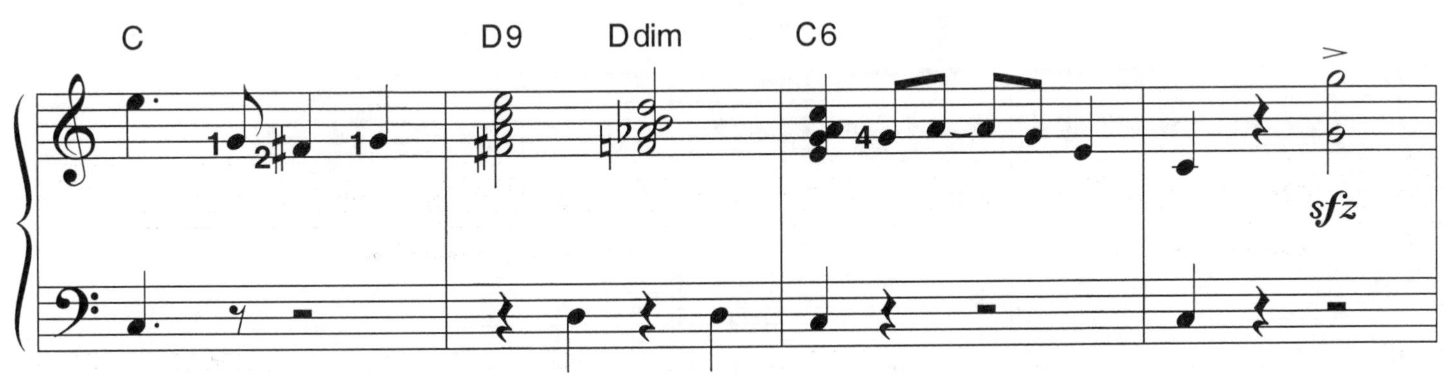
C
D9
Ddim
C6
sfz

N.C.
mf

C
2 3 4
1
C/E
Cdim/E♭
Dm7
G7

C

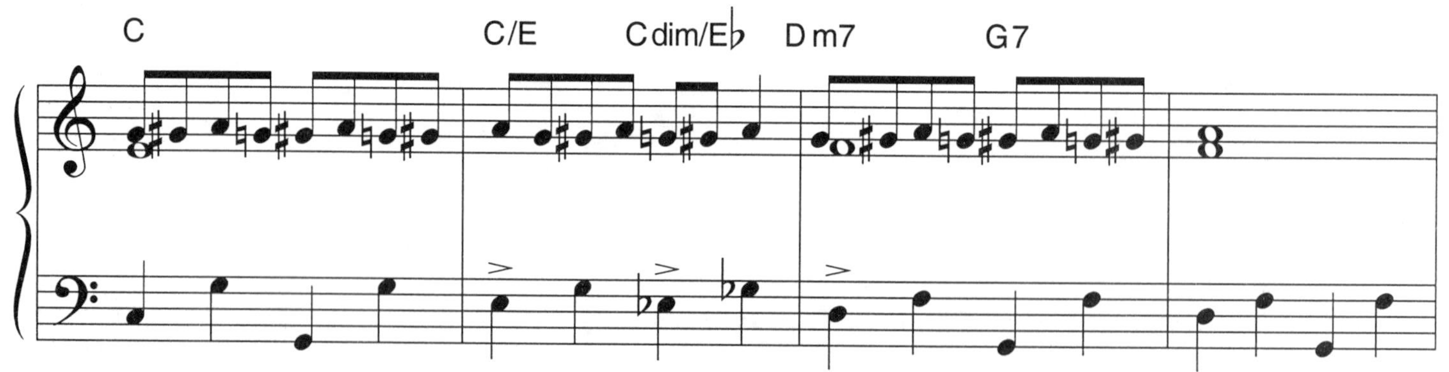
C
C/E
Cdim/E♭
Dm7
G7

D9
D7
D9
Gm
1
G

C
C/E
Cdim/E♭
Dm7
G7
C
C6
C7
F6
Fm6
C
D9
Ddim
C6
sfz

Mountain Greenery

Ella Fitzgerald and Mel Tormé are two of the jazz artists who have recorded this standard from *Garrick Gaieties*.

Words by LORENZ HART
Music by RICHARD RODGERS
Arranged by Richard Bradley

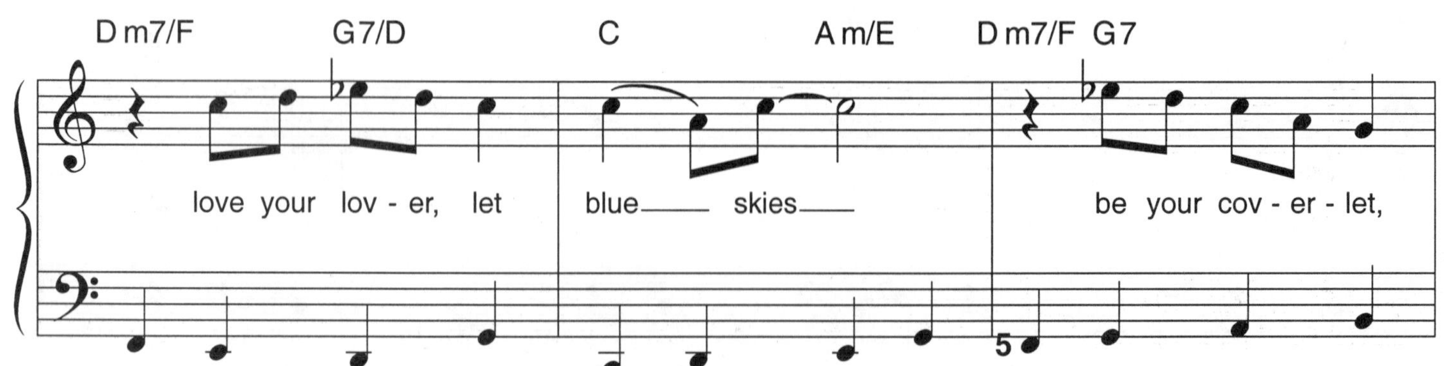

C
Am
D7/F♯
G
Gdim/B♭
when it
rains we'll laugh at the
weath - er.

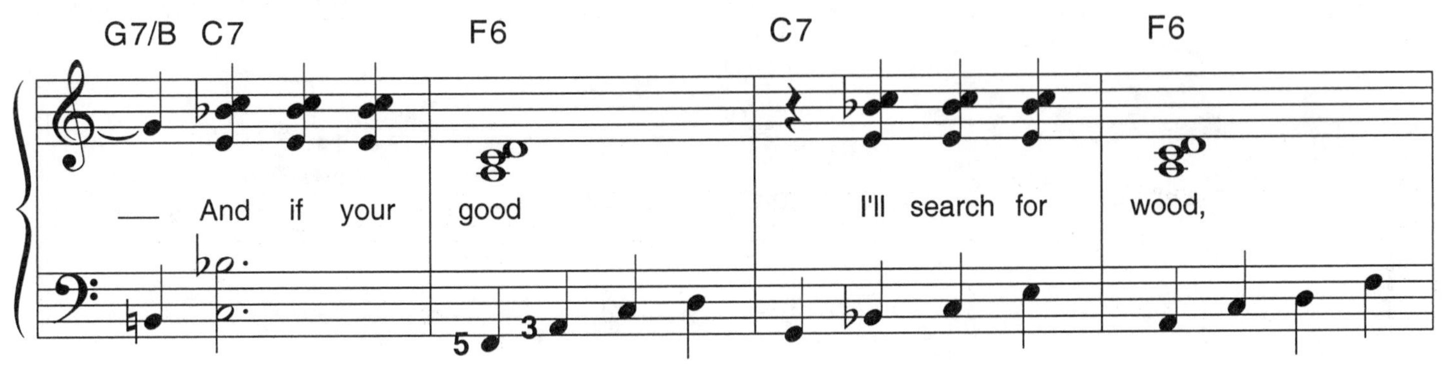
G7/B
C7
F6
C7
F6
And if your
good
I'll search for
wood,

Dm7(♭5)
G
D7
Dm7
so you can
cook
while I stand
look -

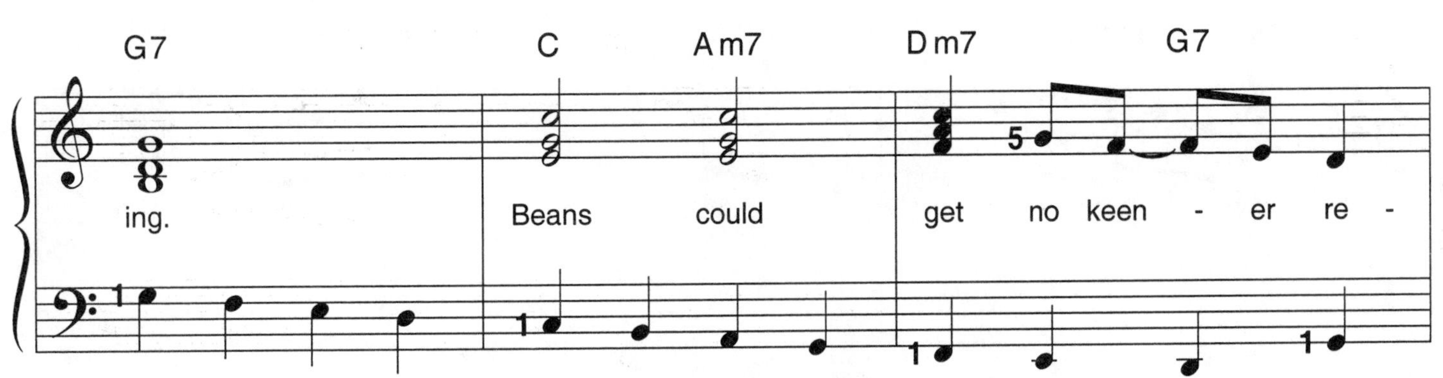
G7
C
Am7
Dm7
G7
ing.
Beans could
get no keen - er re -

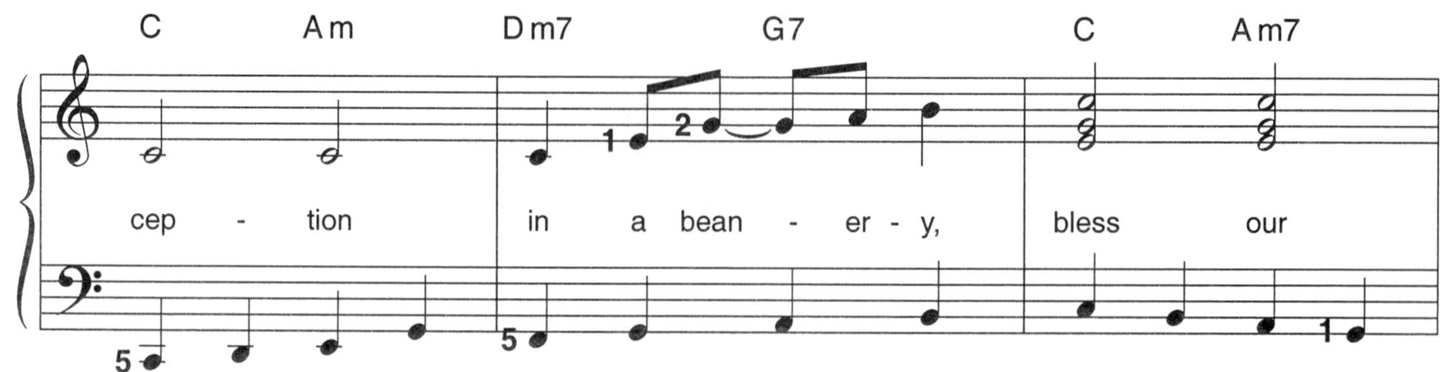
C
Am
Dm7
G7
C
Am7
cep - tion
in a bean - er - y,
bless our

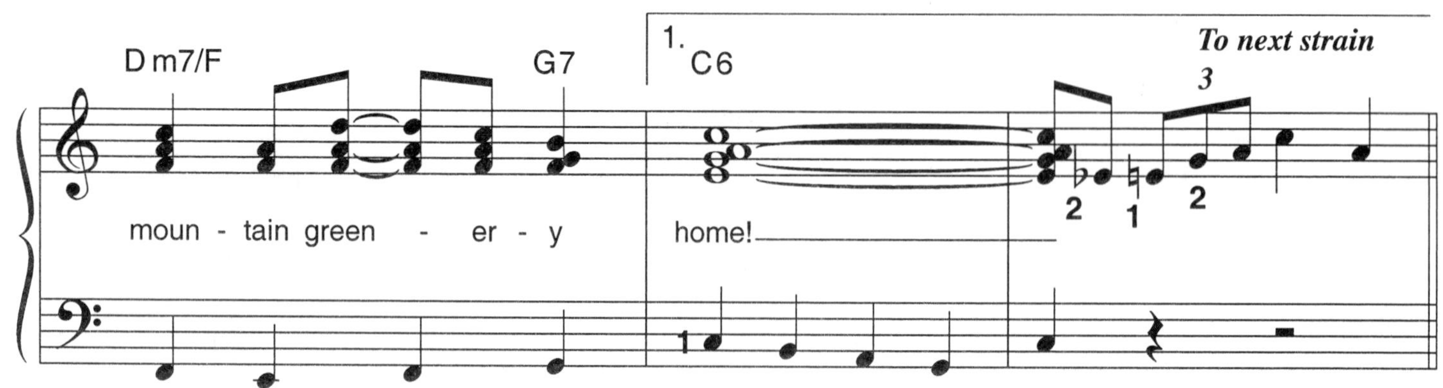
Dm7/F
G7
1. C6
To next strain
mountain green - er - y
home!

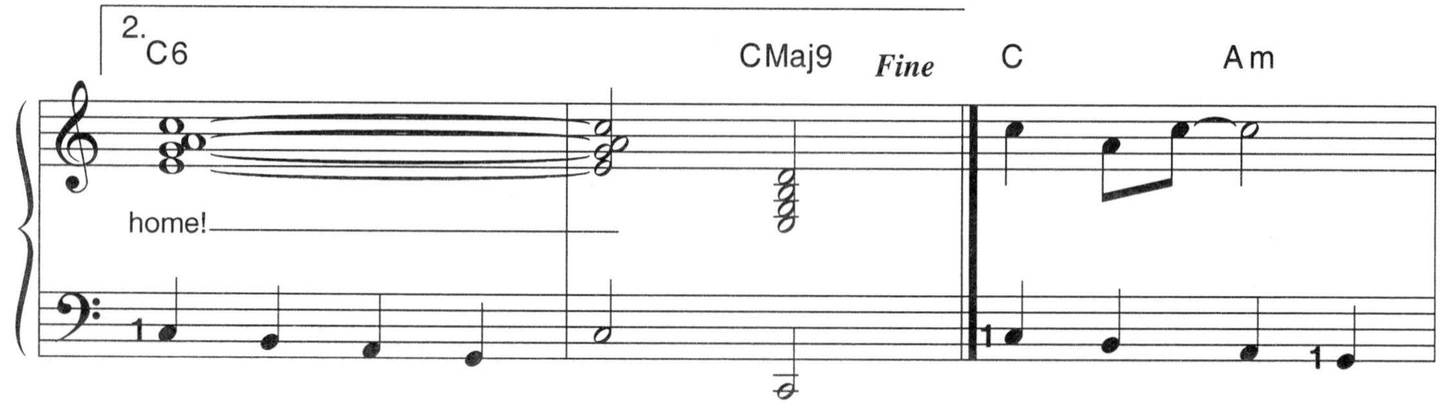
2. C6
CMaj9
Fine
C
Am
home!

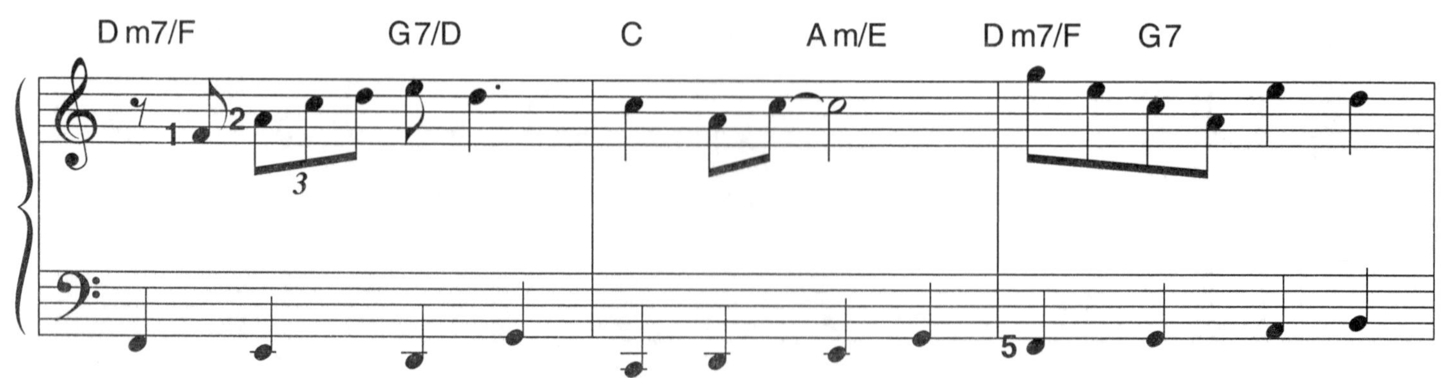
Dm7/F
G7/D
C
Am/E
Dm7/F
G7

C
Am
D7/F♯
G7
Dm7/A
3
1
1
5

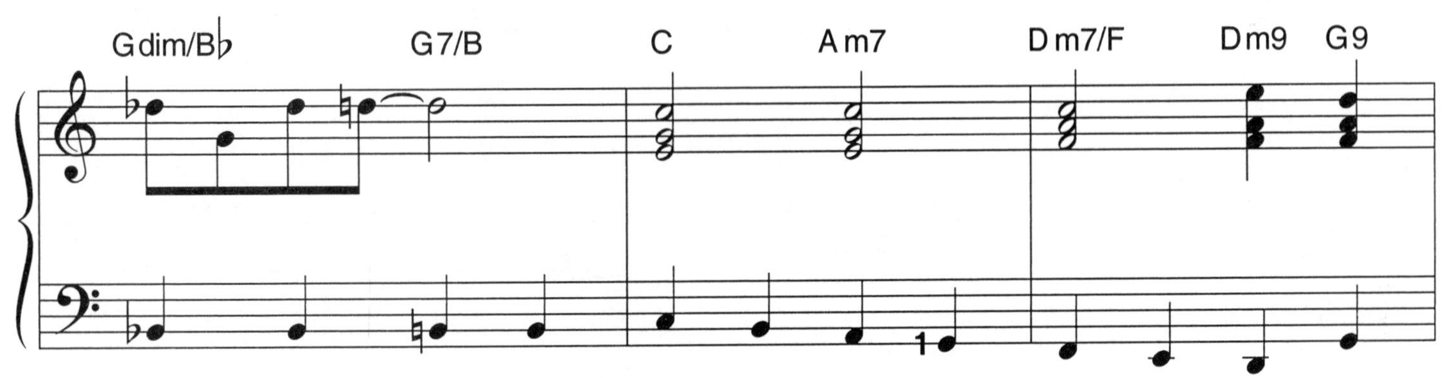
Gdim/B♭
G7/B
C
Am7
Dm7/F
Dm9
G9
1

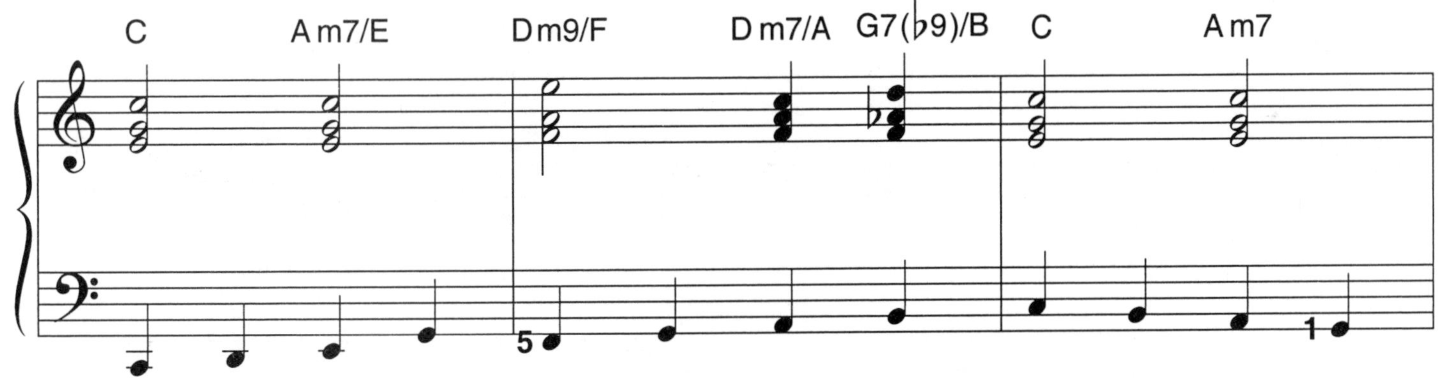
C
Am7/E
Dm9/F
Dm7/A
G7(♭9)/B
C
Am7
5
1

D.C. al Fine

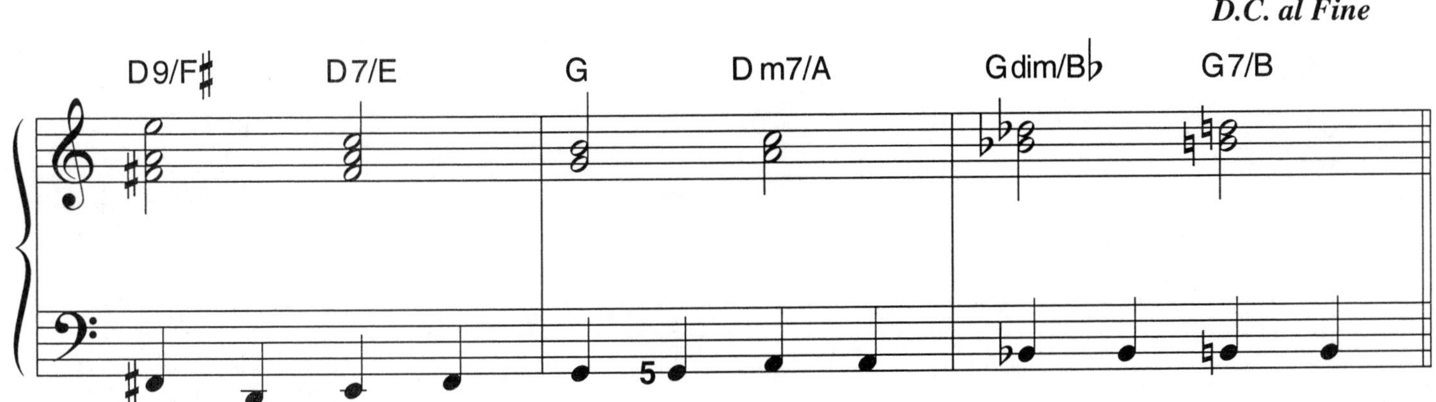
D9/F♯
D7/E
G
Dm7/A
Gdim/B♭
G7/B
5

Five Foot Two, Eyes Of Blue

Early recordings include The California Ramblers, The Savoy Orpheans and The King Brothers.

Words by JOE YOUNG and SAM LEWIS
Music by RAY HENDERSON
Arranged by Richard Bradley

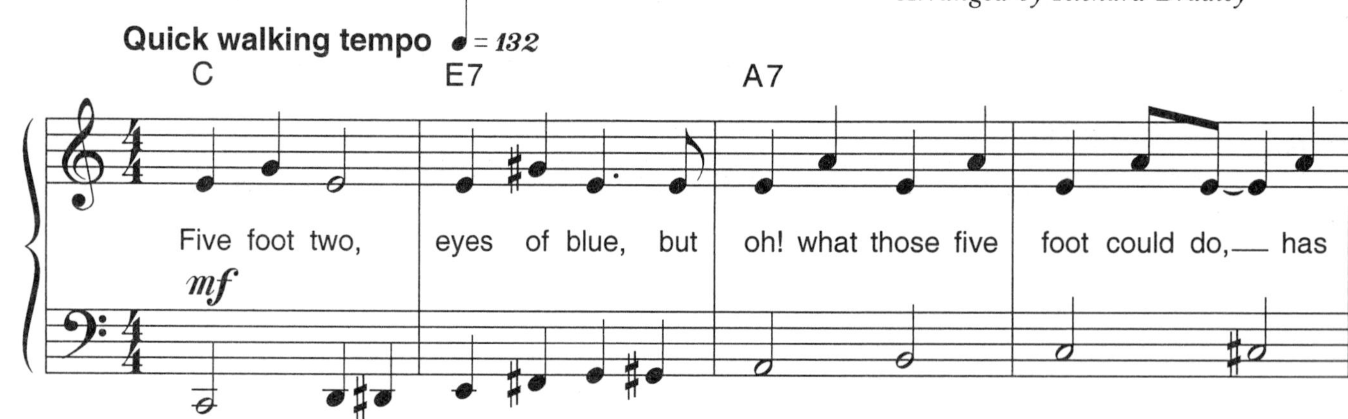

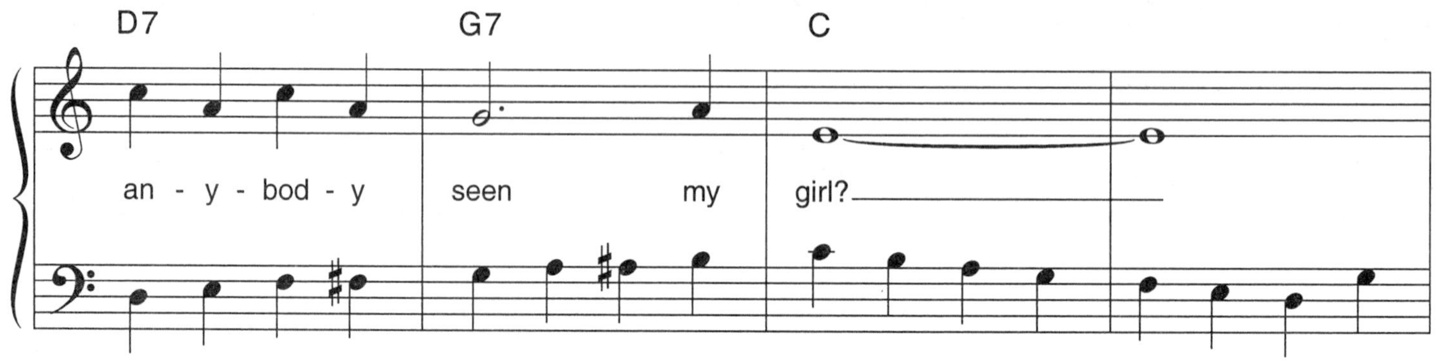

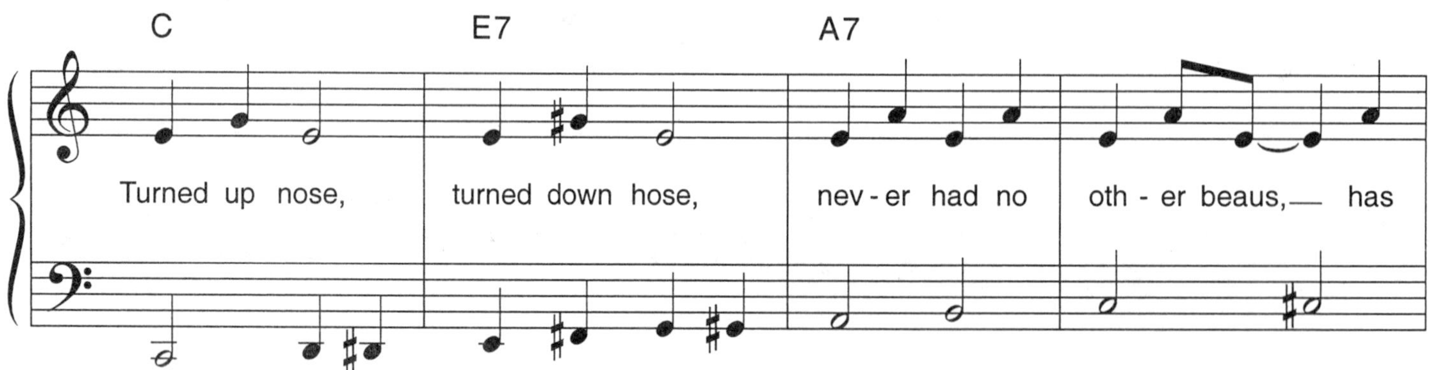

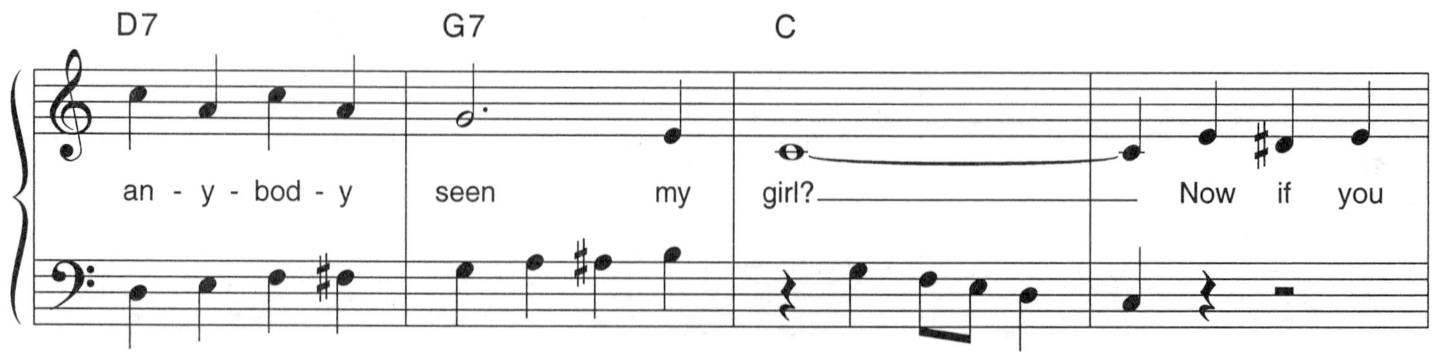

E7
A7
run in - to a five foot two, cov - ered with fur,

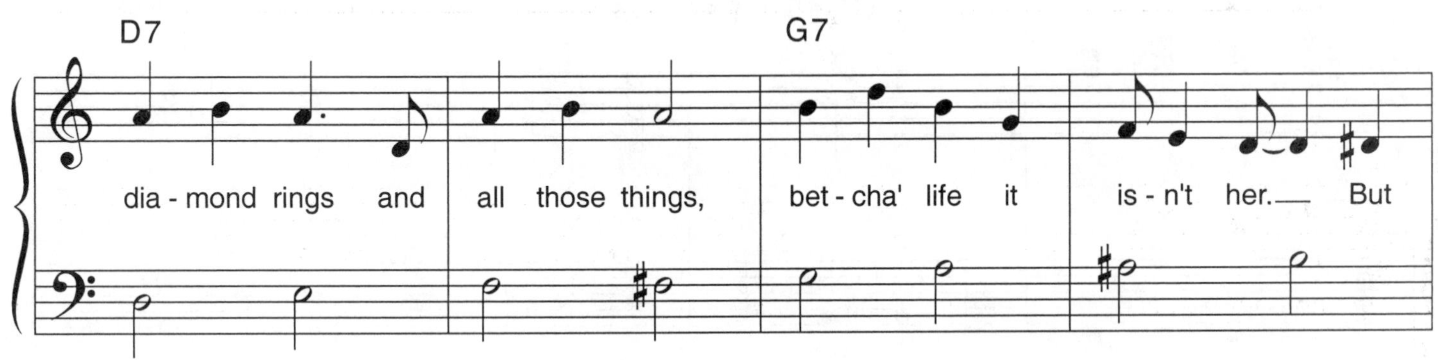
D7
G7
dia - mond rings and all those things, bet - cha' life it is - n't her. But

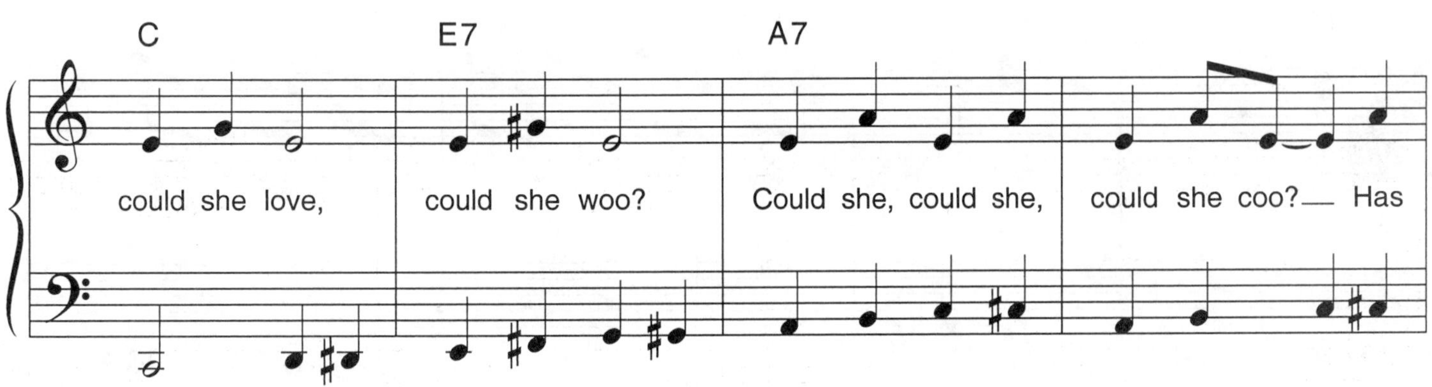
C
E7
A7
could she love, could she woo? Could she, could she, could she coo? Has

D7
G7
C
G7(♯5)
an - y - bod - y seen my girl?

C
E7
A7
D7
G7
G7(♯5)
C6
C♯dim
Dm9
G7(♭9)
C
E7
A7
D7
G7
G7(♯5)
C6

E7
A7
8va
D7
G7
G7(♯5)
8va
C
E7
A7
D7
G7
G7(♯5)
C6
CMaj9

I Got Rhythm

Ella Fitzgerald is among the jazz artists who have recorded this standard from *Girl Crazy*.

Music and Lyrics by
GEORGE GERSHWIN and IRA GERSHWIN
Arranged by Richard Bradley

Moderately (in 2) ♩ = 142

B♭ B♭6/D Cm7/E♭ F7 B♭6/9/D Edim7/D♭ Cm7 F7

mf

I got rhy - thm, I got mu - sic,

with pedal

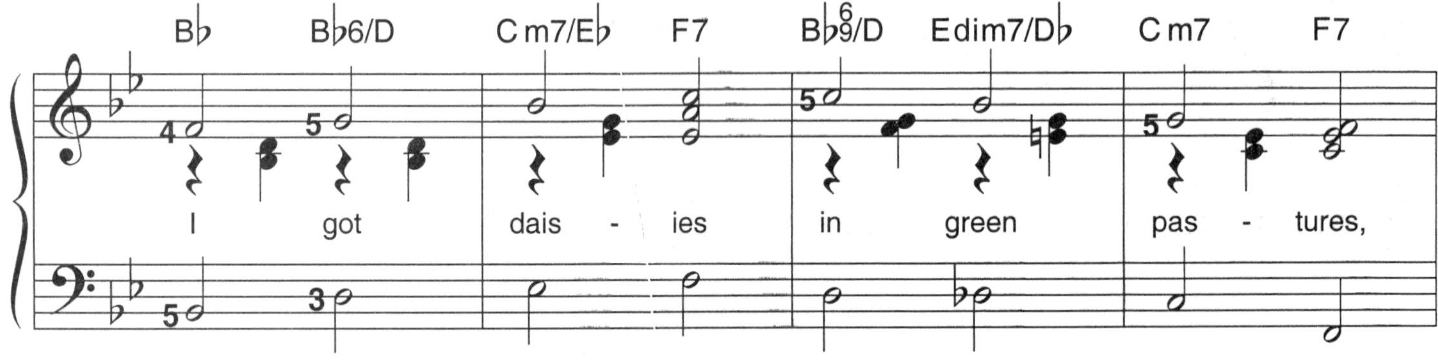

D7 Am7/E Fm6 D9/F♯ G G♭+ G9/F G7/D
Old Man___ Troub - le,___ I don't___ mind him,___

C Dm7 Cdim/E♭C9/E C7(♭5)/G♭ F7 8va
you won't___ find him___ *f* hang-in' round my door.

B♭ B♭6/D Cm7/E♭ F7 B♭6/9/D Edim7/D♭ Cm7 F7
mf I got star - light, I got sweet dreams,

B♭ B♭6/D Cm7/E♭ F7 B♭ Fm7/A♭ G7
I got my man who could ask for an - y - thing more? Who could

C9
F7
B♭6
B♭
B♭6
Cm7
F7
ask for an-y-thing more?

B♭6/9
Edim
Cm7
F7
B♭
B♭6
Cm7
F7

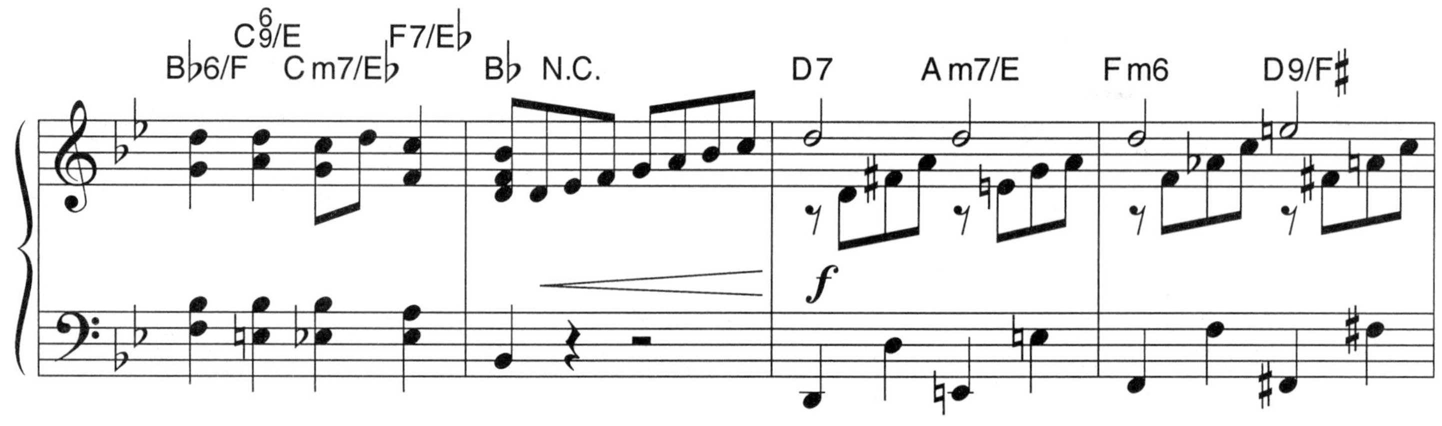
B♭6/F
C6/9/E
Cm7/E♭
F7/E♭
B♭ N.C.
D7
Am7/E
Fm6
D9/F♯

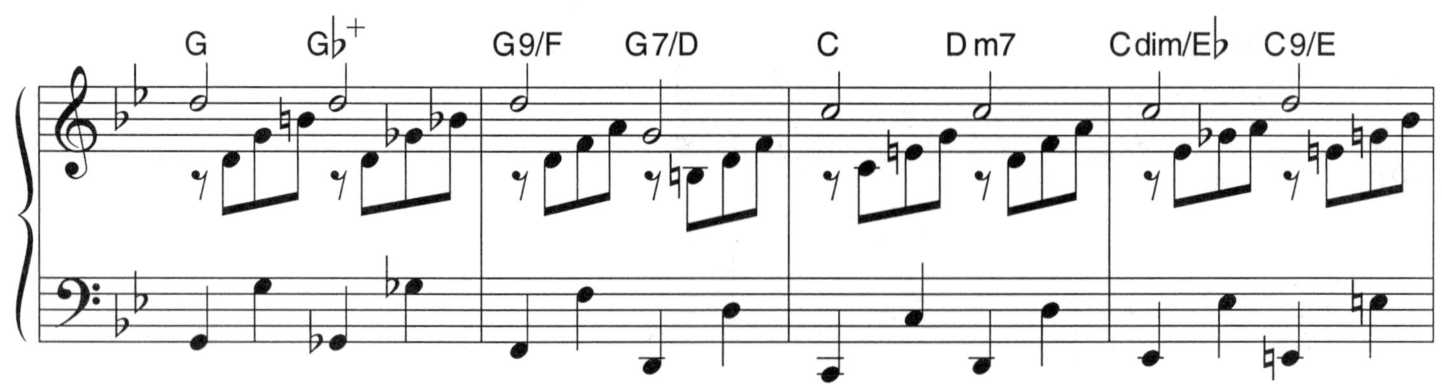
G
G♭+
G9/F
G7/D
C
Dm7
Cdim/E♭
C9/E

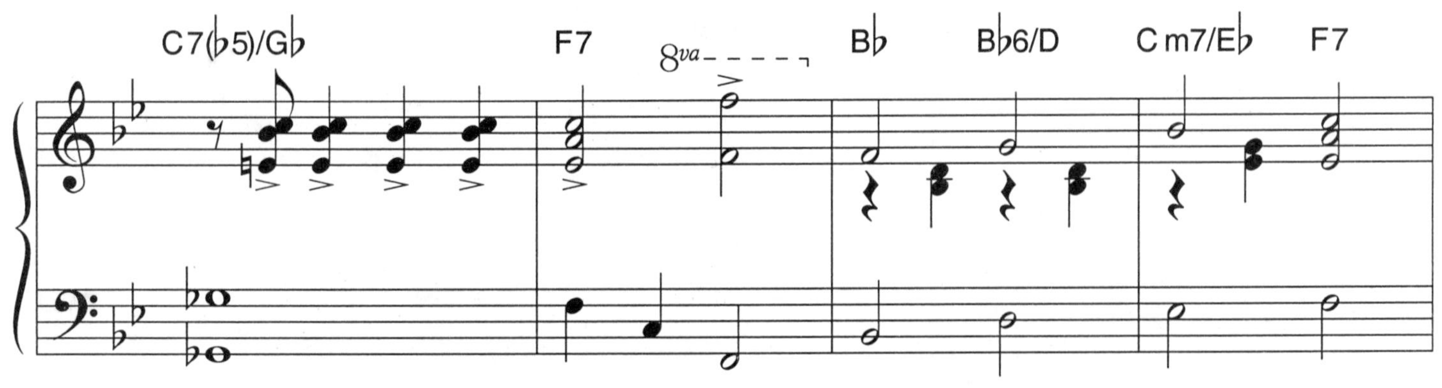
C7(♭5)/G♭
F7
8va
B♭
B♭6/D
Cm7/E♭
F7

B♭6/9/D
Edim7/D♭
Cm7
F7
B♭
B♭6/D
Cm7/E♭
F7

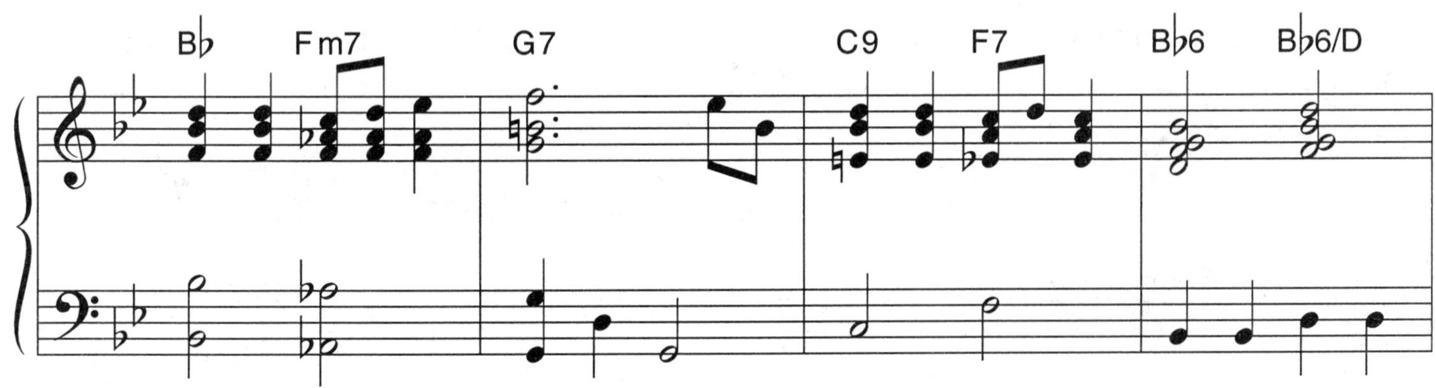
B♭
Fm7
G7
C9
F7
B♭6
B♭6/D

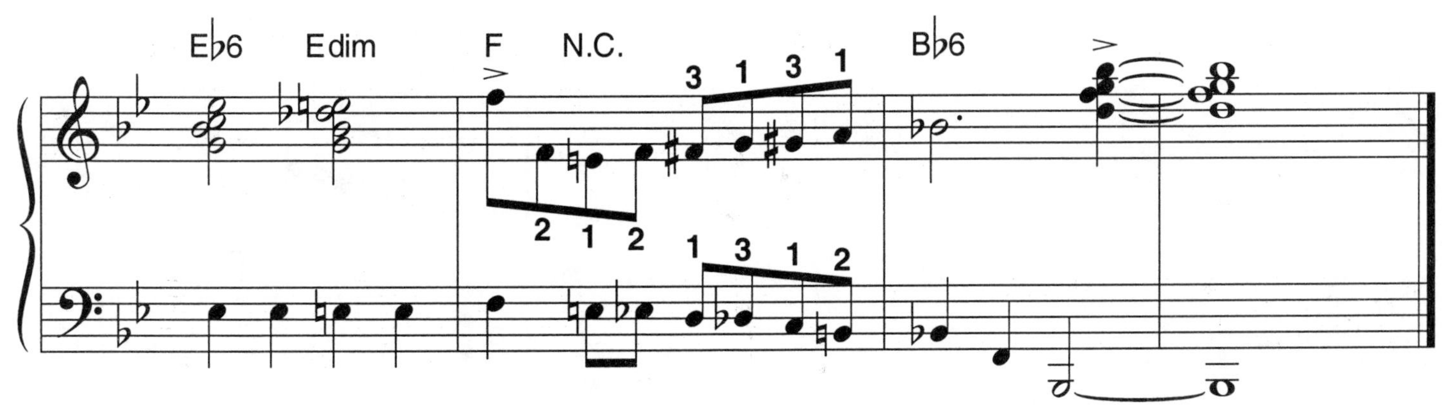
E♭6
Edim
F
N.C.
B♭6

Saint Louis Blues

Jazz great Bessie Smith sang this song in the 1928 film *Saint Louis Blues*.

By
W.C. HANDY
Arranged by Richard Bradley

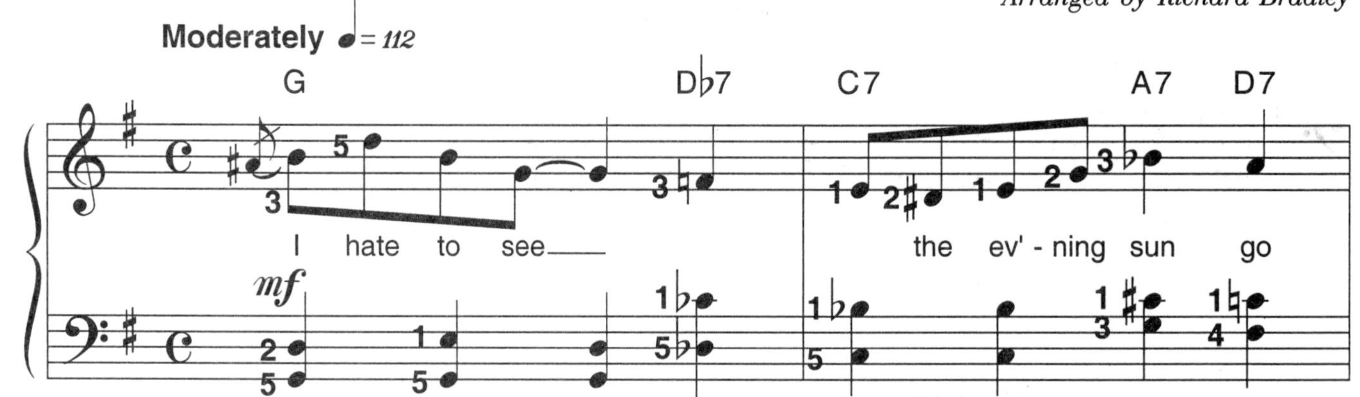

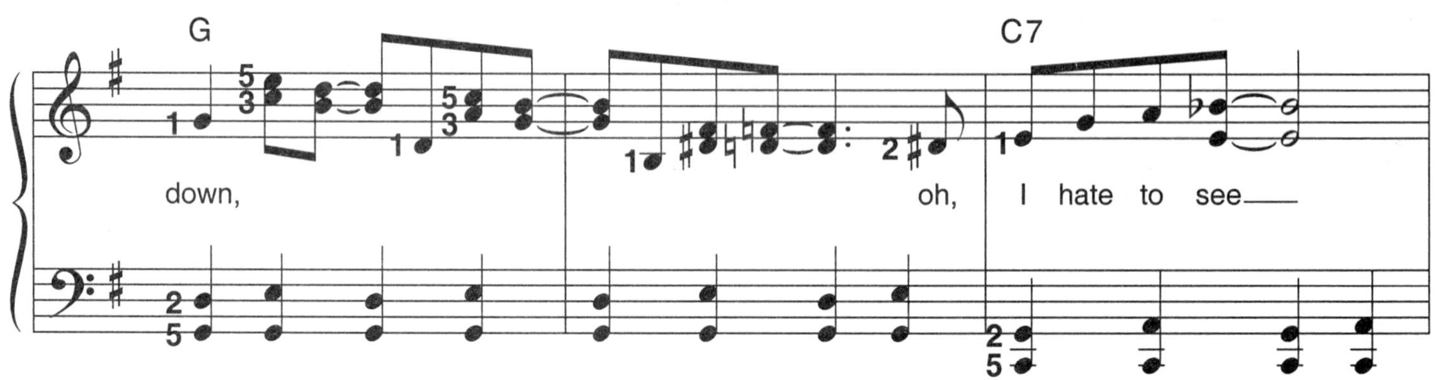

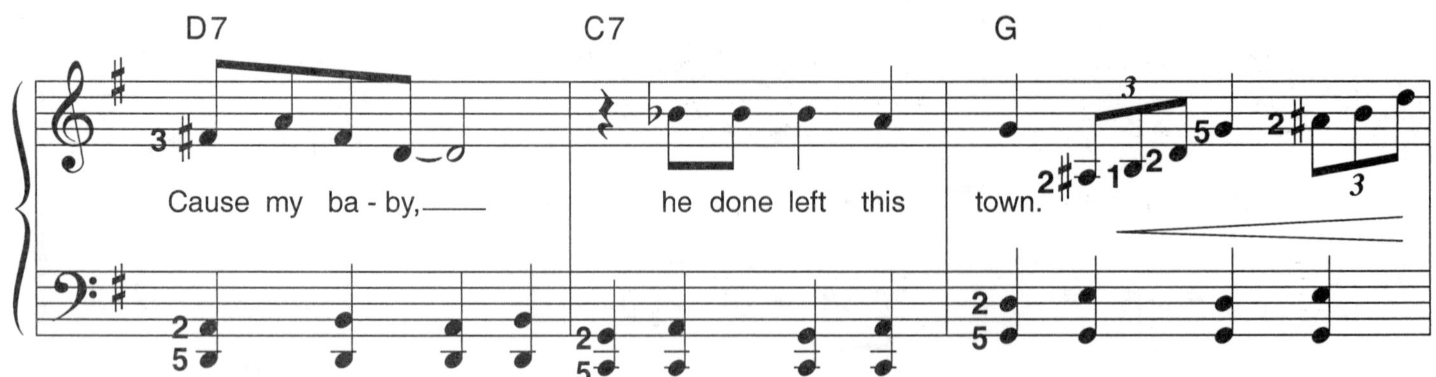

G
D♭7
C7
A7
D7
Feel - ing to - mor - row
like I feel to -

G
C7
day,
feel to - mor - row

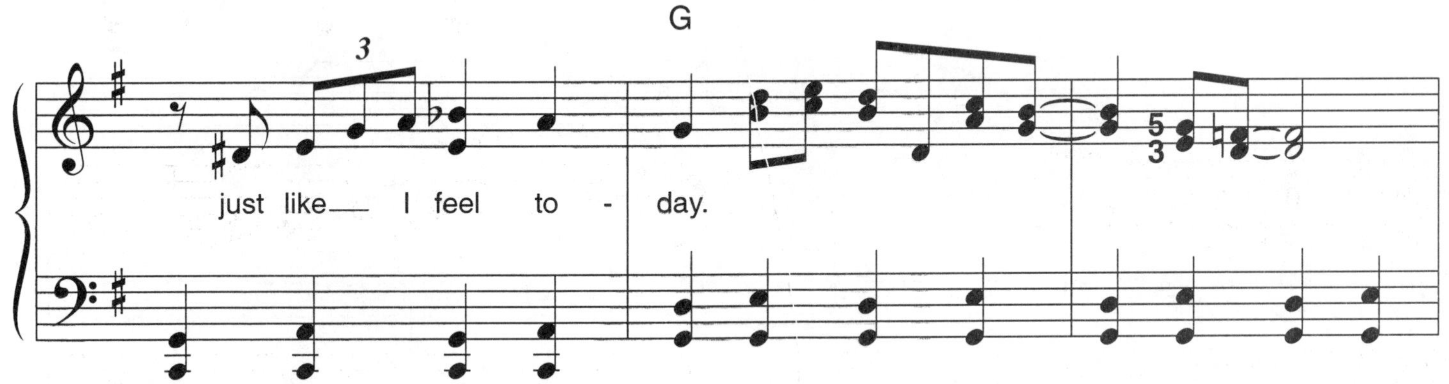
G
just like I feel to - day.

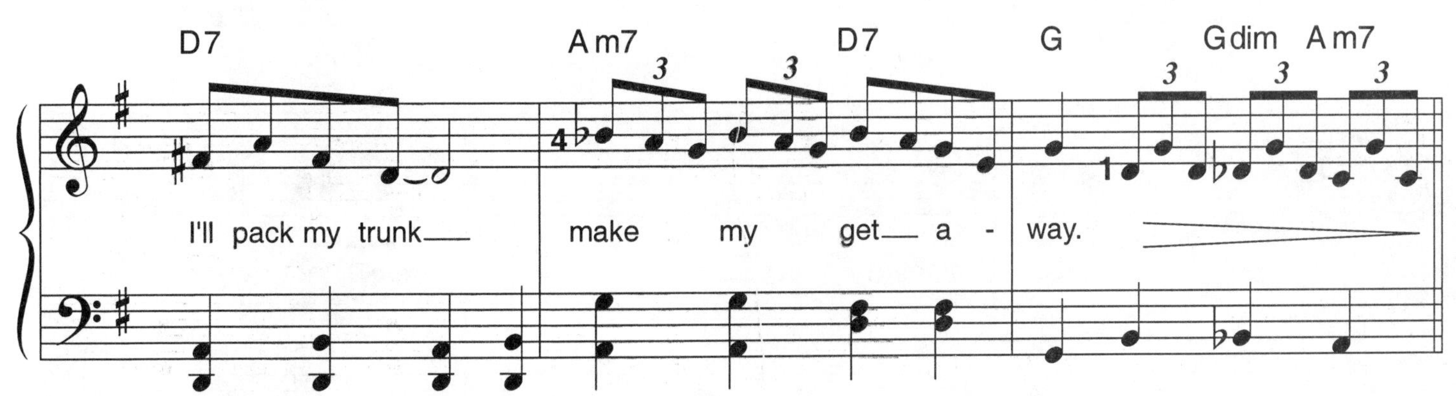
D7
Am7
D7
G
Gdim
Am7
I'll pack my trunk make my get a - way.

G
D
Gm
St. Lou - is
wo-man,
mf
with her dia - mond
D
rings,
pulls that man
a-round
by her a-pron
Gm
strings.
Weren't for
pow-der
and for store bought
D
hair
the
man I love
would not go no -

Gm
A7
D
G
where.
Got the
St. Lou - is blues just as
blue as I can be
That
C
man got a heart like a
rock cast in the
G
sea.
Or
D7
G6
else he would - n't have gone - so far from
me.

G
D♭7
C7
A7
D7
mf
1
5
G
C7
3
G
D7
A m7
3
3
D7
G6
C6
C♯dim
D7
1 2 1
2 1 2 3
G
A7
G7
ff
2 3 1 3
1
3
1

Don't Get Around Much Anymore

Artists who have recorded this standard include Duke Ellington & his Orchestra, The Ink Spots, Eydie Gormé and The King Sisters.

Lyric by BOB RUSSELL
Music by DUKE ELLINGTON
Arranged by Richard Bradley

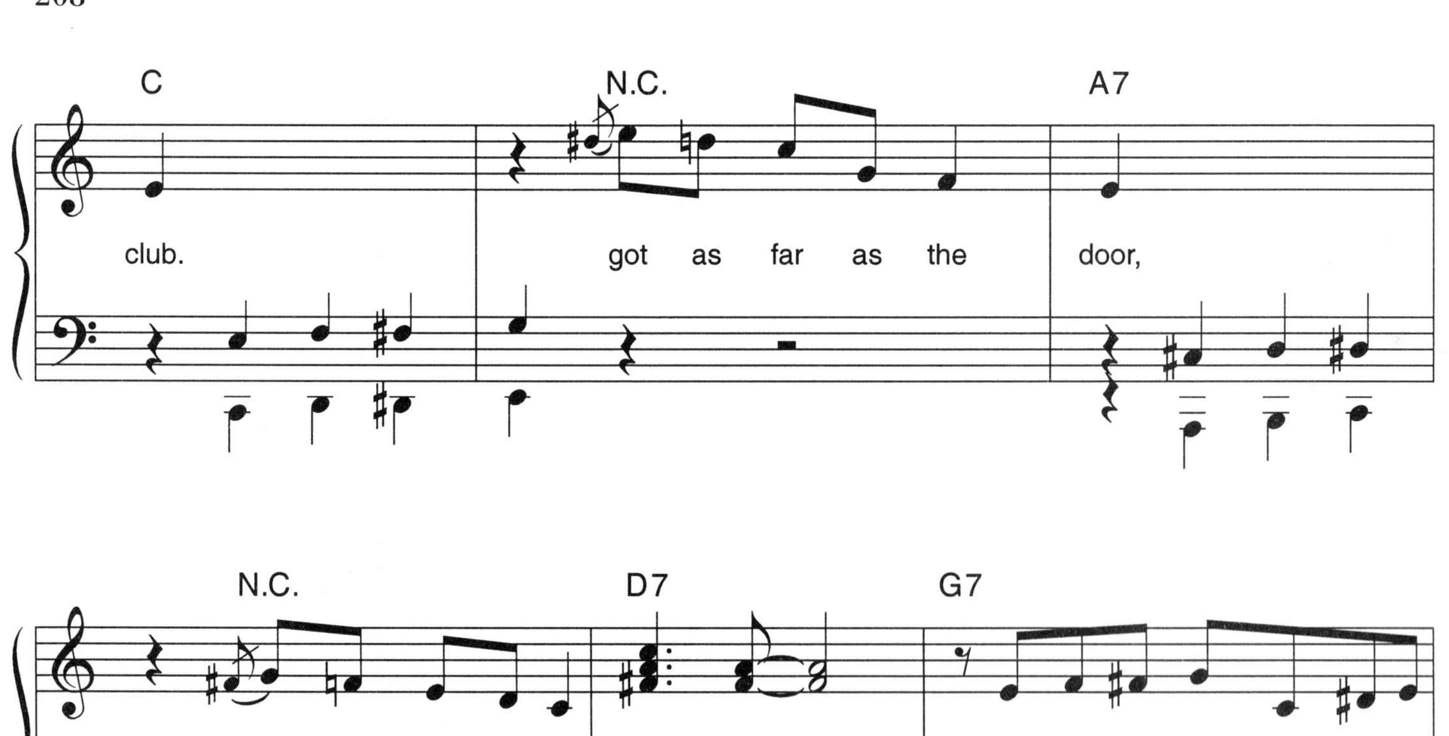
C
N.C.
A7
club.
got as far as the
door,

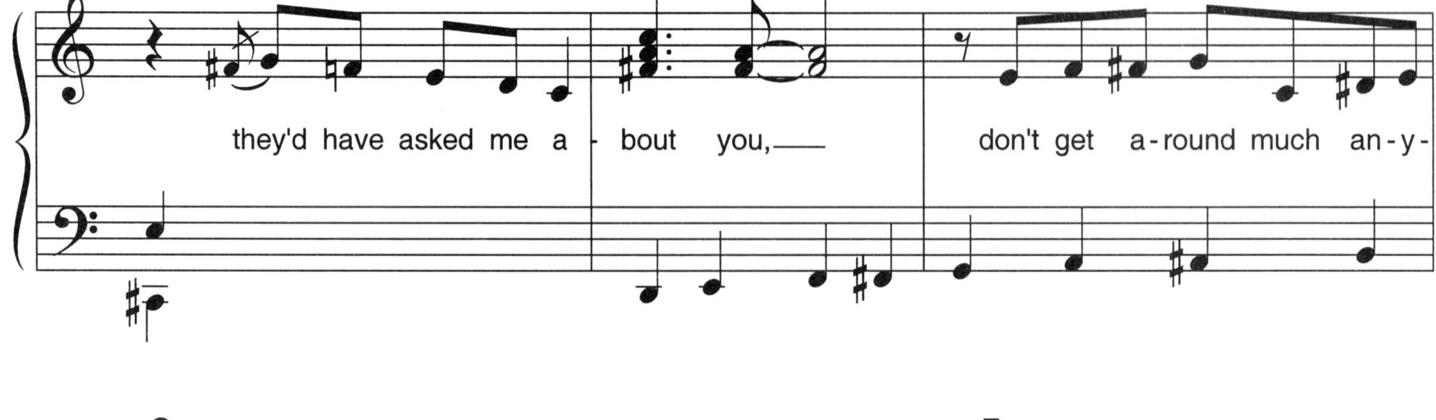
N.C.
D7
G7
they'd have asked me a - bout you,
don't get a-round much an-y-

C
F
more.
Dar - ling, I

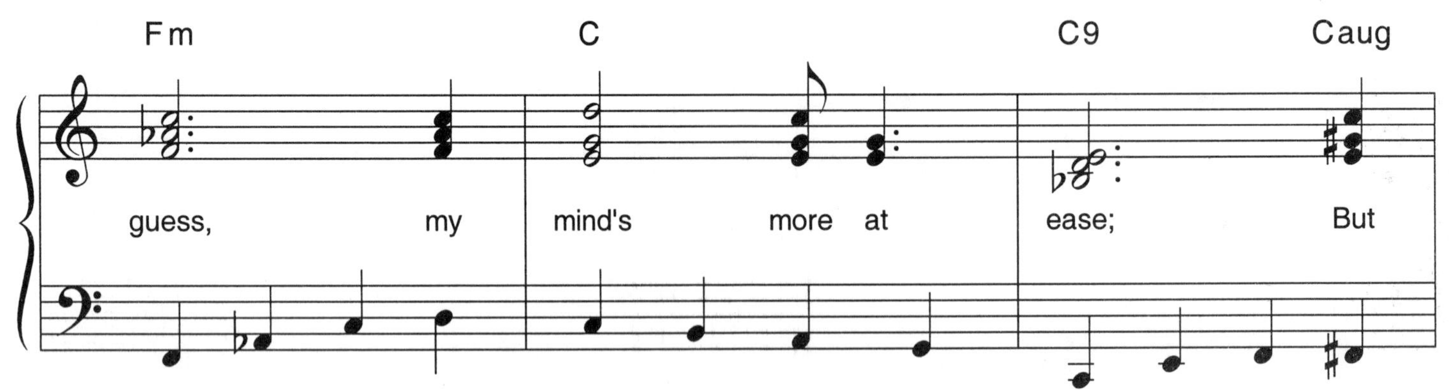
Fm
C
C9
Caug
guess, my
mind's more at
ease; But

F
B♭13
Am9
A♭7
nev - er - the - less,
why stir up mem - o -

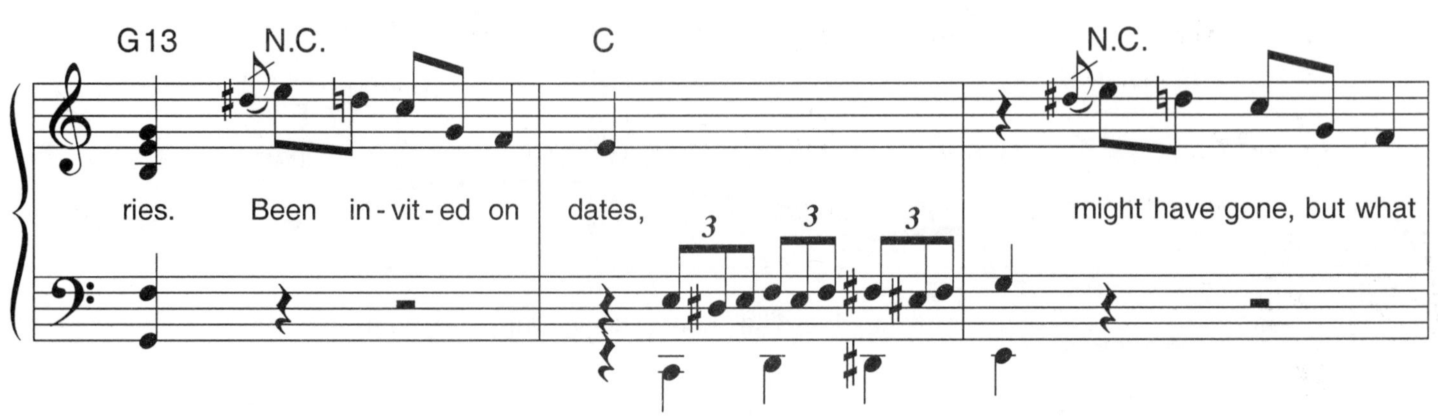
G13
N.C.
C
N.C.
ries. Been in - vit - ed on dates,
might have gone, but what
3 3 3

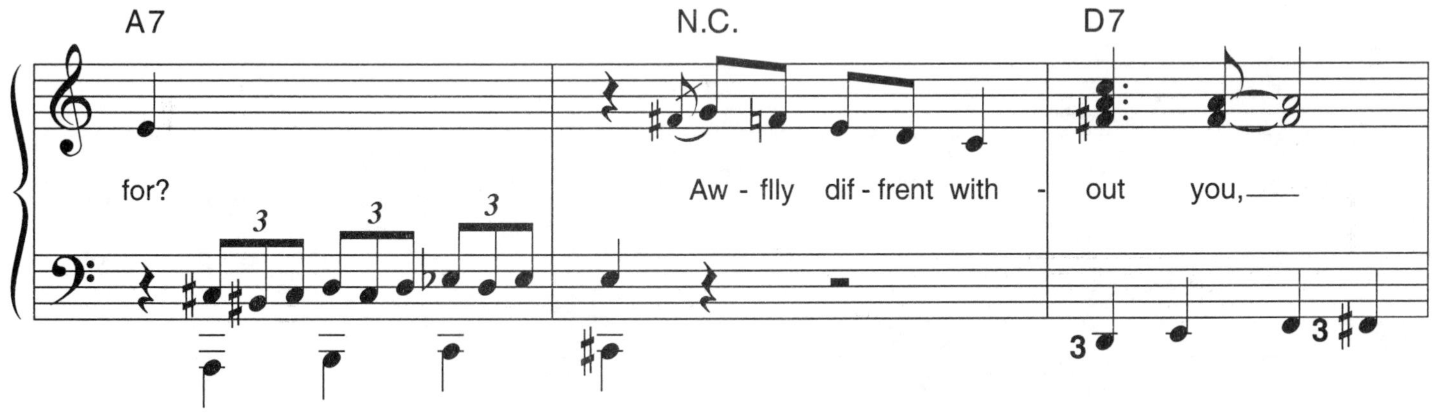
A7
N.C.
D7
for?
Aw - flly dif - frent with - out you,
3 3 3

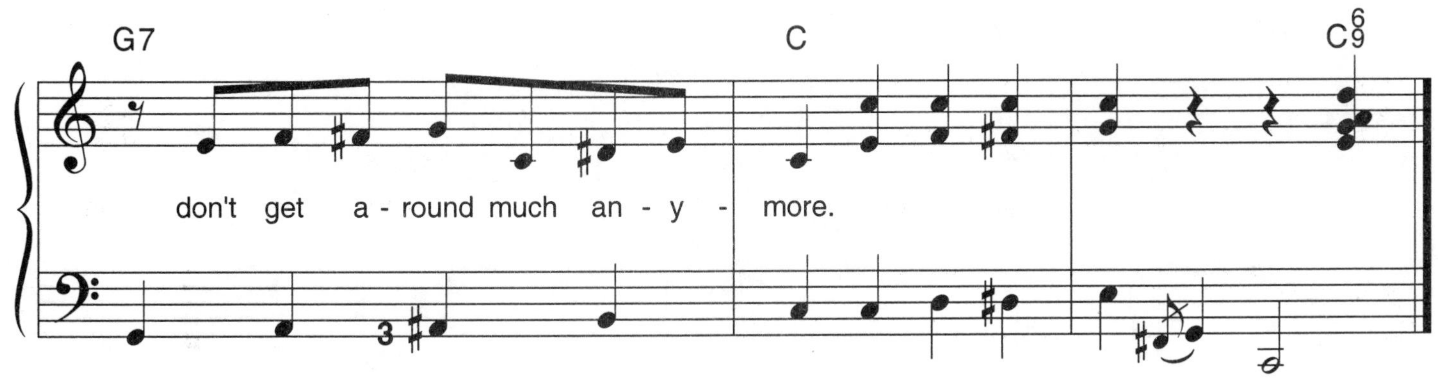
G7
C
C6/9
don't get a - round much an - y - more.

Misty

The Erroll Garner Trio were the first to record this jazz standard.
Johnny Mathis had the pop hit.

Lyric by JOHNNY BURKE
Music by ERROLL GARNER
Arranged by Richard Bradley

F♯7
FMaj7
Cm7
F7/E♭
way, and a thou-sand vi - o - lins be - gin to
B♭Maj7
B♭6
B♭m/G
F
E♭
play, or it might be the sound of your hel - lo, that
F
Dm
Gm
C7
To Coda
mu - sic I hear, I get mist - y the mo - ment you're
F
A♭
G
G♭
N.C.
near. You can say that you're
Cm7
Cm7/G
F/C
lead - ing me on, but it's just what I

Verse 3:
On my own, would I wander through this wonderland alone,
Never knowing my right foot from my left,
My hat from my glove, I'm too misty and too much in love.

The Sorcerer's Apprentice

French composer
1865 - 1935

PAUL DUKAS
Arranged by Richard Bradley

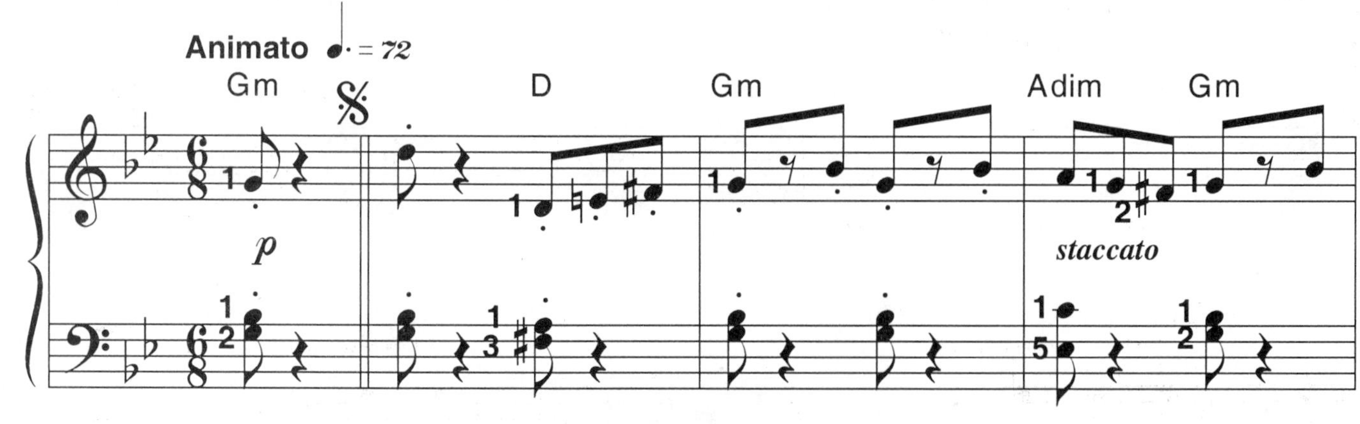

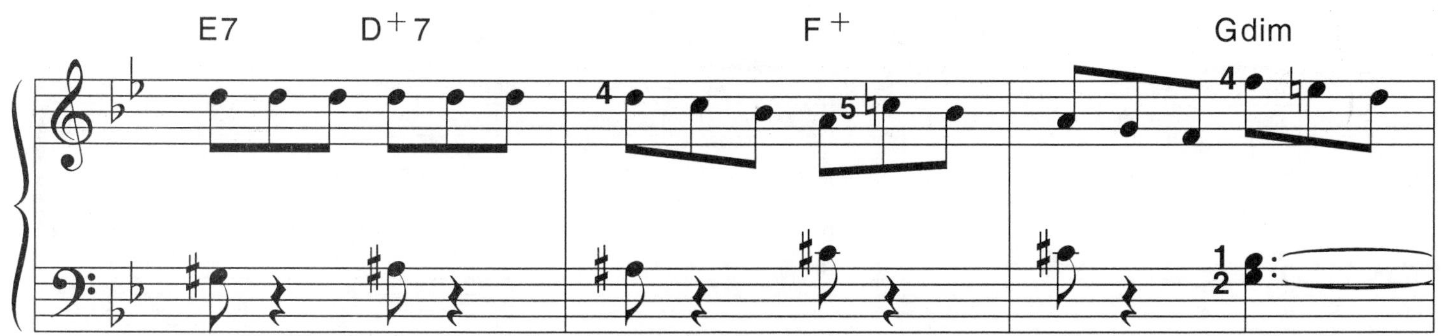

D
E♭
D
Gm

F♯m
Fm
D
Cm
Gm

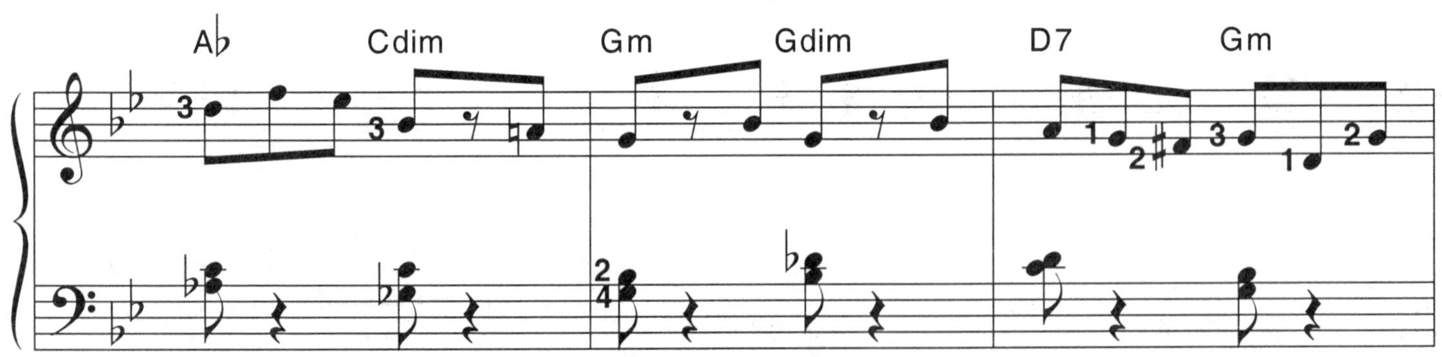
A♭
Cdim
Gm
Gdim
D7
Gm

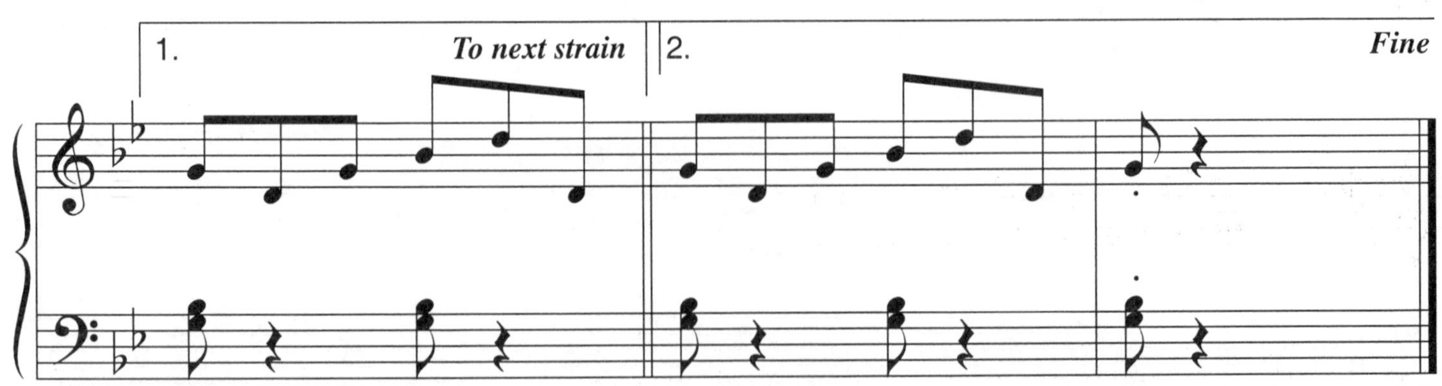
1.
To next strain
2.
Fine

E♭
E♭+
E♭6
f legato
mp
staccato
E♭+
E♭6
E♭+
E♭
legato
E♭+
staccato
legato
D7
staccato
Gm D.S. 𝄋 al Fine

Eighteenth Variation

From "Rhapsody On A Theme Of Paganini"

Russian pianist-composer
1873 - 1943

SERGEI RACHMANINOFF
Arranged by Richard Bradley

Bm
F♯m
AMaj7
3
Bm7
DMaj7
Dm7
E7
f
A
D
mf
f
dim.
cresc
dim.
F♯m
Bm7
A7
p

Em7
A7
cresc
F♯m
DMaj7
Em7
3
Bm
Gm7(♭5)
A7
D
f
ff
3
dim.
f
3
F♯m
dim.
mf
dim.

D7
B7
Em7
Bdim
Gm♯7
dolce
dim.
C♯dim
Dsus4
C♯dim
DMaj7
D7
C♯dim
C7
B7
Gm
dim.
Dm
A♯6
Dm
A♯7
N.C.
A9
p
D
A7
D
A9
D
rit.
pp

Für Elise
(Main Theme)

German composer
1770 - 1827

LUDWIG van BEETHOVEN
Edited by Richard Bradley

E
8va
NC
Am
E
pp
Am
NC
Am
1.
E
Am
2.
E
Am
dim. e rit.

Peter And The Wolf
(Peter's Theme)

Russian composer
1891 - 1953

SERGEI PROKOFIEV
Arranged by Richard Bradley

F
1
2
3
4
1
mf
5

D♭
A♭
4
5

1
2
3
4
3

Em
G7
C
5
1
1
f
5
5

Also Sprach Zarathustra

German composer
1864 - 1949

RICHARD STRAUSS
1864 - 1949
Arranged by Richard Bradley

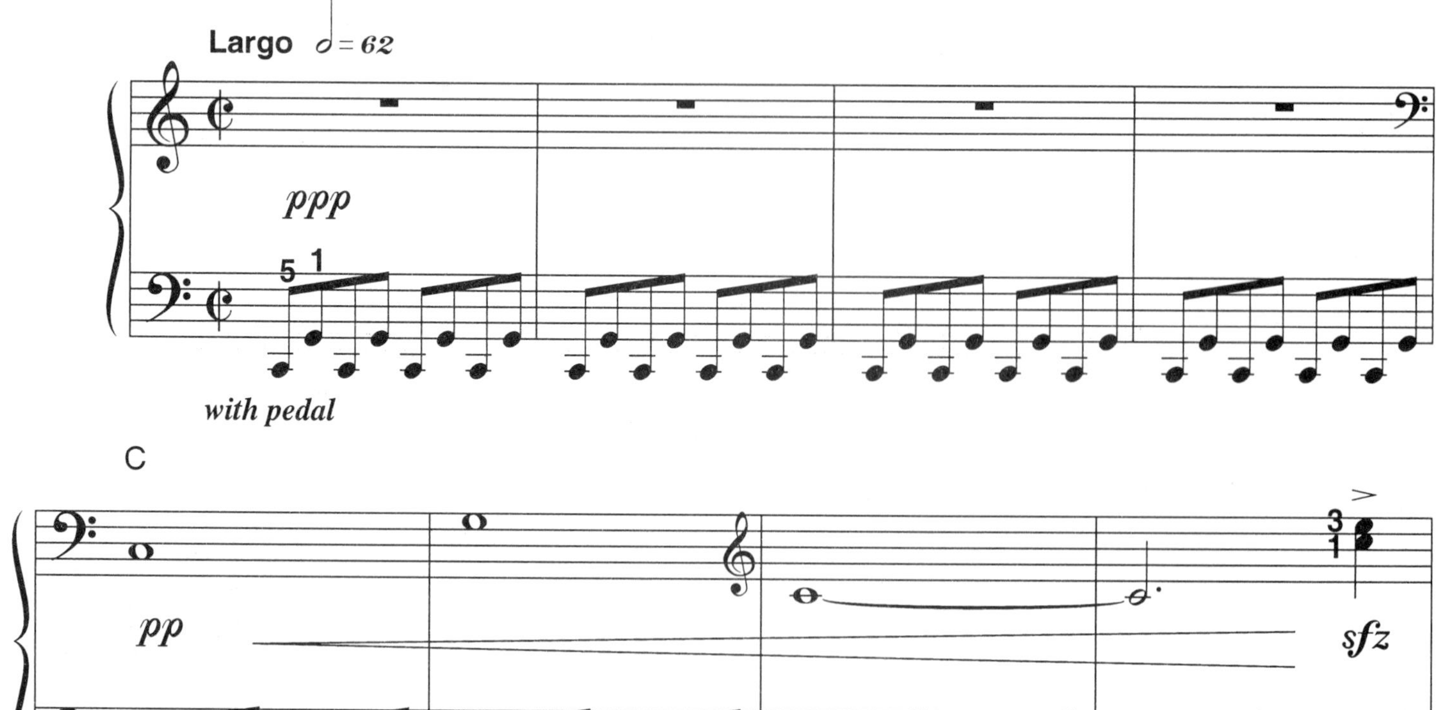

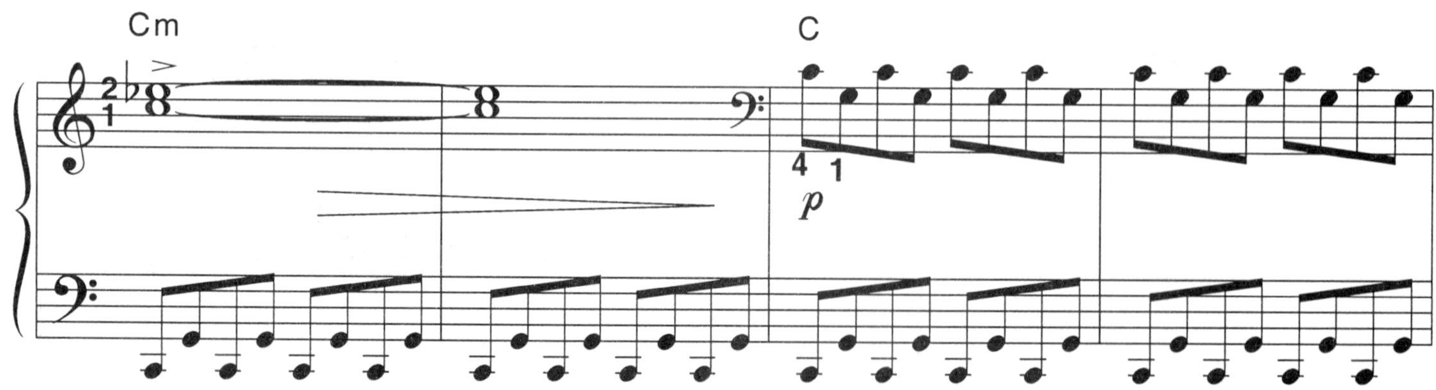

C
3
1
4 1
p
sfz
F
mf
Fm6
C Dm7 C
f
Dm7 C
Am7
G
C

Moonlight Sonata

(Op. 27, No. 2)

German composer
1770 - 1827

LUDWIG van BEETHOVEN
Arranged by Richard Bradley

F
C
p
F/C
A/C♯
Dm
A/C♯
Dm
E♭
A7/E
Dm
D
Gm/D
D

Gm/D
D
Gm/D
C
F/C
5
Gm/D
Edim
A/C♯
Dm
Gm/D
Dm
A/C♯
Dm
A
1
2

Dm
A7(♭9)
Dm
A7(♭9)
Dm/A
Dm
Dm/A
Dm
p
pp

Sonata Pathétique
(Theme From The Second Movement)

German composer
1770 - 1827

LUDWIG van BEETHOVEN
Arranged by Richard Bradley

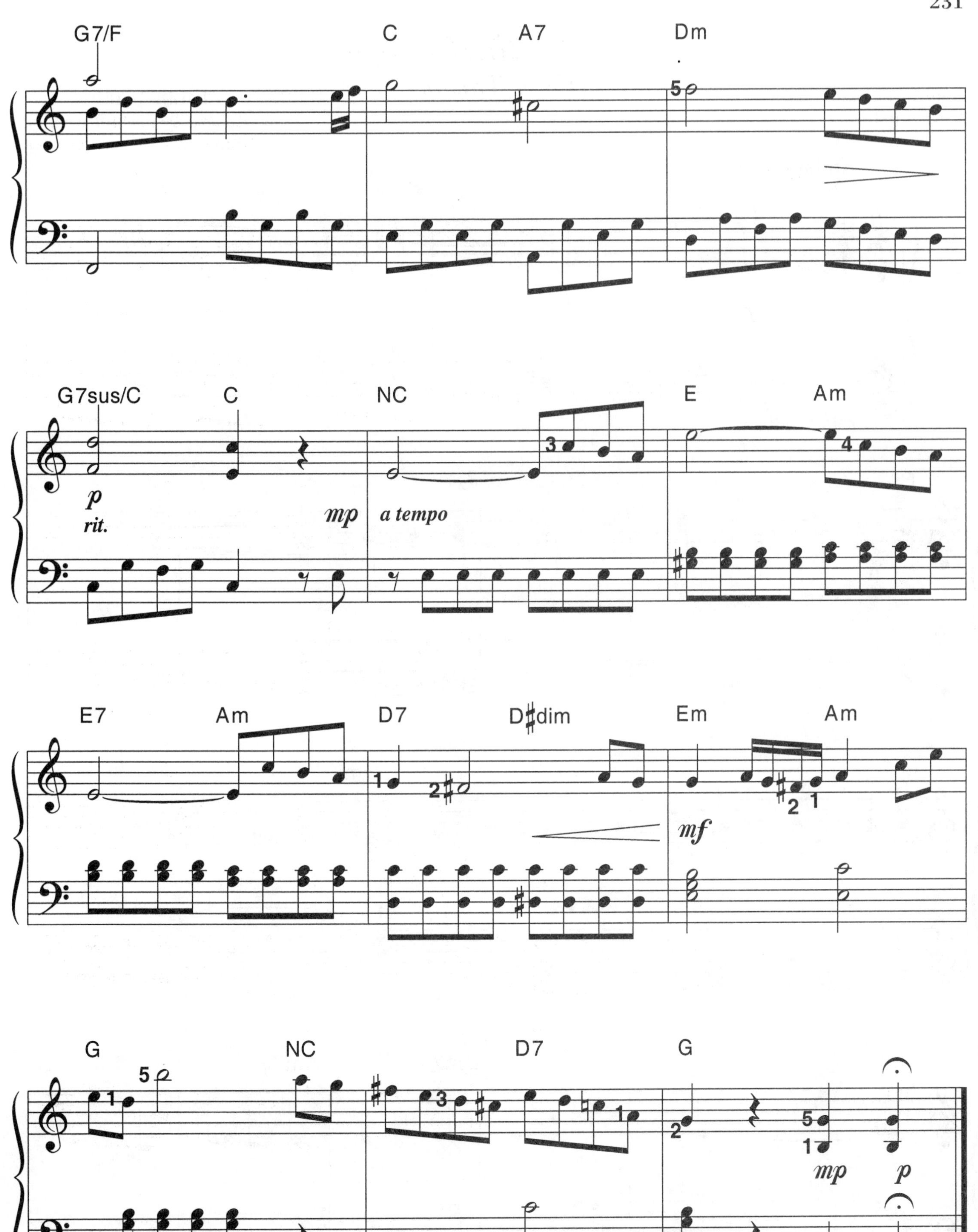
G7/F
C
A7
Dm
5
G7sus/C
C
NC
E
Am
3
4
p
rit.
mp
a tempo
E7
Am
D7
D♯dim
Em
Am
1
2
2
1
mf
G
NC
D7
G
1
5
3
1
2
5
1
mp
p

Clair de Lune
(First Theme)

Fremch composer
1862 - 1918

CLAUDE DEBUSSY
Arranged by Richard Bradley

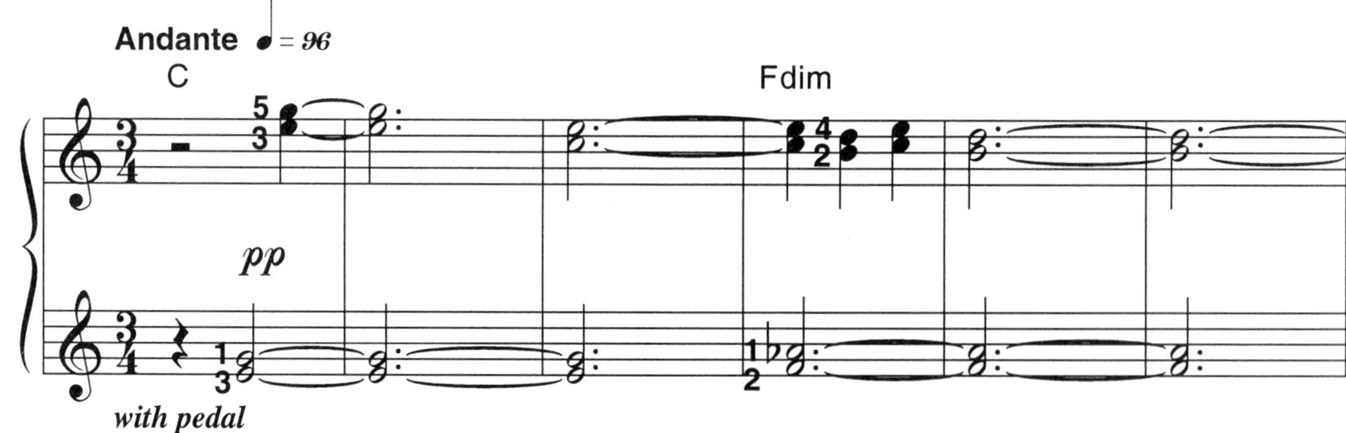

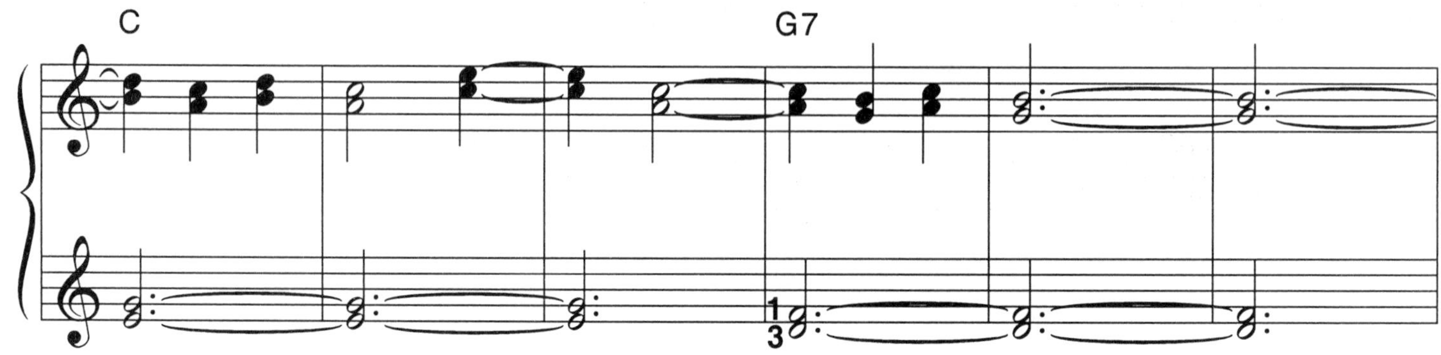

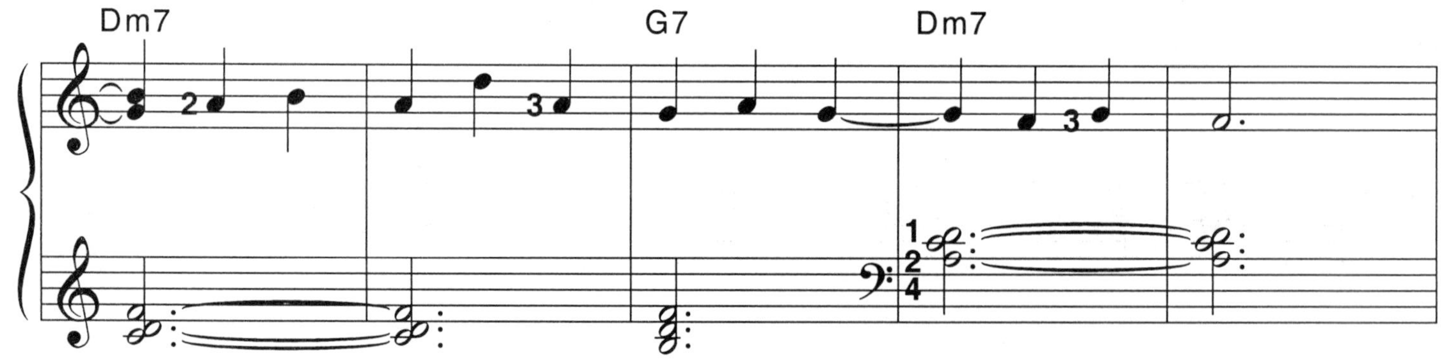

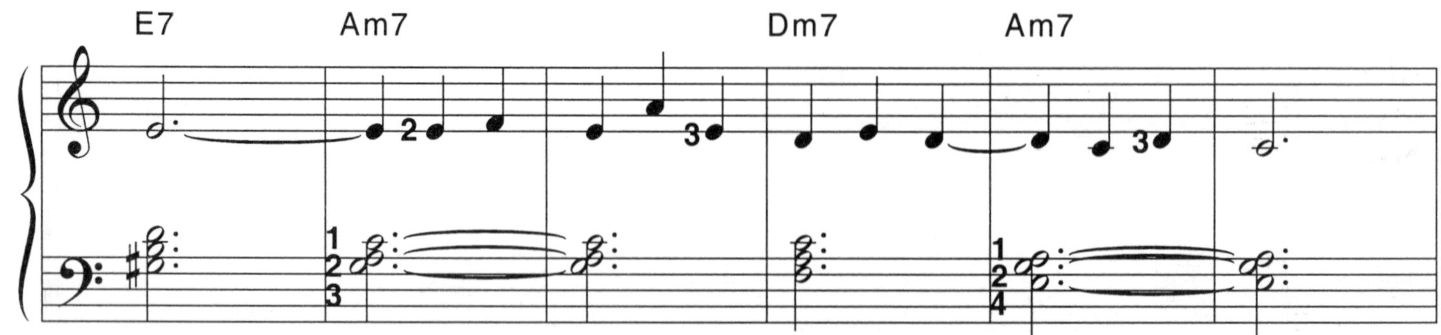

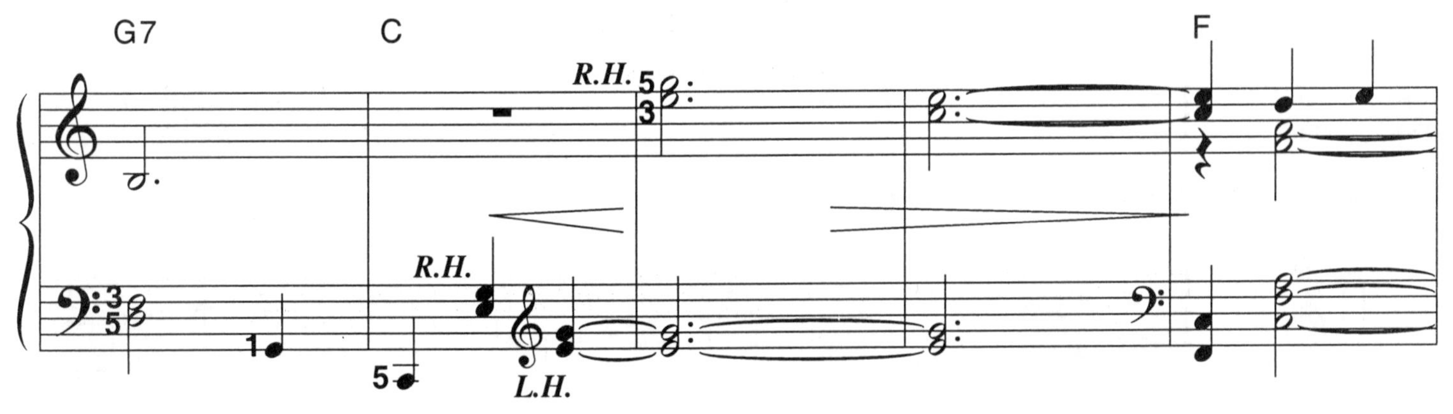
G7
C
F
R.H.
L.H.

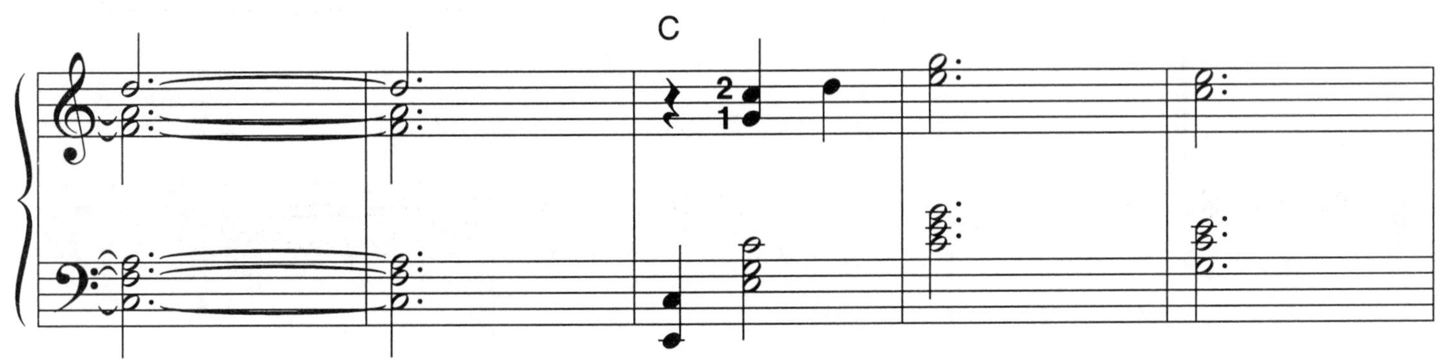
C

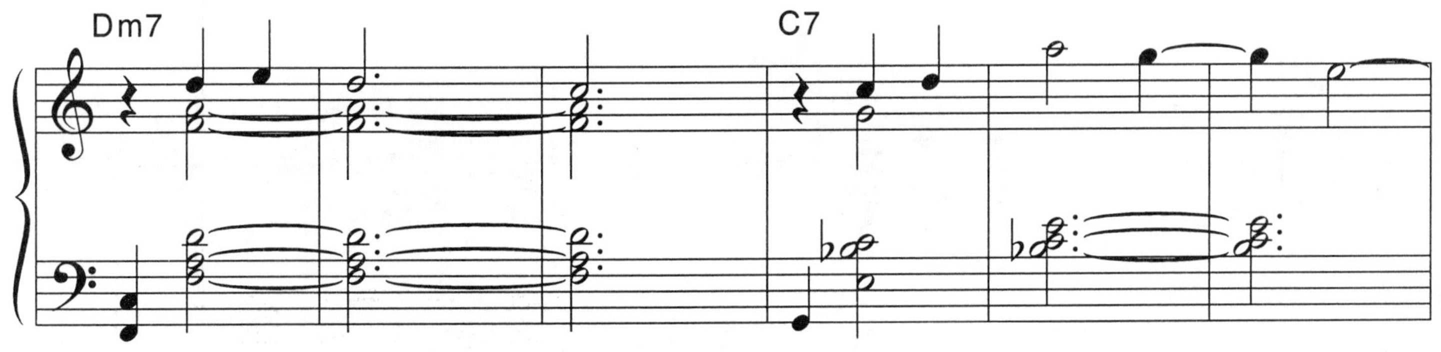
Dm7
C7

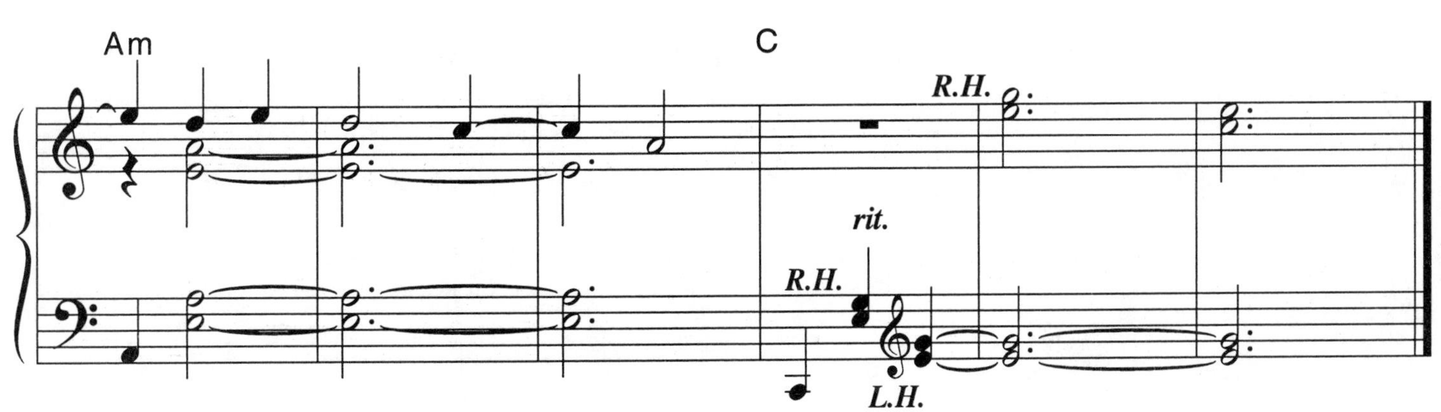
Am
C
R.H.
rit.
L.H.

The Flight Of The Bumble-Bee

Russian composer
1844 - 1908

N. RIMSKY-KORSAKOV
Arranged by Richard Bradley

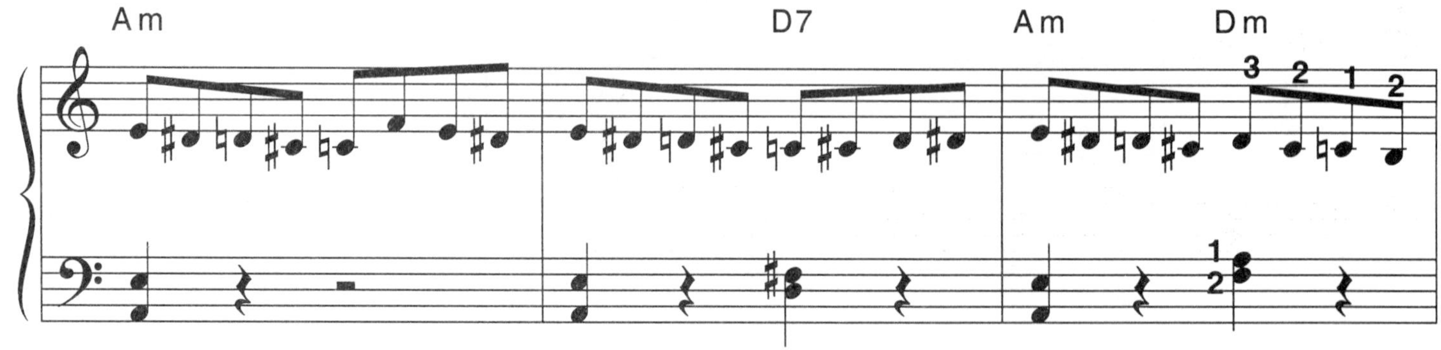

A7
Dm
G7
Dm
3 2 1 2 1 4 3 2

G7
Dm
Gm
Dm
A7
3 2 1 2
1 2 1 2

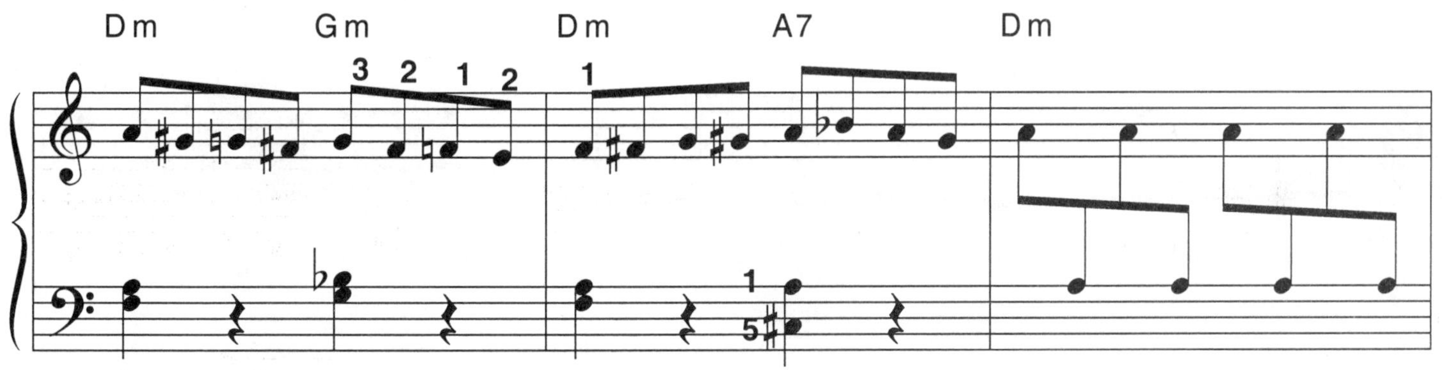
Dm
Gm
Dm
A7
Dm
3 2 1 2
1
1
5

B♭7
Dm
B♭7

A7
F+

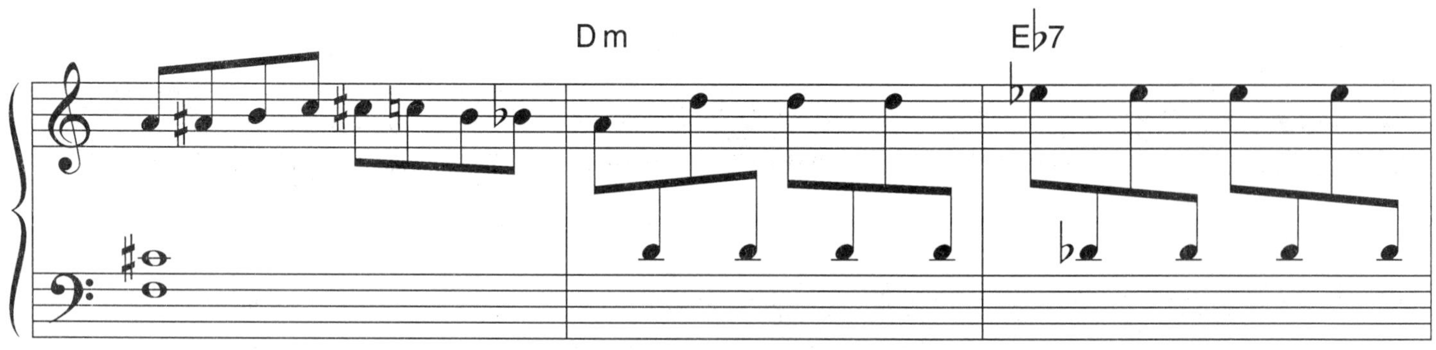
Dm
E♭7

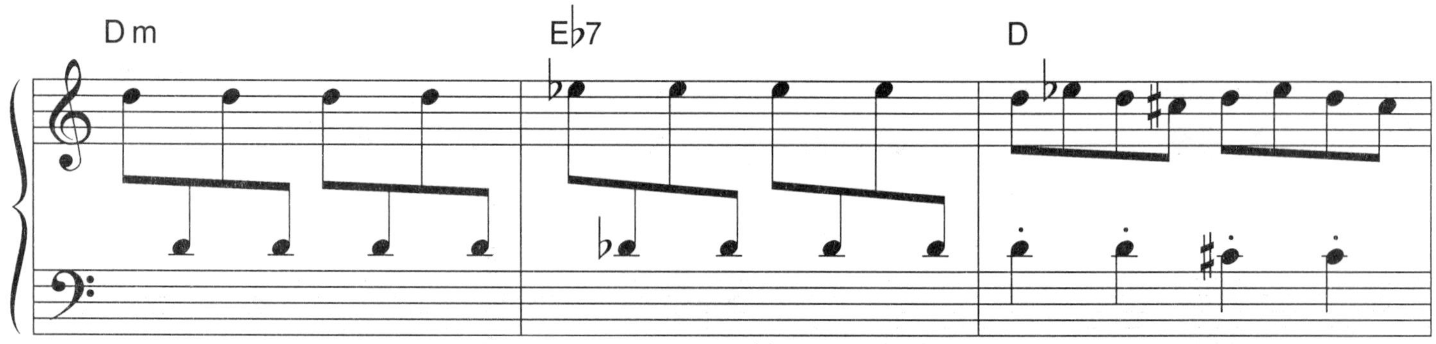
Dm
E♭7
D

B♭+
1 2 1 2 3 2 1 2
mf

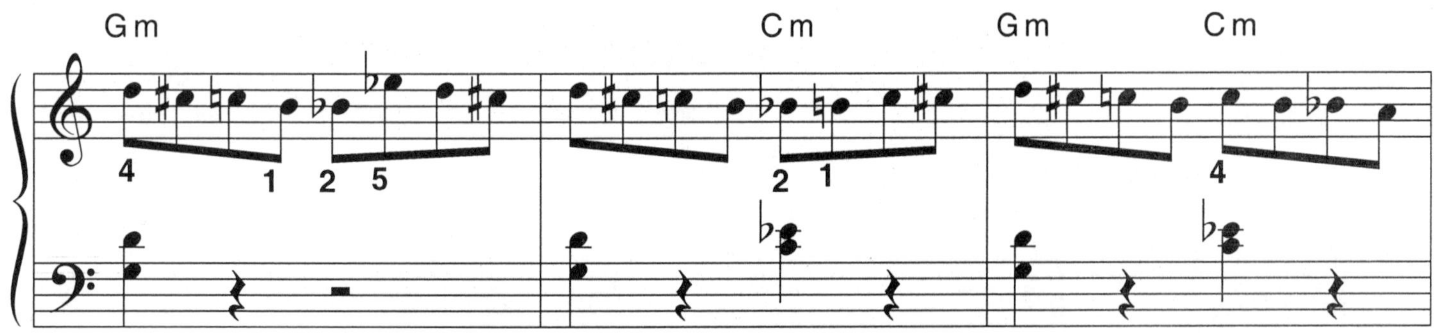
Gm
Cm
Gm
Cm
4
1 2 5
2 1
4

Gm
Dm
E7
N.C.

1.
2.

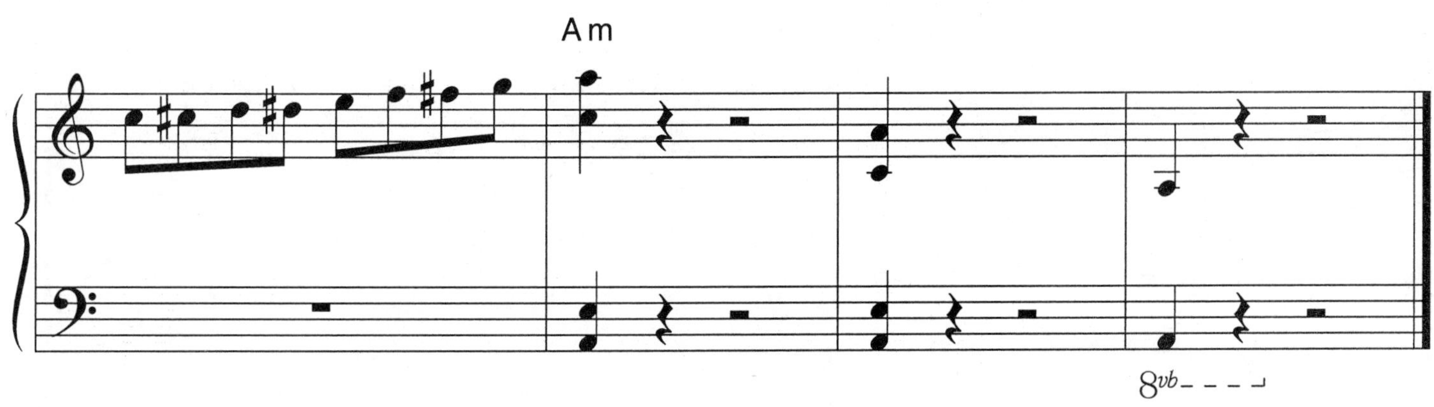
Am
8vb

Un Bel Di

(From "Madame Butterfly")

Italian opera composer
1858 - 1924

GIACOMO PUCCINI
Arranged by Richard Bradley

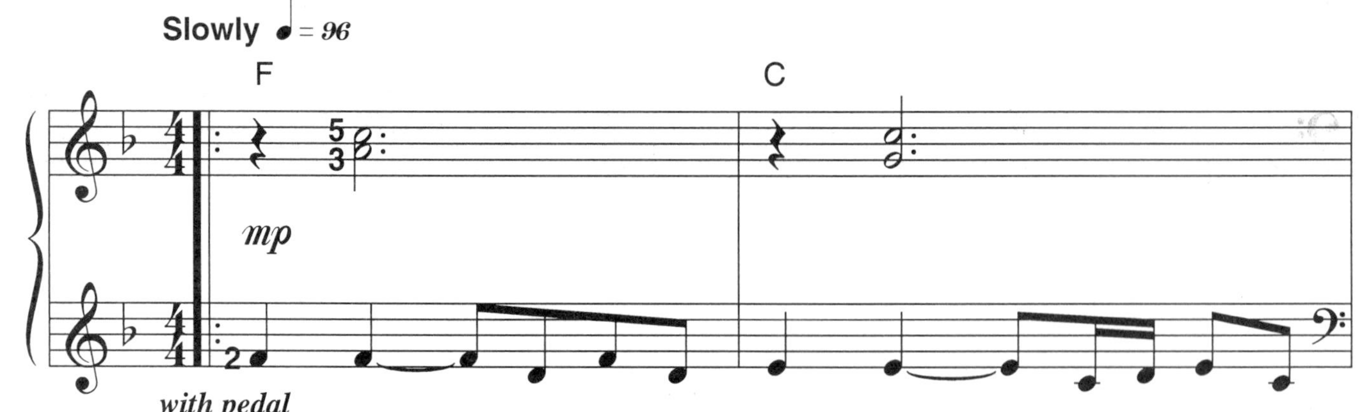

2.
Dm
Am
D/F♯
Am
D/F♯
mf
cresc.

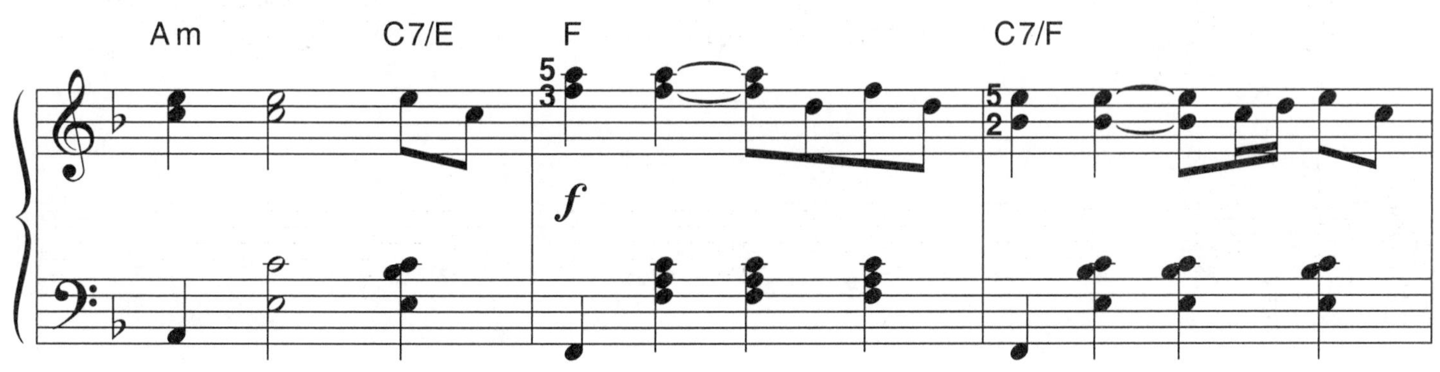
Am
C7/E
F
C7/F
f

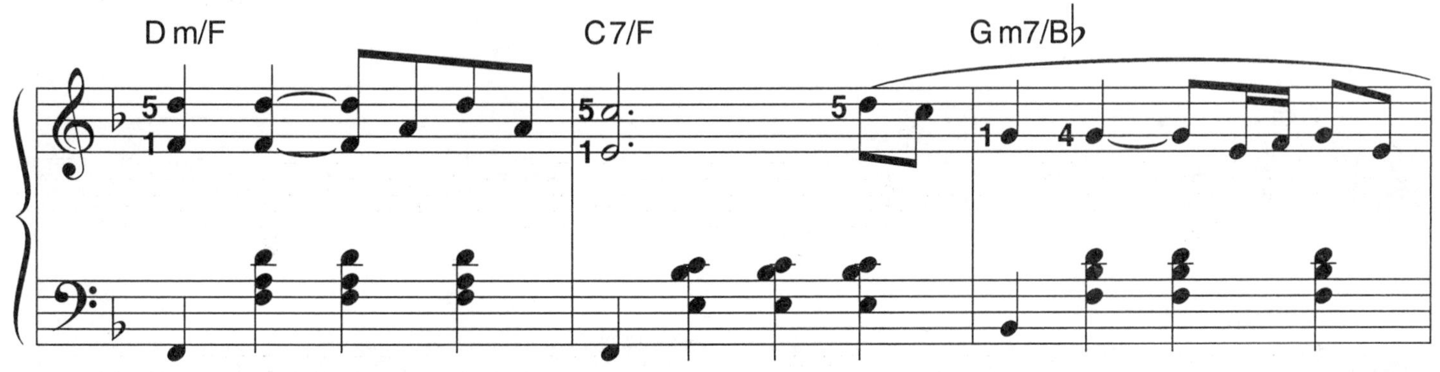
Dm/F
C7/F
Gm7/B♭

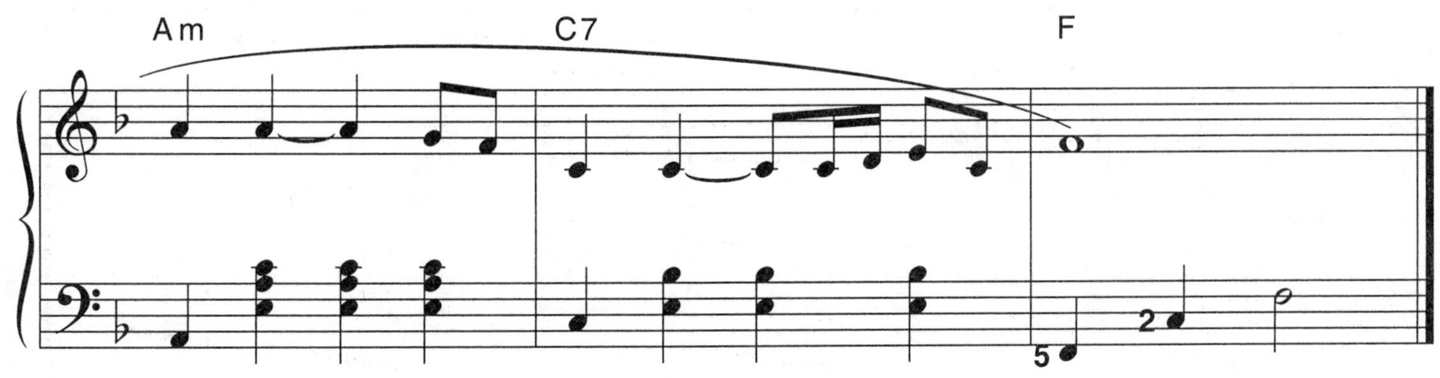
Am
C7
F

Funeral March Of The Marionettes

French composer
1818 - 1893

CHARLES GOUNOD
Arranged by Richard Bradley

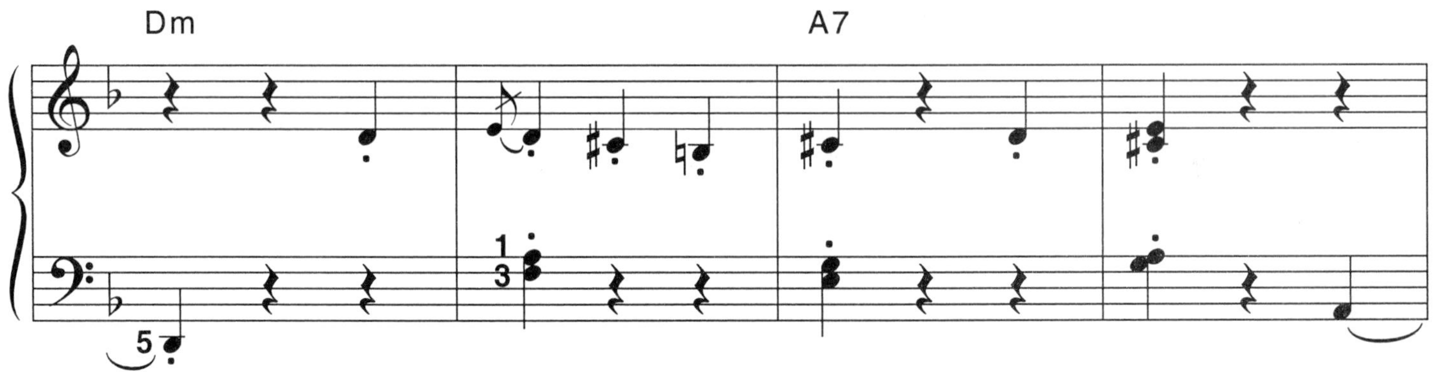

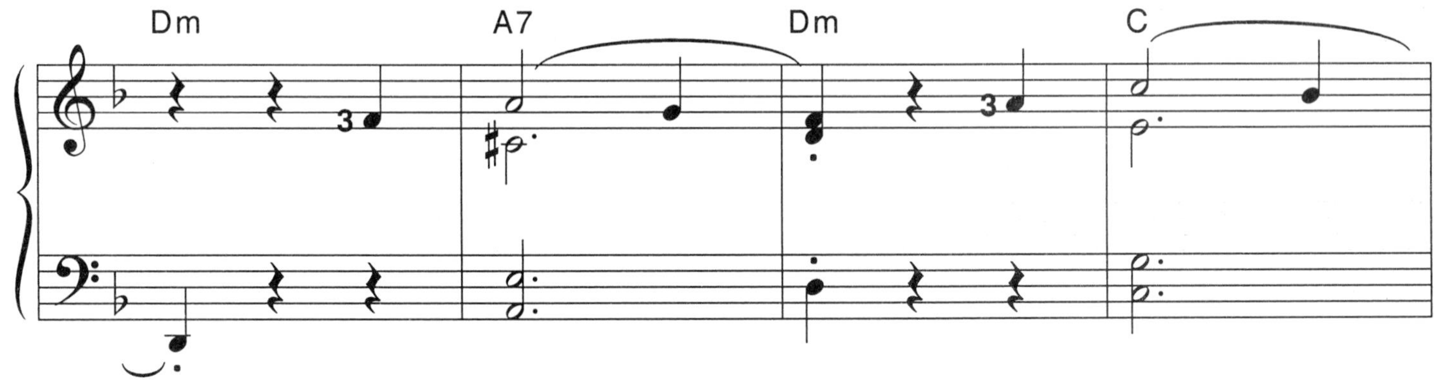

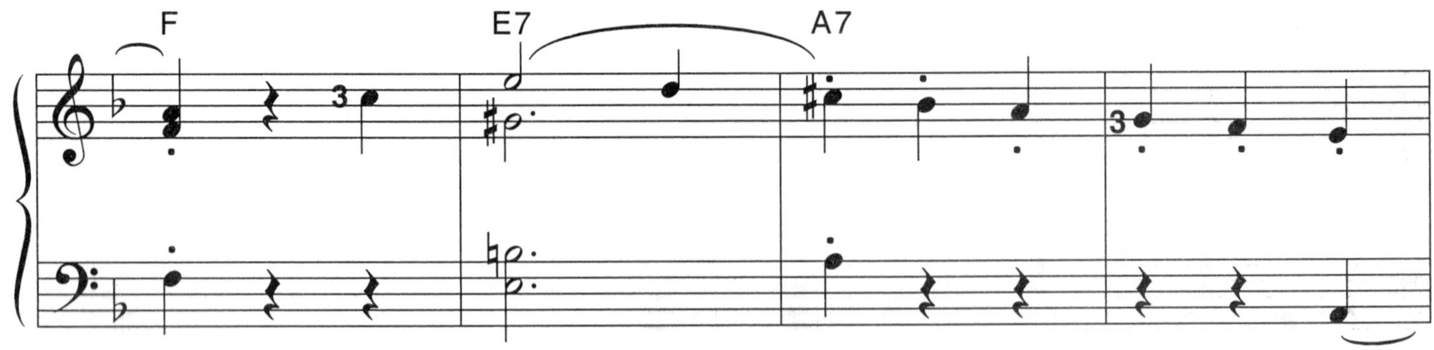

Dm
A7
3

Dm
A7
1
5
1
2
2

Dm
C
F
E♭
Dm
3
1
3
1
2
1

A7
Dm
4
3
1
2

Lullaby

German composer
1833 - 1897

JOHANNES BRAHMS
Arranged by Richard Bradley

C
G7
C
G7
C
8va

Canon In D

German organist - composer
1653 - 1706

JOHANN PACHELBEL
Arranged by Richard Bradley

Bm
F♯m
G
D
G
A
D
A
Bm
F♯m
G
D
G
A
D
A
Bm
F♯m
G
D

G
A
D
A
mf
Bm
F♯m
G
D
G
A
D
A
mp
Bm
F♯m
G
D
G
A

D
A
Bm
F♯m
G
D
G
A
D
A
Bm
F♯m
G
D
G
A
D
A
Bm
F♯m
G
D
G
A
D

Serenade
(Eine Kleine Nachtmusik)

Austrian pianist - composer
1756 - 1791

WOLFGANG AMADEUS MOZART
Arranged by Richard Bradley

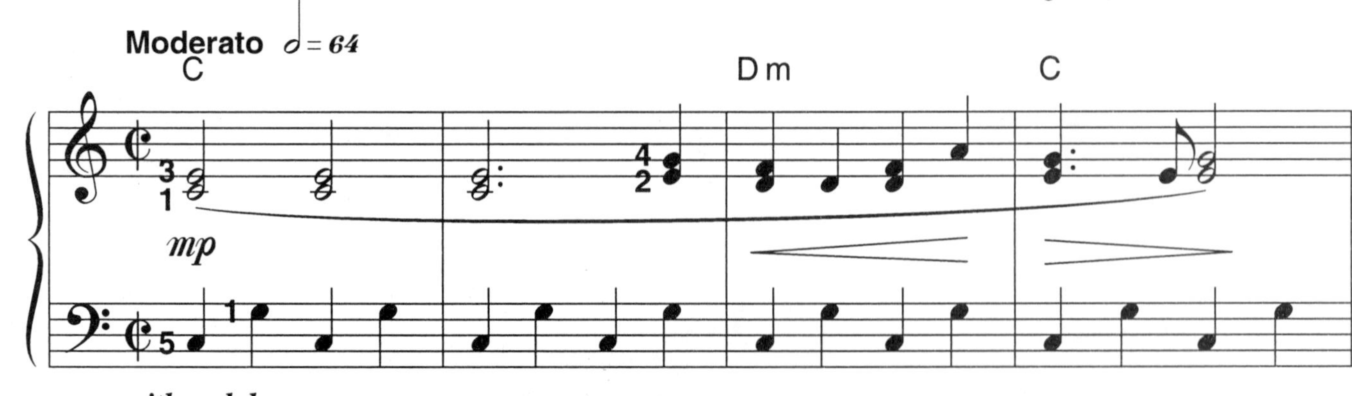

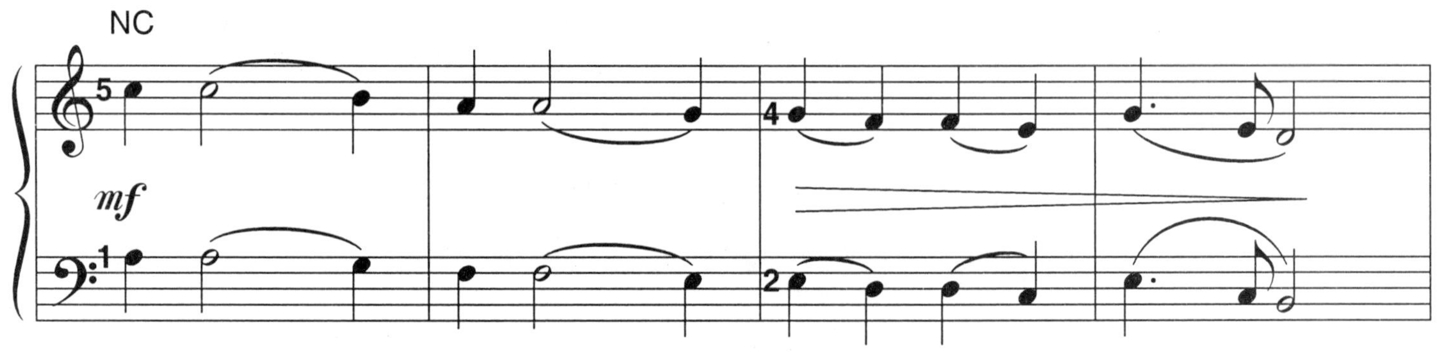

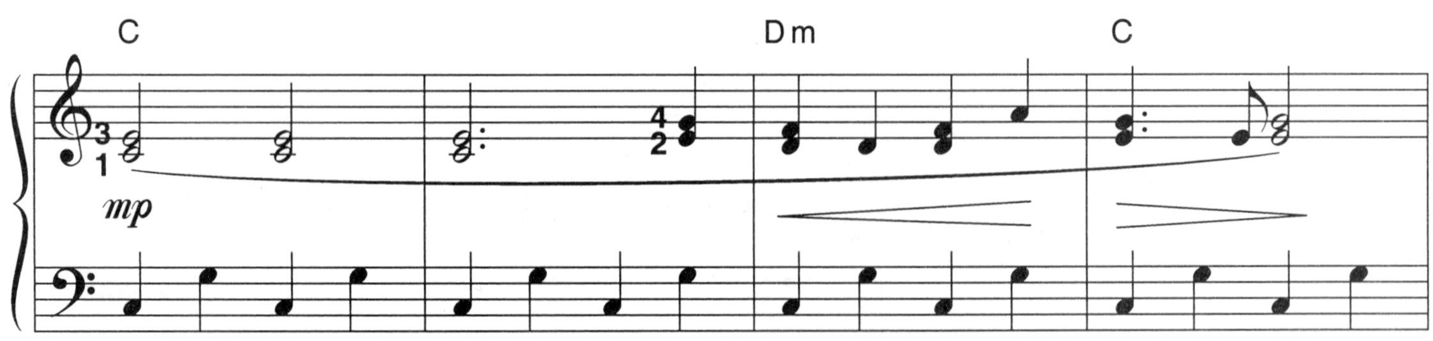

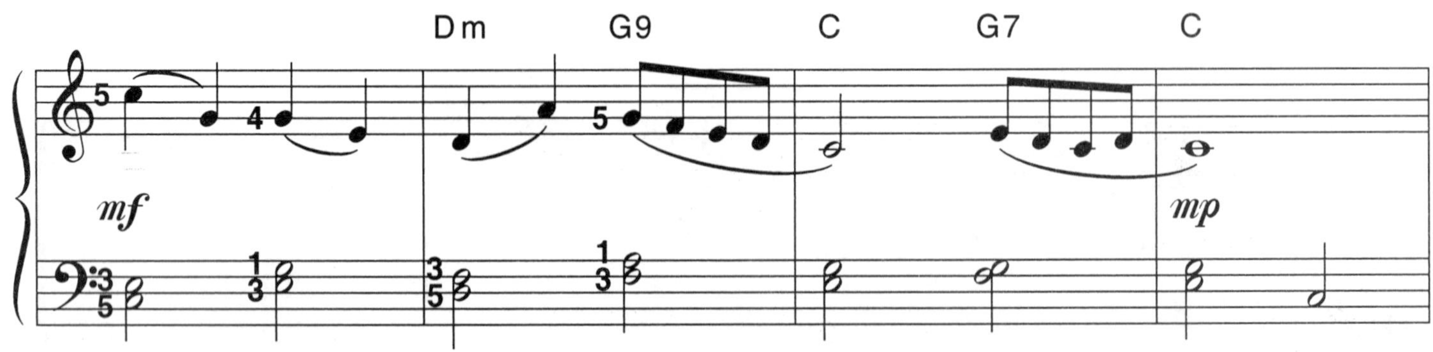

NC
G7
C
F
mf
C
G7
NC
G7
C
D7
G
C
ritard
mp
a tempo
A7
Dm
G9
C
C
Dm
mf
Em
F
C
G7
C
mp
ritard
p

Norwegian Dance

Norwegian composer
1843 - 1907

EDVARD GRIEG
Arranged by Richard Bradley

C7
F
C7
F
G7/F
C7/E
C7
Dm7/F
D7/F♯
Gm
C7/E C7
Dm7/F
D7/F♯
Gm
C7/E C7
F
C7
F
mp
mf
C7
F
C7
F
C7
F

Hungarian Rhapsody No. 2

Hungarian pianist - composer
1811 - 1886

FRANZ LISZT
Arranged by Richard Bradley

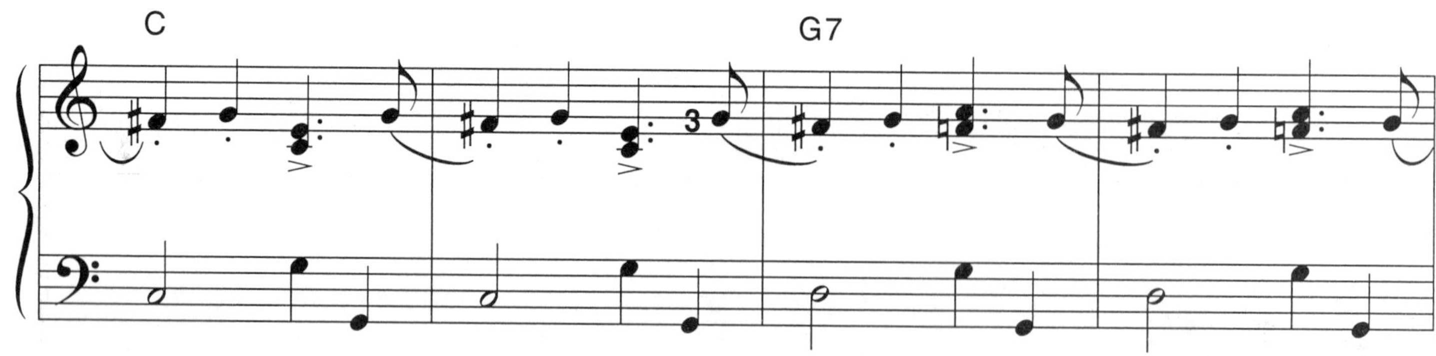

C
G7
mp
C
mf
G7
C
G7
f
C
G7
C
G7
C
ff

Comedians' Gallop

Russian composer
1904 - 1987

DMITRI KABALEVSKY
Arranged by Richard Bradley

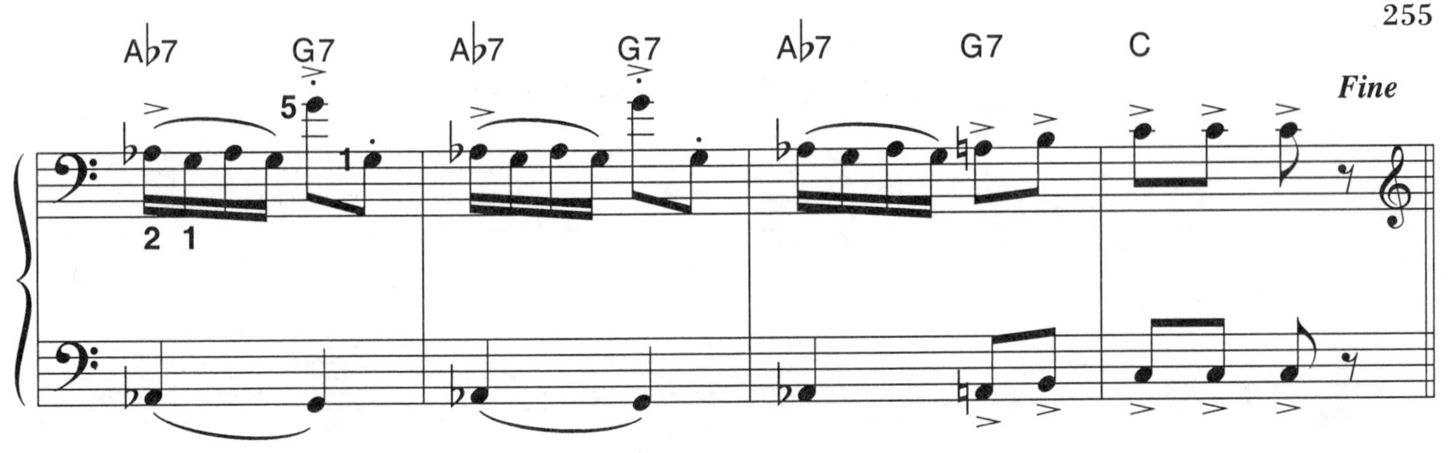
A♭7
G7
A♭7
G7
A♭7
G7
C
Fine

N.C.

Am
mf

B♭
Am
B♭
E7
Am
C
D.S. 𝄋 al Fine